The South West COAST PATH

2004 GUIDE

THE COMPLETE GUIDE TO THE LONGEST NATIONAL TRAIL BY THE SOUTH WEST COAST PATH ASSOCIATION

(FORMERLY THE SOUTH WEST WAY ASSOCIATION)

The South West Coast Path Association

Promoting the interests of South West Coast Path walkers

THE SOUTH WEST COAST PATH ASSOCIATION

Registered as a charity (No. 266754)

The Association formed to promote the interest of users of the South West Coast Path

Visit our Website at www.swcp.org.uk

CHAIRMAN

Bryan Cath, Harwill House, Victoria Street,
Combe Martin EX34 0JS
Tel: 01271 883487 Fax: 01271 883964
E-mail: bryan@combewalks.com

TREASURER

David Richardson, J.P.
44 Whitchurch Avenue
Exeter EX2 5NT
Tel/Fax: 01392 430985

SECRETARY

Eric Wallis
'Windlestraw', Penquit, Ermington,
Devon PL21 0LU
Tel/Fax: 01752 896237
e-mail: info@swcp.org.uk

ADMINISTRATOR

Liz Wallis
'Windlestraw', Penquit, Ermington,
Devon PL21 0LU
Tel/Fax: 01752 896237
e-mail: info@swcp.org.uk

Published by:
The South West Coast Path Association

Trade Sales and Distribution:
Halsgrove Publishing, Halsgrove House, Lower Moor Way,
Tiverton Business Park, Tiverton, Devon. EX16 6SS
Contact: Marie Lewis 01884 243242

Printed in England by Swift Print, Dawlish

ISBN 0 907055 07 9

Jacket photograph:
Main - Stanbury Mouth, North Cornwall, *Insert* - Western Blackapit & Willapark, North Cornwall, both by Fiona Barltrop

South West
Coast Path

CONTENTS

THE SOUTH WEST COAST PATH ASSOCIATION

Dedicated to helping everyone enjoy the path

The South West Coast Path is a National Trail funded by the Countryside Agency (formerly the Countryside Commission) and maintained on its behalf by County Councils, the National Trust, Exmoor National Park, and the unitary authorities of Plymouth and Torbay. The route is waymarked by the distinctive acorn symbol. It is by far the longest of all the Long Distance trails and runs from Minehead in Somerset right round the South West peninsula to South Haven Point on the south side of Poole Harbour in Dorset.

As a result of the 1999/2000 survey of the coast path end to end using a global positioning system, we now have access to very precise distances - the coast path is 630 miles (1014 km) long. The survey, carried out by the South West Coast Path Team, included the Isle of Portland. It is interesting to note that in a contour count undertaken by this Association, it was calculated that the walker completing the South West Coast Path will climb over 91 000 feet (27 737 m), which is three times Mount Everest.

This Guide attempts to provide in one single book all the basic information you need to walk the path. The information is updated annually and members are advised by newsletters of important changes during the year. We try to provide the basic information in one book.

A survey established that one of the chief joys of those accomplishing the Pennine Way was the sense of achievement; of a challenge met. What of our path which is twice as long and requires far more total effort? Because of its length, few will be able to undertake to walk it as a whole, which is why as much as possible of this guide is written to be just as useful to those who only wish to walk parts of the path.

Thirty-one years ago the Association was formed by a group of enthusiasts to encourage the development and improvement of the South West Coast Path. This is still one of the main aims of the Association, and it works closely with the Countryside Agency, local authorities and other more general user groups such as the Ramblers' Association and the Long Distance Walkers' Association.

Over those thirty-one years the Association has continuously campaigned for maintenance, signing and alignment improvements. Of primary importance is to have the coast path removed from roads. There have been many improvements as long-standing members know, and we like to think we have strongly influenced the implementation of these.

Today one of the Association's functions is to assist and advise all those who wish to walk along this wonderful coastline - whether in short, relaxing strolls around a headland, or by more demanding long distance walks lasting several days, or by heroic attempts at covering the whole length of 630 miles (1014 km)!

The path passes along some of the finest coastal scenery in Europe, and with its enormous variety and contrast between bustling resort and quiet cove is a never-ceasing source of delight. This path is the longest National Trail in the country. We think it is the finest, and hope you will too. We certainly know of no other that has as much contrast and variety as ours; try it!

Members receive a free Annual Guide and two Newsletters a year, with up-to-date information on the state of the path.

So here it is - Britain's longest and most beautiful walking trail - read about it, then go for it!

MEMBERSHIP

Subscriptions: Single: £11.00; Joint: £12.50; Associations & Local Authorities: £18.50;

Life Membership: £160.00;   Joint Life Membership: £185.00;   Non-UK
Membership: £16.00.

Payment may be made using a cheque or postal order made payable to the South West Coast
Path Association. We can accept the credit/debit cards shown below, providing we have the
following information:

Card Number   Expiry Date
Full name as it appears on the card
Issue Number (Switch Cards Only)

We welcome...

WEATHER

The South West Coast Path is more exposed to wind than any other long distance trail, so please
pay attention to gale forecasts as well as rain. Along some sections, strong winds can be
dangerous, especially when rounding exposed headlands and crossing bridges; a high backpack
can act like a sail. Detailed forecasts are available on 09068 400105 for Somerset, 09068 400104
for Devon and Cornwall, and on 09068 400103 for Dorset.

A WORD TO BEGINNERS

Long Distance Path Walking

These words are not for those hardy veterans who have all the gear, have done several paths
already, and know all about it. We will only say to them at least read the second paragraph of
'Grading' near the beginning of the 'Trail Description' section. However, we do get a number of
letters each year from those who have not ventured before on long distance paths and need
some advice. This we are pleased to try and provide and we do hope those who read this will
find it helpful. However, it is easy to miss out things that folk wish to know, so if you who are
new read this, and are still baffled, please write to us and we will try to provide the answers. As
well as perhaps helping you, it will enable us to improve this section for another year and so be
of help to more people.

Newcomers to the coast path

To get the feel of the coast path you are advised to take some day walks along it - there are
some very good ones on the coast. Better still, look for the sections marked 'Easy' - start at one
end and stop and turn back before you have half had enough. We say before half because it is
always better to do a bit less and really enjoy it.
You can soon progress to setting out to walk a whole section either by using two cars or using
public transport. One point here - if possible use the public transport to go out and walk back to
your car or base. This means that you do not get yourself in a position of having to race the clock
if you should take a bit more time than you thought.

If you are walking on your own, do please take additional care for, as you will appreciate, if you
fall or twist an ankle there can be problems. If you are on your own therefore, you should leave
a note with someone to make sure that you arrive at your destination. Not everyone is happy
walking on their own and can feel lonely. There is also an added problem that you may try to do
too much, so please bear this in mind.

There is no need to buy expensive equipment for the easy sections at the start; a pair of stout
shoes and a rainproof is all you need. As you progress, a small rucksack or haversack for 'eats'
will be needed next.

Obviously if you can join a walking club and go out with them you will collect lots of friendly
advice on all sorts of gear you may care to purchase as you become more serious about walking.
Maps, guides, etc., are all listed in their appropriate sections.

For Those Who Have Walked, But Not On Long Distance Trails

Day walking on long distance trails is really no different from any other kind of day walking. It is only when you contemplate several days' continuous walking that other considerations arise and there are some pitfalls which even quite experienced day walkers often overlook.

Do not be too ambitious in the distance you plan. Do not carry too much weight of gear.

Having stated the two big points, we will elaborate. You will not be able to accomplish in daily distance the same amount you normally cover in a day walk; you will have to settle for less. The first reason is that you will be carrying more equipment; you must for instance, have a complete change of clothing and footwear, possibly nightwear and toilet kit. For this you need a bigger rucksack so you will be carrying quite a bit more weight than you normally do. Secondly, there is what we call the 'wear' factor. For the first few days until you are really fit, it is just simply more tiring having to walk each day. The last point could be called the 'interest' factor. Usually, if you are walking a long distance path, you are further from your home base, in fresh fields and pastures new; there is more to see so you will need more time to look around.

If you usually accomplish 15 miles (24 km) a day, aim, say, for 12 (19 km). This is particularly important if you are booking ahead. You can find yourself tied to a treadmill which you cannot get off. Booking ahead has the advantage that you know there is a bed ahead. On the other hand, it does mean even if you are tired, have developed blisters, and the weather is diabolical, you have to go on. Be guided too by our 'Trail Description' section and the terrain you are tackling. 6 miles (10 km), say, of a 'Severe' section can equal in effort 10-12 miles (16-19 km) of an 'Easy' one.

We have stated you must carry more gear and this is true. Having said that, think long and hard about every item you imagine you may need. You will be surprised - you may find you will not want it at all. Watch particularly those extras such as cameras and binoculars - they are often a source of considerable weight. One little additional point, many rucksacks, even modern ones, are not as waterproof as you think. A plastic liner, which can be obtained quite cheaply from rambling shops, etc., as an additional inner layer, may save you that most unpleasant discovery after a long day spent in the rain that your only change of clothing is no longer dry. We would also recommend that in addition to this liner, your dry clothing should then be enclosed in further plastic bags to ensure dryness. Trainer shoes are useful for wearing at the end of the day and can be worn on some parts of the path.

A sensible idea before undertaking a long walking holiday is to take, say, a weekend of two or three days first, walking continuously as a practice.

Another point to watch especially on our coast path is the availability of refreshment. At main holiday times, you will get it nearly everywhere, except for the few places we especially mention in our 'Trail Description' section. Out of season, you will find it in surprisingly few places on long stretches of coast. The usual remarks about carrying stand-by supplies, therefore, certainly apply; better to carry an extra couple of bars of chocolate than to go hungry.

Walking Alone

The Association has a scheme that enables single female members who are a little nervous about walking alone to team up with other single female members. Contact the Administrator for information.

Easing The Load

On long trips it is a good idea to:

a)   Send guides, maps etc. ahead to larger post offices Poste Restante. The only snag is if you arrive on a Saturday evening.

b)   Start out with a few map-sized envelopes and the smallest available roll of sellotape so that you can despatch finished guides, maps, books etc. home.

c)   many of our B & B proprietors will transfer your kit to your next destination (see p 93).

SOUTH WEST COAST PATH ASSOCIATION PUBLICATIONS

Path Descriptions by our Association are detailed accounts on all aspects of short sections of the coast path and include maps and illustrations. They cover in great detail what cannot be included in the guide book.

These Path Descriptions are all priced at £1.00 including postage. All are available from the Administrator (see page 2).

PATH DESCRIPTIONS

(Please note that as each Path Description is revised, we shall be using the new accurate distances accordingly)

Minehead to Porlock Weir (9.5 miles/15.3 km)
Porlock Weir to Lynmouth (12.3 miles/19.8 km)
Lynmouth to Ilfracombe (18 miles/30 km)
Ilfracombe to Croyde Bay (13.6 miles/21.9 km)
Croyde Bay to Barnstaple (16 miles/25 km)
Barnstaple to Westward Ho! (19.1 miles/30.7 km)
Westward Ho! to Clovelly (11.2 miles/18 km)
Clovelly to Hartland Quay (10.3 miles/16.6 km)
Hartland Quay to Bude (15.4 miles/24.8 km)
Bude to Crackington Haven (9 miles/15 km)
Crackington Haven to Tintagel (12 miles/20 km)
Tintagel to Port Isaac (8 miles/13 km)
Port Isaac to Padstow (11.7 miles/18.9 km)
Padstow to Porthcothan (12 miles/20 km)
Porthcothan to Newquay (11.1 miles/17.9 km)
Newquay to Perranporth (11 miles/18 km)
Perranporth to Portreath (12.2 miles/19.7km)
Portreath to Hayle (12.4 miles/19.9 km)
Hayle to Pendeen Watch (19.5 miles/31.3 km)
Pendeen Watch to Porthcurno (15.6 miles/25.2 km)
Porthcurno to Penzance (11.5 miles/18.5 km)
Penzance to Porthleven (14 miles/22.5 km)
Porthleven to The Lizard (13.9 miles/22.3 km)
The Lizard to Coverack (10.6 miles/17.1 km)
Coverack to Helford (13.1 miles/21.1 km)

Helford to Falmouth (10 miles/ 16 km)
Falmouth to Portloe (13 miles/22 km)
Portloe to Mevagissey (12.3 miles/19.8 km)
Mevagissey to Fowey (17 miles/ 27 km)
Fowey to Polperro (7.1 miles/11.5 km)
Polperro to Looe (5.0 miles/8.0 km)
Looe to Portwrinkle (7.6 miles/12.2 km)
Portwrinkle to Plymouth (13.3 miles/21.4 km)
Plymouth (River Tamar) to Wembury (River Yealm) (14.8 miles/23.8 km)
Warren Point (Wembury) to Bigbury-on-Sea (14 miles/22 km)
Bigbury-on-Sea to Salcombe (13 miles/21 km)
Salcombe to Torcross (12.9 miles/20.8 km)
Torcross to Dartmouth (10 miles/16 km)
Dartmouth to Brixham (10.8 miles/17.3 km)
Brixham to Shaldon (19 miles/30 km)
Shaldon to Sidmouth (21 miles/32 km)
Sidmouth to Lyme Regis (17 miles/27 km)
Lyme Regis to Abbotsbury (18 miles/30 km)
Abbotsbury to Weymouth (14 miles/23 km)
Isle of Portland (14 miles/22 km)
Weymouth to Lulworth Cove (11 miles/18 km)
Lulworth to Kimmeridge, Lulworth Range (7 miles/11 km)
Kimmeridge to South Haven Point, Poole Harbour (20 miles/31 km)
Alternative Inland Route, West Bexington to Osmington Mills (18 miles/28 km)

A History of the South West Coast Path

The Association has written a history of the origins of the coast path. This book also includes an account of walking the coast path in 1854, and an account of a protracted legal case involving access to the coast path on the Devon / Dorset border in the mid 19th century.

Price £2.50 including postage.

The Reverse Guide

The Association has written a description of the Trail for those walking in the Poole to Minehead direction. It deals only with the path so this Annual Guide will be necessary for all the other information. Our Reverse Guide supplement was comprehensively revised in 2002.

Price £3.50 including postage.

THE ASSOCIATION'S SHOP

Log Book

Why not keep a day by day record of your walk in an easy to carry, pocket size booklet, with a page per section in which to record your daily journey round the coast path (all 630 miles / 1014 km!). Whether you do it all in one go or over a period of time, you will have a permanent record of your walks round some of the most beautiful country in the British Isles.

Price £3.50 including postage

Polo Shirt

In an attractive jade green, with the Association logo embroidered on the shirt, with 'SOUTH WEST COAST PATH' embroidered around the logo.

A good quality garment, easy to wash (65% polyester / 35% cotton), in Small, Medium, Large, Extra Large and Extra Extra Large.

Price £18.25 including postage

Sweat Shirt

In bottle green or jade embroidered with the Association logo on the left side, and 'SOUTH WEST COAST PATH' around the logo (70% polyester / 30% cotton). It comes in five sizes, Small, Medium, Large, Extra Large and Extra Extra Large.

Price £25.00 including postage

Sleeveless Artic Fleece

In bottle green with the Association logo on the left side and two zip pockets. 100% pill resistant polyester and unlined. Sizes small, medium, large, extra large, and extra extra large.

Price £25.00 including postage

Polar Fleece Jacket

In bottle green with the Association logo on the left side and two zip pockets. 100% pill resistant, unlined, elasticated hem and cuffs. Sizes small, medium, large, extra large, and extra extra large.

Price £27.50 including postage

Cloth Badge

Good quality cloth badge, showing the Association logo, with 'SOUTH WEST COAST PATH' embroidered below, approximate size 4" x 3" (10 x 8 cm). Suitable for sewing onto shirt or rucksack, coloured logo in green and yellow on a blue background.

Price £2.70 including postage

Coast Path Embroidery

We have designed this unique counted cross stitch embroidery to celebrate the South West Coast Path. The embroidery kit contains everything you need to complete the project, and a leaflet containing full details can be obtained from the Administrator. Guidance is also given on how to personalise your embroidery to include your own completion date of the coast path.

Price £25.00 including postage

Notelets

The coast path Embroidery has been used as the cover design for notelets, which come in packs of 10.

Price £7.50 including postage

Whisky Tumblers

Cut glass whisky tumblers with the Association logo sand-blasted on the glass. In a presentation box.

Price £16.00, £32.00 for a pair in a presentation box, including postage.
PLEASE ALLOW 28 DAYS FOR DELIVERY

Glass Beer Tankards

Glass beer tankards, plain glass with the Association logo sand-blasted onto the glass. Suitably packaged.

Price £12.99 including postage. PLEASE ALLOW 28 DAYS FOR DELIVERY

CD-ROM

Our CD-Rom is cut straight from the master files used on our web site. It contains over 350 pictures from along the path in our acclaimed Photo Tour. It also has 33 stunning pictures especially prepared for use as computer wallpaper. It will work with Linux, Apple MACs and all versions of Microsoft Windows. If you require more technical details, check our web site.

Price £6.50 including postage

Illustrated Coast Path Walk, by Sue Jeffreys

Sue Jeffreys started her walk along the coast path in May 1994. Sue likes to walk alone and finds that she can see more by doing so. Sue is also an accomplished artist and she took with her a sketch-pad and some colouring crayons with which she was able to write and illustrate a diary of her walk.

Between 1994 and 1997 Sue walked the path in four stages each of roughly two weeks, sketching and recording her experiences. As well as drawing the many places visited, Sue also drew the plants she encountered.

When completed Sue approached the Association to ask if it might be suitable for publishing. Sadly, no one was willing to take up the offer, so the Association has decided to publish all 134 pages of the diary itself, not on paper but on CDROM.

'I was very surprised to learn of the Association's plan to publish my diary on CDROM, but also very interested' said Sue. Working with us, Sue allowed the Association to scan the original diaries to produce very high-quality images for the CDROM, which are provided at two resolutions to suite all popular screen sizes. The disc is designed for all types of computer (Linux/MAC/Windows) and requires a web browser. The CDROM costs £6.00.

TO ORDER:- Please send details of the sizes of garments and / or quantity required, together with a cheque made payable to: **The South West Coast Path Association** to the Administrator.

We can also accept the credit/debit cards shown below, providing we have the following information:

Card Number   Expiry Date
Full name as it appears on the card
Issue Number (Switch Cards Only)

We welcome...

Non UK Orders: Please add £1.00 to cover extra postage.

Certificates

These are now available to persons who have walked the whole path. To members - £1.50 and to non-members - £2.50 including postage. Contact the Administrator.

BOOKS

These publications are available from bookshops. This list is not exhaustive; there are a number of other books available but we have tried hard to list all those which are really useful and even those not really useful that you might think would be.

South West Coast Path - Minehead to South Haven Point (ISBN 1-85284-379-9)

An excellent pocket sized book is by Paddy Dillon. We can recommend it as most useful. It has stunning photographs and OS maps. Available from Cicerone Press, 2 Police Square, Milnthorpe, Cumbria, LA7 7PY at £12.95 and bookshops.

National Trail Guides - published by Aurum Press in association with the Countryside Agency. They are available from bookshops, or in case of difficulty, from Aurum Press, 25 Bedford Avenue, London WC1B 3AT. These are good guide books with good maps. An excellent venture by those involved.

Minehead to Padstow by Roland Tarr (6th Edition - due out in Spring)

Padstow to Falmouth by John Macadam (4th Edition 2002)

Falmouth to Exmouth by Brian Le Messurier (5th Edition 2003)

Exmouth to Poole by Roland Tarr (5th Edition - due out in Spring)

LANDFALL WALKS BOOKS - Bob Acton of Devoran has written twelve splendid books that contain well over 100 circular walks in Cornwall. These feature sections of the coast path throughout the county. They will enable walkers to progress along the coast path by basing themselves at one location. Write to Landfall Publications, Landfall, Penpol, Devoran, Truro, TR3 6NW for full list, or Tel: 01872 862581.

Footpath Touring with Ken Ward. Land's End and The Lizard. Price £3.75 including postage. Available direct from 'Sea Chimney', South Down, Beer, EX12 3AE. An excellent guide to this section of the path by one of the co-authors of the well-known Letts Guides.

Two Moors Way (now illustrated) - by Devon Area Ramblers' Association - Price £3.00. This is not our path: one is enough! This describes the path from Lynmouth in North Devon to Ivybridge near Plymouth - and very well done it is too.

Two Moors Way by John Macadam. This is a new recreational guide published by Aurum Press and Ordnance Survey. £12.99.

Classic Walks Cornwall - 56 half day circular walks involving the coast path. From Cornish Publications Ltd, PO Box 12, Camborne, TR14 0YG. £4.99 plus 75p P&P, (£2 outside the UK).

Most Tourist Information Centres (see our Accommodation section) have good supplies of leaflets and books relating to their local areas. We suggest you telephone or write to them and ask what is available.

Other Walking Routes

We recommend the Long Distance Walker's Handbook: 6th Edition: Completely revised and updated. Contact - Brian Smith, 10 Temple Park Close, Leeds, West Yorkshire LS15 0JJ (Tel: 0113 264 2205). (£11.99 inc postage)

Information on Long Distance Routes can also be obtained from the Ramblers' Association, see page 17.

THE NATIONAL TRUST 'COAST OF DEVON' LEAFLETS

A series of detailed leaflets with maps is available covering much of the coastline owned by the National Trust in Devon. Each leaflet contains good maps and information on the history, flora and fauna and general information of the areas.

They are available from National Trust shops in Devon or from the Devon Regional Office, Killerton House, Broadclyst, Exeter, EX5 3LE, Tel: 01392 881691; Fax: 01392 881954 at 75p each plus post and packing: (see guidelines overleaf).

The West Exmoor Coast	Wembury and Aymer Cove
Watersmeet and Countisbury	Salcombe Estuary
Bideford Bay to Welcombe Mouth	Dartmouth and South Devon
	Ilfracombe to Croyde

THE NATIONAL TRUST 'COAST OF CORNWALL' LEAFLETS

A series of detailed leaflets with maps, covering the coastline owned by the National Trust in Cornwall. Each leaflet contains information of the history, flora and fauna of the area as well as general information on points of interest. Available from National Trust shops in Cornwall or from Lanhydrock House Shop, Lanhydrock, Bodmin, Cornwall PL30 4DE. Tel: 01208 265952.

Please make cheques payable to The National Trust and include postage & packing (see guidelines below).

No 1	Bude to Morwenstow	£1
No 2	Crackington Haven	£1
No 3	Boscastle	£1
No 4	Tintagel	£1
No 5	Polzeath to Port Quin	£1
No 6	Trevose to Watergate Bay, including Bedruthan Steps (not NT)	£1
No 7	Crantock to Holywell Bay	£1

No 8	St. Agnes and Chapel Porth	£1
No 9	Godrevy to Portreath	£1
No 10	West Penwith: St. Ives to Pendeen	£1
No 11	West Penwith: Levant to Penberth	£1
No 12	Loe Pool and Mount's Bay	£1
No 13	Lizard, West Coast	£1
No 14	Lizard, Kynance, Lizard Point & Bass Point	£1
No 15	Lizard, East Coast, Landewednack to St. Keverne	£1
No 16	Helford River	£1
No 17	Trelissick	£1
No 18/19	The Roseland and St Anthony Head	£1
No 20	Nare Head and the Dodman	£1
No 21	Fowey	£1
No 22	East Cornwall	£1

Country Walks Leaflet : Cotehele Estate	90p
Country Walks Leaflet : Lanhydrock	£1.00
Godolphin	£1.00
Focus on Wildlife Booklet	£1.99

When ordering, please add the following rates for postage and packaging:

Quantity	1st Class
1-3	50p
4-8	75p
9-11	£1.00
12 & over	£2.00

THE NATIONAL TRUST WESSEX REGION

The following illustrated guided walks leaflets are available from the Wessex Regional Office. To order copies, please write to: The Box Office, The National Trust, Wessex Regional Office, Eastleigh Court, Bishopstrow, Warminster, Wiltshire, BA12 9HW enclosing a cheque or postal order to include 50p towards postage and packing. Cheques should be made payable to 'the National Trust (Enterprises) Ltd.' Alternatively, you may call 01985 843601 and pay by credit card.

Isle of Purbeck (5 walks) - telephone for current price	
Holnicote (Horner Wood)	
- Valley Walk	£0.60
- Hill Walk	£0.60
Golden Cap - Walks from Stonebarrow	£0.50
Golden Cap - Walks from Langdon Hill Wood	£0.50
Explore Holnicote	£1.00
Holnicote - Bossington and Coastline Walk	£0.60
Holnicote - Allerford and Selworthy woods walk	£0.60
Exploring Corfe Common	£0.50
Holnicote - Dunkery and Horner Wood	£0.60
Holnicote - Luccombe and Woodland	£0.60
Holnicote - Selworthy and Bury Castle	£0.60
Holnicote - Upland Archaeology	£0.60
Holnicote - Selworthy	£0.60

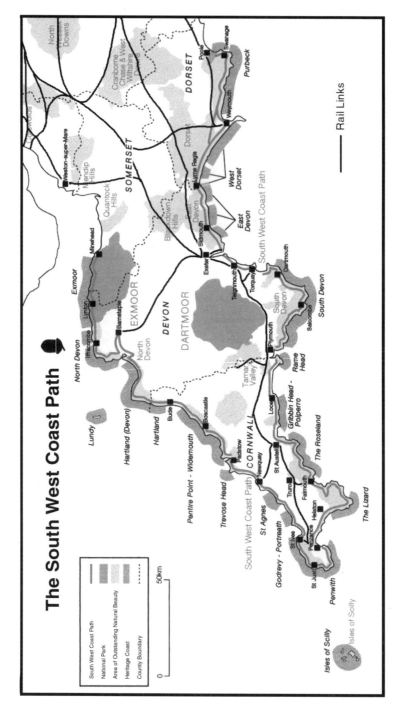

The South West Coast Path

Rail Links

South West Coast Path
National Park
Area of Outstanding Natural Beauty
Heritage Coast
County Boundary

0   50km

DORSET
SOMERSET
DEVON
CORNWALL
EXMOOR
DARTMOOR

North Wessex Downs
Cranborne Chase & West Wiltshire
Cotswolds
Mendip Hills
Quantock Hills
Blackdown Hills
North Devon
Tamar Valley

Dorset
West Dorset
East Devon
South Devon
South West Coast Path

Purbeck
Poole
Swanage
Weymouth
Lyme Regis
Weston-super-Mare
Sidmouth
Exeter
Teignmouth
Torquay
Dartmouth
South Devon
Salcombe
Plymouth
Rame Head
Looe
Gribbin Head - Polperro
The Roseland
St Austell
Newquay
Padstow
Boscastle
Bude
Hartland
Hartland (Devon)
Pentire Point - Widemouth
Trevose Head
St Agnes
Godrevy - Portreath
St Ives
Penzance
Helston
Falmouth
Truro
St Just
Penwith
The Lizard
Minehead
Lynton
Ilfracombe
Barnstaple

Lundy

Isles of Scilly

NATIONAL TRUST REGIONAL MARKETING AND COMMUNICATIONS MANAGERS

Devon and Cornwall Regional Office, Killerton House, Broadclyst, Exeter, Devon EX5 3LE (Tel: 01392 881691).

Wessex Regional Office, (for Dorset and Somerset) Eastleigh Court, Bishopstrow, Warminster, Wilts. BA12 9HW (Tel: 01985 843600).

Cornwall Regional Office, Lanhydrock, Bodmin, Cornwall PL30 4DE (Tel: 01208 74281)

RAILWAYS

Throughout the year there is a regular service of direct First Great Western Trains linking London Paddington with Taunton, Exeter St. David's, Newton Abbot, Plymouth and Cornwall. There are also regular Virgin Cross Country Trains' services linking Birmingham, the North West, North East and Scotland with Taunton, Exeter St. David's, Plymouth, Cornwall, Bournemouth and Poole. All these services offer a range of on-train facilities including catering and on most First Great Western services during the school holidays, coach E is dedicated for the use of families. During the high season (May to September), demand for seats is high so it is recommended that seats are reserved in advance to ensure a comfortable journey. On Saturdays, additional services run to and from the West Country to the Midlands, North of England and London with a direct service operated between London and Newquay during the summer only.

There is a regular South West Trains' service linking London Waterloo with Bournemouth, Poole, Wareham (for Swanage), and Weymouth for those who intend to walk the Dorset end of The South West Coast Path. East Devon is served by an approximate two hourly service from London Waterloo to Axminster (for Lyme Regis and Seaton) and Honiton (for Sidmouth). In addition to these services South West Trains also offer a service of trains linking London Waterloo, Basingstoke, Salisbury, Exeter Central and Paignton.

Wales & Borders Trains offers long distance trains in the South West. They link Cardiff, Manchester, and Bristol with Penzance, Plymouth, Paignton and Exeter. A wide variety of attractive reduced-rate fares is often available, details of which can be obtained at Stations and Travel Centres. To obtain train information, call the National Rail Enquiries Service on 08457 484950 (24 hours a day), and to book tickets and reserve seats call 0870 9000 773 (0800-2000 Mon-Sat, 0900-1700 Sun). The web address is www.walesandborderstrains.co.uk

Wessex Trains offers long distance and most local trains in the South West. The long distance trains link Cardiff and Bristol with Exeter, Penzance, Plymouth, Portsmouth, Salisbury, Southampton and Weymouth. The local services on the branch lines of Devon and Cornwall offer connections into and out of First Great Western, Wales and Borders, South West Trains and Virgin Train services. Most Wessex Trains local routes also operate on Sundays during the summer months with the first five asterisked * below operating a Sunday service during the winter months too.

* Westbury - Yeovil - Weymouth	Liskeard - Looe
* Exeter - Barnstaple	Par - Newquay
* Exeter - Exmouth	Truro - Falmouth
* Newton Abbot -Torquay - Paignton	St Erth - St Ives
* Plymouth - Gunnislake	

To obtain train information, call the National Rail Enquiries Service on 08457 484950 (24 hours a day), and to book tickets and reserve seats call 0870 9000 773 (0800-2000 Mon-Sat, 0900-1700 Sun). The web address is www.wessextrains.co.uk

Private Branch Line Railways

Bishops Lydeard to Minehead - The West Somerset Railway PLC runs steam trains through 20 scenic miles (32 km) to Minehead. Bishops Lydeard is 4 miles (6 km) outside Taunton and easily accessible by bus. The service operates between March and October. For details contact the company at 'The Station', Minehead TA24 5BG (Tel: 01643 704996).

Paignton to Kingswear (Dartmouth) - For the rambler who is also a railway enthusiast, the Paignton and Dartmouth Railway is a `must'. This most attractive line runs from Paignton to Goodrington, Churston and Kingswear and operates preserved Great Western steam locomotives and rolling-stock. The line passes through some delightful coastal and river scenery, and a trip on the railway could easily be combined with a walk to make a very pleasant day out. It operates from March to December. For details contact - Queens Park Station, Torbay Road, Paignton TQ4 6AF (Tel: 01803 555872).

Bodmin Parkway to Bodmin Town is a service that could prove useful for those requiring bus transport to the coast. (Tel: 01208 73666).

BUS SERVICES

A new National Transport Enquiry Service has been established. For all timetable enquiries in South West England, call Traveline on 0870 6082608

Tourist Information Centres can help with bus enquiries. For details of all coastal TICs see our Accommodation section of the back of this book.

ACCESS TO THE START OF THE PATH:
Access to the start of the path can be made locally and from outside the region, with First's bus service 28 linking Minehead to the Great Western Rail Line at Taunton.

Service 28 Taunton-Minehead currently operates on an hourly frequency up to the early evenings from Monday to Saturdays. On Sundays service 28 operates less frequently. For service 28 timetable enquiries telephone First - Taunton. (Tel: 01823 272033).

National Express operates direct services to Minehead. For more information about national coach services to the South West, telephone National Express (Tel: 0990 808080) (this is charged at local call rates).

BUS INFORMATION:
Listed below, in path order, are details of services and information available from County Councils and local bus operators; it is intended for guidance use only. All information provided is correct at the time of going to print; responsibility for any inaccuracies or changes cannot be accepted by County Councils or bus operators. For up to date bus service information, telephone the relevant numbers given in the following paragraphs.

SOMERSET:
For service 28 from Taunton to Minehead and services 30/30A from Taunton to Lyme Regis and Weymouth via Axminster (change buses) contact First, The Bus Station, Tower Street, Taunton, TA1 4AF (Tel: 01823 272033).

Somerset County Council produces timetable booklets twice a year in Spring and Autumn. The 5 booklets are based on the District Council areas and are available from Libraries and TIC offices. A countywide bus map is also produced annually listing all the services in the county. In addition a leaflet showing the network of Sunday services is now also available. All literature can be obtained from The Integrated Passenger Transport Unit, Somerset County Council, Room A1, County Hall, Taunton, TA1 4DY. T: 01823 356700 E: transport@somerset.gov.uk

NORTH DEVON:
The North Devon coast has a range of bus services which may be of use to coastal walkers. The greatest choice of coastal destinations is provided from Barnstaple. The principal services are: 309/310 Barnstaple to Lynton; Services 3 & 30 Barnstaple to Ilfracombe; 308 Barnstaple to Georgeham; 303 Barnstaple to Woolacombe; 1, Barnstaple to Bideford and Westward Ho!; 2 Barnstaple to Appledore and 319 Barnstaple to Bideford, Clovelly and Hartland. Note that the number prefix refers to the bus route number. During the summer, service 300 operates daily from Barnstaple to Ilfracombe, Lynton and Minehead, with glorious coastal views along much of the route.

From Bideford there are frequent services to the coast. The principal services are 2, Bideford to Appledore; 1 Bideford to Westward Ho! and 319 Bideford to Clovelly and Hartland.

Those who are not walking the entire path in one go may find the Western National X9 service from Exeter to Bude a useful link to or from the coast.

The above services are operated by First in Devon, First in Cornwall; for timetable enquiries telephone Traveline - 0870 6082608 0700-2100 daily, www.traveline.org.uk

Devon County Council produces timetable guides summer and winter entitled 'North Devon Public Transport Guide'. They are available from Tourist Information Centres, Libraries, bus operators or by telephoning the DevonBus enquiry line Barnstaple: 01271 382500 or Exeter 01392 382800, Monday - Friday 0900-1700. Email: devonbus@devon.gov.uk Website: www.devon.gov.uk/devonbus

CORNWALL:

Cornwall County Council, in conjunction with First, produces a public transport timetable. The booklet is published twice yearly in May and September and covers the whole of Cornwall. It is available from the Passenger Transport Unit, Cornwall County Council, Fal Building, County Hall, Truro, TR1 3AY, T: 01872 322000 price £1.50, with cheques made payable to Cornwall County Council. The timetable can also be obtained free locally from bus stations, Tourist Information Centres and libraries, as can a county public transport map showing all bus and rail routes with a summary of frequencies.

There is no comprehensive county bus enquiry number in Cornwall. First bus information is available from Western House, Tabernacle Street, Truro, TR1 2EJ, W: www.firstgroup.com
Their customer care line is 01209 722625. Details of **Truronian** services can be obtained from 24, Lemon Street, Truro, TR1 2LS, T: 01872 273453, W: www.truronian.co.uk **Western Greyhound** service information is available from 14 East Street, Newquay, TR7 1BH. T: 01637 871871 W: www.westerngreyhound.com **DAC Coaches** information from Rylands Garage, St Ann's Chapel, Gunnislake, PL18 9HW. W: www.daccoaches.co.uk Information on other operators can be obtained from Cornwall County Council's Passenger Transport Unit T: 01872 322000. **For full public transport information on services in Cornwall ring Traveline T: 0870 6082608 W: www.traveline.org.uk**

The principal routes serving coastal areas are:

First Services: 1 Penzance to Land's End, 2 Penzance to Helston to Falmouth, 300 (summer only) Penzance to St Ives to Land's End, 16 & 17 Penzance to St Ives, 87 Truro to Perranporth to Newquay, 88 Truro to Falmouth, 24 St Austell to Fowey (please see important note at the end of section 51), 25 St Austell to Mevagissey, 55 Bodmin Parkway Station to Bodmin to Wadebridge to Padstow, X7 Penzance to Helston to Falmouth to Truro to St Austell, X9 Exeter to Bude, X10 Exeter to Wadebridge and Newquay, 301 (summer only) Newquay to Padstow to St Ives.

Truronian Service T1 Perranporth to St Agnes to Truro to Helston to The Lizard, T34 Redruth to Helston. DAC Coaches service 267 Liskeard to Looe and Polperro. Hambleys Coaches Polperro to Looe to Plymouth. Polruan Bus (summer only) Polruan to Polperro to Looe. Western Greyhound service 522 Wadebridge to Tintagel to Bude, 524 Wadebridge to Port Isaac to Camelford, 526 St Austell to Mevagissey to Gorran Haven, 556 Newquay to Padstow, 592 Truro to St Columb Major to Newquay, 594 Truro to St Columb Major to Wadebridge.

SOUTH DEVON:

The coastline between Plymouth and Exeter is accessible by bus from many inland towns. The principal services are:

80/81 Plymouth to Torpoint; 34 and 34/B Plymouth City Centre and Admirals Hard for Cremyll Ferry (buses meet ferry and through ticket available); 7A Union Street (short walk from Cremyll Ferry) to Mountbatten (54 Bovisand in the summer); 49 Plymouth to Heybrook Bay; 48 Plymouth to Wembury; 94 Plymouth to Noss Mayo; 92 Plymouth to Salcombe; 93 Plymouth to Kingsbridge & Dartmouth; X80 Plymouth to Paignton & Torquay; X38 Plymouth to Exeter; X64, 164 Totnes to Kingsbridge; 111 Totnes to Dartmouth; 162 Kingsbridge to Hope Cove; 606 Kingsbridge to Salcombe; 120 Kingswear to Paignton; 22, 24 Kingswear to Brixham; 12/12A Brixham & Paignton to Torquay and Newton Abbot; 85 Torquay to Teignmouth, Dawlish and Exeter; 85A Newton Abbot to Teignmouth, Dawlish and Exeter.

The above services are operated by First, Tally Ho!, Plymouth Citybus and Stagecoach. For timetable enquiries telephone Traveline on 0870 6082608.

Devon County Council produce timetables, guides summer and winter for the South Hams and Teignbridge areas. They are available from Devon bus on 01392 382800.

Plymouth Citybus map and services are available from the Public Transport Team, Plymouth City Council, Civic Centre, Plymouth, PL1 2EW, or call 01752 307735.

EAST DEVON:

The East Devon coastline is accessible by bus from Exeter, Ottery St. Mary, Honiton and Axminster. The principal services are:

X53 Exeter to Beer, Seaton, Lyme Regis, Bridport, Weymouth; X53 Exeter to Wareham (summer only), 20 Taunton to Seaton; 57 Exeter to Exmouth, change Exmouth for service 157 and 357 (through fares available) to Budleigh Salterton and Sidmouth; 52 Exeter to Sidmouth; 382 Ottery St. Mary to Sidmouth; 340 Honiton to Sidmouth; 885 Axminster to Seaton; 30 Taunton to Axminster change at Axminster for service 31 (through fares available) 31 Taunton to Axminster to Lyme Regis (and continues to Bridport, Dorchester and Weymouth); 899 Sidmouth to Lyme Regis. On Summer Sundays service 378 operates along the East Devon coast from Sidmouth, Seaton and Axminster.

The above services are operated by Stagecoach, Axe Valley Mini-Travel and First Hampshire and Dorset. For timetable enquiries telephone Traveline public transport info. (tel: 0870 6082608) daily 0700-2100.

Devon County Council produces timetable guides summer and winter, entitled 'East Devon Public Transport Guide'- they are available from Tourist Information Centres, libraries, bus operators or by telephoning the DevonBus enquiry line on Exeter (tel: 01392 382800) Monday-Friday 0900-1700.

Bus Map - Other useful information provided by Devon County Council includes the public transport map. This depicts all bus routes and railway lines throughout the county and gives a summary of service frequency. It is available from Tourist Information Centres, libraries and bus stations or by telephoning the DevonBus enquiry line on Barnstaple (tel: 01271 382800) or Exeter (tel: 01392 382800) Monday-Friday 0900-1700.

DORSET:
The Dorset Coast is accessible by bus from various inland points with train connections for the distant traveller. The principal routes are listed below.

Service 31 provides hourly journeys on Mondays to Saturdays between Weymouth - Dorchester - Bridport - Lyme Regis - Axminster. This service also operates until late evening and offers a two hourly Sunday service. Most buses will connect with trains at Axminster and Dorchester South. Passengers benefit from low floor buses that provide easy access and greater comfort. Please contact First Hampshire and Dorset. Tel: 01305 783645.

Service 103 operates a Monday to Saturday service between Dorchester and Lulworth/Durdle Door. It also calls at Wool railway station. For details contact First Hampshire and Dorset, see above.

Service X53 operates between Weymouth - Lyme Regis - Exeter travelling along the coast between Weymouth and Bridport. Operates daily. During the summer months the service is extended from Weymouth to Wareham. This service is operated by First Hampshire and Dorset, see above.

Service 150 operates from Bournemouth - Swanage via Sandbanks Ferry with Service 142/3/4 operating from Poole - Swanage via Wareham and Corfe Castle. Both services run Monday - Saturday and Sundays. Please contact Wilts & Dorset Ltd, Travel Office, Bus Station, Poole BH15 1SN. Tel: 01202 673555.

Service 152 operates from Sandbanks Ferry to Poole Bus Station 5 minutes walk from the railway station. No Sunday service from October to April. Please contact Wilts & Dorset Ltd, as above.

Dorset County Council annually produces a series of local public transport timetables listing bus and rail services and companies by area. A county-wide Bus and Rail Map listing all services in rural Dorset with frequency guide is also produced together with two Heritage Coast maps providing enhanced map details and timetables. These are available from Tourist Information Centres or The Passenger Transport Section, Dorset County Council, County Hall, Dorchester DT1 1XJ. Tel: 01305 225165, d.fiddik@dorsetcc.gov.uk. Timetables are also available at www.dorsetcc.gov.uk/bustimes

SEA TRANSPORT AND COASTAL CRUISES

The famous pleasure steamers Waverley and Balmoral provide both cruises and transport, to and from the Exmoor Coast.

From May until late September these big and fast sea-going ships provide transport between South Wales, Bristol, North Somerset, and the Exmoor Coast.

Sailings are to and from Ilfracombe, Lynmouth & Minehead. The timetable is subject to the Bristol Channel tides which have the second highest rise and fall in the world. Free copies of the full programme are available from Waverley Excursions Ltd., The Waverley Terminal, Anderston Quay, Glasgow G3 8HA www.waverleyexcursions.co.uk - telephone 0845 1304647, or from Tourist Information Centres in West Somerset and North Devon.

AIRPORTS

There are airports in or near towns close to the coast path.

In path order, they are:

Newquay Airport (for flights to and from Plymouth and flights to and from the Isles of Scilly): St Mawgan, NEWQUAY, TR8 4EQ.
Tel: 0845 7105555.

Land's End (for flights to the Isles of Scilly): Information from Isles of Scilly Travel, Steamship House, Quay Street, PENZANCE, TR18 4BZ.
Tel: 0845 7105555.

Penzance (for flights to the Isles of Scilly): British International, Eastern Green, Jelbert Way, PENZANCE, TR18 3AP.
Tel: 01736 363871

Plymouth: Plymouth City Airport, North Quay House, Sutton Harbour, PLYMOUTH. PL4 0RA. Tel: 01752 204090.

Exeter: Exeter International Airport, EXETER, EX5 2BD.
Tel: 01392 367433.

Bournemouth: Bournemouth Airport Ltd., CHRISTCHURCH, BH23 6SE.
Tel: 01202 364000.

USEFUL ADDRESSES

Countryside Agency, 2nd Floor, 11-15 Dix's Field, Exeter, EX1 1QA T: 01392 477150.
Countrywide Holidays, Miry Lane, Wigan, Lancs. WN3 4AG. T: 01942 823456; F: 01942 825034 E: countrywidewalking@shearingsholidays.co.uk
Exmoor National Park Authority, Exmoor House, Dulverton, Somerset TA22 9HL T: 01398 323665 F: 01398 323150 E: info@exmoor-nationalpark.gov.uk W: www.exmoor-nationalpark.gov.uk
HF Holidays Ltd, Imperial House, Edgware Road, Colindale, London NW9 5AL
T: 020 8905 9558 F: 0208 205 0506 E: info@hfholidays.co.uk W: www.hfholidays.co.uk
Ramblers' Association, Second Floor, Camelford House, 87-90 Albert Embankment, London, SE1 7TW T: 0207 339 8500 F: 0207 339 8501 E: ramblers@london.ramblers.org.uk
W: www.ramblers.org.uk

COUNTY COUNCILS

Somerset County Council, County Hall, Taunton, TA1 4DY (Tel: 01823 355455).
Devon County Council, County Hall, Exeter, EX2 4QW (Tel: 01392 382000).
Cornwall County Council, County Hall, Truro, TR1 3BE (Tel: 01872 322000).
Dorset County Council, County Hall, Dorchester, DT1 1XJ (Tel: 01305 251000).

Addresses of Ramblers' Association contacts in the West Country

Devon - Mrs E. M. Linfoot, 14 Bladen Cottages, Blackborough, Cullompton, EX15 2HJ. 01884 266435
Cornwall - Mrs C. James, Chy-vean, Tresillian, Truro, TR2 4BN. 01872 520368
Dorset - Mr D. Riches, 43 Wyke Road, Weymouth, DT4 9QQ. 01305 784672
Somerset - Mrs M Henry, 22 Linden Grove, Taunton, TA1 1EF. 01823 333369

MAPS

We are sometimes asked if you require a map sheet as well as a guide book and our advice is certainly yes. One does not get as badly lost on the coast path as you can on inland paths, but a map is an asset nonetheless. Furthermore many walkers derive much interest from looking at their route in relation to the rest of the countryside on ordinary walks, and the same applies just as much, if not more so, on our coast path. The National Trail Guides offer a partial solution with their maps, but even these are not as useful as a map sheet.

1:50 000 Map. Ordnance Survey

The Metric 1:50 000 Landranger Series needed to cover the coast from Minehead in Somerset to Studland in Dorset are as follows, working round the coast from Minehead.

181	Minehead & Brendon Hills	200	Newquay & Bodmin
180	Barnstaple & Ilfracombe	201	Plymouth & Launceston
190	Bude & Clovelly	202	Torbay & South Dartmoor
200	Newquay & Bodmin	192	Exeter & Sidmouth
204	Truro & Falmouth	193	Taunton & Lyme Regis
203	Land's End & The Lizard	194	Dorchester & Weymouth
204	Truro & Falmouth	195	Bournemouth & Purbeck

The two tourist 1" maps of Dartmoor and Exmoor available are of no advantage except that Exmoor could be used instead of Map 181 and nearly all 180.

1:25 000 Maps. Ordnance Survey

In path order, from Minehead the coast path on $2^1/_2$" maps.

Outdoor Leisure 9	- Exmoor
Explorer 139	- Bideford, Ilfracombe and Barnstaple
Explorer 126	- Clovelly, Hartland and Bideford
Explorer 111	- Bude, Boscastle and Tintagel
Explorer 109	- Bodmin Moor (depicts coast path from Boscastle to Portgaverne)
Explorer 106	- Newquay, Padstow, Wadebridge and Port Isaac
Explorer 104	- Redruth, St Agnes, Camborne and Perranporth
Explorer 102	- Land's End, Penzance, St Ives
Explorer 103	- The Lizard
Explorer 105	- Falmouth and Mevagissey
Explorer 107	- St Austell, Fowey and Looe
Explorer 108	- Looe, Rame Head
Outdoor Leisure 20	- Plymouth and South Devon
Explorer 110	- Torquay and Dawlish
Explorer 115	- Exmouth and Sidmouth
Explorer 116	- Lyme Regis and Bridport
Outdoor Leisure 15	- Purbeck and South Dorset

All these maps may be obtained from bookshops. They may also be obtained from KenRoy Thompson Limited, 25 Cobourg Street, Plymouth, PL1 1SR (Tel: 01752 227693) POST FREE TO UK MEMBERS OF THE SOUTH WEST COAST PATH ASSOCIATION (Credit cards accepted).

TAXIS

Coast path walking can be arduous in places but some of the hard work can be eliminated. We have been informed that the use of local taxis can ease the muscles. Transport is not for the walker, naturally, but for rucksack transfer from B&B to B&B. Local taxi firms will be pleased to give a price for the service. Consult yellow pages or ask the locals for details of taxi operators.

NATIONAL TAXI HOTLINE
Many taxi operators subscribe to the 'National Taxi Hotline' which works on a Freephone number - 0800 654321. When you dial that number your call will be automatically routed through to the subscribing taxi operator nearest to your location and you have your taxi.

MARCH 2004		
LOW WATER		
From 28th, add 1 hour for BST		
Days	Morning Time	Afternoon Time
1 Mo	0627	1908
2 Tu	0757	2031
3 We	0919	2141
4 Th	1017	2235
5 Fr	1104	2320
6 Sa	1146	------
7 Su	0001	1226
8 Mo	0041	1304
9 Tu	0117	1339
10 We	0151	1413
11 Th	0224	1445
12 Fr	0259	1520
13 Sa	0338	1601
14 Su	0427	1658
15 Mo	0544	1837
16 Tu	0749	2036
17 We	0918	2146
18 Th	1016	2238
19 Fr	1104	2323
20 Sa	1148	-----
21 Su	0005	1228
22 Mo	0044	1305
23 Tu	0119	1338
24 We	0149	1406
25 Th	0216	1430
26 Fr	0238	1451
27 Sa	0258	1510
28 Su	0320	1534
29 Mo	0357	1620
30 Tu	0537	1828
31 We	0721	1956

APRIL 2004		
LOW WATER		
add 1 hour for BST		
Days	Morning Time	Afternoon Time
1 Th	0841	2106
2 Fr	0941	2201
3 Sa	1030	2249
4 Su	1115	2333
5 Mo	1157	------
6 Tu	0014	1238
7 We	0054	1317
8 Th	0132	1353
9 Fr	0209	1429
10 Sa	0246	1506
11 Su	0328	1550
12 Mo	0422	1651
13 Tu	0544	1836
14 We	0744	2021
15 Th	0859	2123
16 Fr	0952	2213
17 Sa	1038	2257
18 Su	1120	2338
19 Mo	1159	------
20 Tu	0015	1234
21 We	0048	1305
22 Th	0118	1332
23 Fr	0143	1355
24 Sa	0206	1416
25 Su	0227	1437
26 Mo	0253	1506
27 Tu	0334	1554
28 We	0500	1748
29 Th	0644	1918
30 Fr	0757	2024

MAY 2004		
LOW WATER		
add 1 hour for BST		
Days	Morning Time	Afternoon Time
1 Sa	0857	2121
2 Su	0950	2212
3 Mo	1039	2300
4 Tu	1126	2347
5 We	------	1211
6 Th	0031	1255
7 Fr	0114	1337
8 Sa	0157	1418
9 Su	0240	1501
10 Mo	0328	1549
11 Tu	0424	1651
12 We	0540	1817
13 Th	0712	1943
14 Fr	0822	2046
15 Sa	0917	2138
16 Su	1004	2224
17 Mo	1047	2306
18 Tu	1126	2343
19 We	------	1201
20 Th	0018	1233
21 Fr	0049	1302
22 Sa	0117	1328
23 Su	0144	1355
24 Mo	0212	1423
25 Tu	0245	1458
26 We	0329	1548
27 Th	0434	1705
28 Fr	0558	1831
29 Sa	0711	1939
30 Su	0812	2039
31 Mo	0909	2135

JUNE 2004					
LOW WATER					
add 1 hour for BST					
Days	Morning Time	Afternoon Time	Days	Morning Time	Afternoon Time
1 Tu	1004	2229	16 We	1053	2313
2 We	1057	2322	17 Th	1131	2351
3 Th	1148	------	18 Fr	------	1206
4 Fr	0012	1237	19 Sa	0026	1240
5 Sa	0102	1325	20 Su	0059	1312
6 Su	0150	1412	21 Mo	0132	1344
7 Mo	0238	1458	22 Tu	0205	1418
8 Tu	0327	1547	23 We	0241	1453
9 We	0419	1639	24 Th	0320	1535
10 Th	0517	1741	25 Fr	0407	1626
11 Fr	0623	1850	26 Sa	0506	1733
12 Sa	0730	1955	27 Su	0617	1848
13 Su	0829	2053	28 Mo	0726	1958
14 Mo	0922	2145	29 Tu	0832	2103
15 Tu	1010	2232	30 We	0935	2205

JULY 2004					
LOW WATER					
add 1 hour for BST					
Days	Morning Time	Afternoon Time	Days	Morning Time	Afternoon Time
1 Th	1035	2304	16 Fr	1107	2331
2 Fr	1132	------	17 Sa	1147	------
3 Sa	0000	1226	18 Su	0010	1226
4 Su	0053	1317	19 Mo	0047	1301
5 Mo	0144	1405	20 Tu	0122	1335
6 Tu	0231	1449	21 We	0156	1408
7 We	0316	1532	22 Th	0229	1440
8 Th	0359	1614	23 Fr	0303	1514
9 Fr	0442	1659	24 Sa	0339	1554
10 Sa	0529	1751	25 Su	0423	1645
11 Su	0623	1851	26 Mo	0521	1755
12 Mo	0725	1958	27 Tu	0639	1923
13 Tu	0829	2102	28 We	0804	2043
14 We	0929	2200	29 Th	0919	2154
15 Th	1022	2249	30 Fr	1026	2257
			31 Sa	1124	2353

AUGUST 2004
LOW WATER
add 1 hour for BST

Days	Morning Time	Afternoon Time
1 Su	------	1217
2 Mo	0044	1306
3 Tu	0131	1350
4 We	0214	1430
5 Th	0254	1507
6 Fr	0329	1542
7 Sa	0403	1616
8 Su	0437	1654
9 Mo	0519	1747
10 Tu	0618	1900
11 We	0732	2021
12 Th	0852	2135
13 Fr	0958	2230
14 Sa	1048	2314
15 Su	1130	2354
16 Mo	------	1209
17 Tu	0031	1245
18 We	0106	1319
19 Th	0139	1350
20 Fr	0210	1420
21 Sa	0240	1452
22 Su	0313	1528
23 Mo	0351	1613
24 Tu	0442	1719
25 We	0603	1906
26 Th	0755	2042
27 Fr	0919	2154
28 Sa	1022	2251
29 Su	1115	2341
30 Mo	------	1203
31 Tu	0027	1247

SEPTEMBER 2004
LOW WATER
add 1 hour for BST

Days	Morning Time	Afternoon Time
1 We	0110	1327
2 Th	0149	1403
3 Fr	0223	1436
4 Sa	0253	1504
5 Su	0320	1531
6 Mo	0346	1600
7 Tu	0416	1643
8 We	0514	1808
9 Th	0647	1945
10 Fr	0821	2112
11 Sa	0934	2205
12 Su	1023	2248
13 Mo	1105	2327
14 Tu	1144	------
15 We	0005	1221
16 Th	0041	1255
17 Fr	0114	1328
18 Sa	0146	1359
19 Su	0217	1432
20 Mo	0250	1508
21 Tu	0328	1554
22 We	0419	1704
23 Th	0551	1910
24 Fr	0802	2045
25 Sa	0916	2146
26 Su	1010	2236
27 Mo	1058	2321
28 Tu	1141	------
29 We	0003	1222
30 Th	0042	1259

OCTOBER 2004
LOW WATER
until 31st, add 1 hour for BST

Days	Morning Time	Afternoon Time
1 Fr	0117	1332
2 Sa	0148	1401
3 Su	0214	1426
4 Mo	0237	1449
5 Tu	0257	1510
6 We	0317	1541
7 Th	0355	1717
8 Fr	0605	1908
9 Sa	0744	2032
10 Su	0856	2126
11 Mo	0946	2210
12 Tu	1030	2252
13 We	1111	2332
14 Th	1151	------
15 Fr	0011	1229
16 Sa	0048	1306
17 Su	0124	1341
18 Mo	0159	1418
19 Tu	0235	1459
20 We	0318	1550
21 Th	0414	1707
22 Fr	0553	1908
23 Sa	0749	2028
24 Su	0855	2123
25 Mo	0946	2211
26 Tu	1032	2254
27 We	1114	2334
28 Th	1153	------
29 Fr	0011	1229
30 Sa	0045	1301
31 Su	0113	1329

NOVEMBER 2004
LOW WATER

Days	Morning Time	Afternoon Time	Days	Morning Time	Afternoon Time
1 Mo	0139	1354	16 Tu	0149	1414
2 Tu	0201	1417	17 We	0232	1501
3 We	0222	1442	18 Th	0319	1555
4 Th	0248	1518	19 Fr	0417	1705
5 Fr	0330	1631	20 Sa	0537	1835
6 Sa	0512	1819	21 Su	0709	1950
7 Su	0654	1938	22 Mo	0817	2048
8 Mo	0805	2036	23 Tu	0912	2138
9 Tu	0900	2126	24 We	1001	2223
10 We	0949	2213	25 Th	1044	2304
11 Th	1036	2258	26 Fr	1124	2341
12 Fr	1121	2342	27 Sa	------	1201
13 Sa	------	1204	28 Su	0015	1234
14 Su	0025	1248	29 Mo	0045	1305
15 Mo	0107	1330	30 Tu	0113	1333

DECEMBER 2004
LOW WATER

Days	Morning Time	Afternoon Time	Days	Morning Time	Afternoon Time
1 We	0141	1402	16 Th	0232	1502
2 Th	0209	1433	17 Fr	0319	1551
3 Fr	0241	1511	18 Sa	0409	1644
4 Sa	0322	1604	19 Su	0504	1746
5 Su	0423	1719	20 Mo	0610	1853
6 Mo	0549	1838	21 Tu	0722	1959
7 Tu	0707	1943	22 We	0827	2058
8 We	0811	2041	23 Th	0925	2150
9 Th	0908	2136	24 Fr	1015	2236
10 Fr	1003	2228	25 Sa	1100	2316
11 Sa	1056	2320	26 Su	1140	2353
12 Su	1146	------	27 Mo	------	1217
13 Mo	0009	1236	28 Tu	0027	1251
14 Tu	0058	1325	29 We	0100	1323
15 We	0145	1414	30 Th	0132	1355
			31 Fr	0203	1427

We think it a grand scheme. It is free so no worries about having the appropriate coins when you are tired, wet through and fed up. You may find that your mobile phone cannot make contact with the hotline: our experiments show that some can and some cannot.

BANKS

We suggest you contact your own bank for a list of where their branches along the trail are located. Probably a Girobank account or Post Office National Savings account would prove to be the most convenient as there are small Post Offices in most villages. Overseas visitors, we suggest, will find their cashpoint cards very useful.

TELEPHONES

We urge you to consider buying BT Phonecards or BT Chargecards. Life is easier when you do not have to seek change for a call box.

MOBILE PHONES

These are always useful to have whilst on the coast path. However, do not rely on them as coverage is not always good in the South West. You may also have difficulty in obtaining top-up cards in some areas.

ORGANISED WALKING HOLIDAYS

We have compiled a list of organisations that run either self-guided or guided coast path holidays. Some also provide baggage transfer services. For a copy of this list please write to the Administrator and enclose £1.50 to cover printing, postage and administration time.

RIVER CROSSINGS

The walker tends to view that feet are the only certain method of progress - and why not? Unfortunately, the absolute purist would need to be an olympic-class swimmer not to have to use ferries on the South West Coast Path. However, a certain amount of scepticism is helpful, absolute reliance on ferries is not advised.

There are other ferries available on the path which walkers may wish to use for diversions or shortcuts. We have attempted to list those directly necessary.

Tide Tables (see pages 19 and 20)

The tide tables included in this edition refer to the times of low water at Devonport. These tables will act as a guide for those wishing to paddle across the Gannel (Newquay), Gillan Creek, and the Erme and Avon (Bigbury-on-Sea). Please be sure to read the warnings given under each section. We have been criticised for being too cautious over the times we suggest for wading the rivers, and know that some walkers cross at other times. We believe our attitude is correct as there certainly are dangers, but you may wish to try at low tide on other occasions to see if conditions will permit a safe crossing. Variations in barometric pressure can affect tide levels. Remember there are different levels daily of low water; if in doubt seek local knowledge.

Newquay (The Gannel)	Deduct 30 minutes	Gillan Harbour	Deduct 15 minutes
R. Erme	As at Devonport	Bigbury/Bantham (R.Avon)	As at Devonport

DOGS

1. Beaches

For many years most district councils and unitary authorities have implemented dog bans on beaches generally from 1st May to 31st October. Our Association and most of the general public regard this as a sensible measure.

There are several sections of the South West Coast Path that cross beaches and are officially marked as such. These beaches are Croyde Bay in Devon, Harlyn Bay, Constantine, Treyarnon and Perranporth in Cornwall, and Studland in Dorset.

The routing of the coast path (with its designation as a National Trail) across these beaches means that they are public rights of way. Our enquiries reveal that a public right of way DOES carry precedence over seasonal regulations banning dogs, and ultimately any walker in the process of walking along, but not stopping on, these sections of the path may be accompanied by a dog under TOTAL control.

However we strongly recommend the following:-
a) If an alternative route is provided and signposted, that you use it.
b) That residents near to dog ban beaches use other walks and do not use the beach path during the ban period.
c) Total control means that the dog should be on a short (not extendable) lead.
d) That your progress should be as unobtrusive as possible to other beach users. To aid this, close attention should be paid to the actual route marked on the map.
e) Lastly, but most importantly that, should the worst happen, any dog mess MUST be removed from the beach.

2. Along the coast path

Many walk the coast path with their dogs and all have an enjoyable time. We receive many reports of not only humans but dogs completing the whole path.

However we do urge caution because the coast path is very high along many sections and it takes only an excited dog to go chasing after a rabbit, thus causing much grief if it goes over the edge.

If your dog is well-trained and you can trust it, then please enjoy your coast path walk with your four-legged friend. If it is not and you cannot, then do take care.

Many sections along the South West Coast Path will have farm livestock grazing. Again, walkers should maintain proper control of their dogs.

SUGGESTED ITINERARY

For some the fun of planning their own itinerary is a major part of the enjoyment of their holiday. If you are one of these, DO NOT READ THIS SECTION.

On the other hand there are some who have been put off tackling our path because they just could not see how to pack 630 miles' (1014 km) walking into a normal holiday. The answer is, of course, you cannot. Our path, we reckon, needs about eight weeks to accomplish. That being so, we have tried to divide it up sensibly into eight roughly equal sections. Obviously, if we are going to suggest weekly stages, the beginning and end of each one must have reasonable accommodation and public transport. That presents a problem in itself, so after some thought we have broken it down into four 7-day and four 6-day weeks. Obviously not everybody will take a day off per week on their walk. That being the case, some will find they progress further along the coast path than our suggested itinerary. As usual, we would be very glad to hear from anyone who has tried one of our weeks and to hear their comments on it.

If you are a seasoned walker then there is a lot to be said for walking the whole path, albeit at different times, in our usual anticlockwise order. However, if you are not experienced, then obviously we should point out that the North Cornwall week, the third one in our schedule, is much the easiest if you want to start with something less demanding.

To keep the weeks set out below in a simple format the information is only an outline. IT IS ESSENTIAL TO CONSULT THE DETAIL IN THE REST OF THE GUIDE TO EFFECTIVELY PLAN YOUR HOLIDAY. Distances can vary depending on where you actually stay. Furthermore, our distances are only approximate because they are all 'rounded'.

After some of the place names we have added 'River Crossing'. You are advised to consult the appropriate section in this book for ferry and low tide suggestions.

Kilometres	Miles	Week 1 (Seven days)	
		MINEHEAD Rail Services to Taunton & S. National to Minehead Direct Nat. Express coach services.	
15	10	PORLOCK WEIR	
20	12	LYNMOUTH/LYNTON	
21	13	COMBE MARTIN	
20	13	WOOLACOMBE	
27	16	BRAUNTON	
20	12	INSTOW	
18	11	WESTWARD HO! (via Bideford) Filers/Red Bus to Barnstaple & Rail services to Exeter. Direct Nat. Express coach services.	
141	87		
		Week 2 (Seven days)	
		WESTWARD HO! Rail services to Barnstaple & Filers/Red Bus to Westward Ho! Direct Nat. Express coach services	
18	11	CLOVELLY	
16	10	HARTLAND QUAY	
25	15	BUDE	
16	10	CRACKINGTON HAVEN	
18	11	TINTAGEL	
15	9	PORT ISAAC	
19	12	PADSTOW (River Crossing) First Western National bus to Bodmin Parkway Railway Station (Great Western Main Line)	
127	78		
		Week 3 (Six days)	
		PADSTOW Rail services to Bodmin Parkway (Great Western Main Line). First Western National Bus to Padstow	
22	14	PORTHCOTHAN	
18	11	NEWQUAY (River Crossing)	
18	11	PERRANPORTH	
20	12	PORTREATH	
20	12	HAYLE	
9	6	ST IVES Numerous bus services or rail service to St Erth (Great Western Main Line)	
107	66		
		Week 4 (Six days)	
		ST IVES Numerous bus services or rail service from St Erth (Great Western Main Line)	
22	14	PENDEEN	
15	9	SENNEN COVE	
19	12	LAMORNA	
15	9	MARAZION	
17	11	PORTHLEVEN	
22	13	LIZARD TOWN Truronian bus service to Truro Railway Station (Great Western Main Line)	
110	69		

Kilometres	Miles	
		Week 5 (Six days)
		LIZARD TOWN Rail service to Truro (Great Western Main Line)
		Truronian bus service.
17	11	COVERACK
21	13	HELFORD (River Crossing)
16	10	FALMOUTH (River Crossing)
22	14	PORTLOE
20	12	MEVAGISSEY
19	12	PAR Rail services (Great Western Main Line)
115	72	
		Week 6 (Seven days)
		PAR Rail services (Great Western Main Line)
21	13	POLPERRO
20	12	PORTWRINKLE
21	13	PLYMOUTH (River Crossing)
24	15	WEMBURY POINT (River Crossing)
22	14	BIGBURY-ON-SEA (River Crossing)
22	14	SALCOMBE
21	13	TORCROSS First Western National service Dartmouth -
		Kingsbridge - Plymouth
151	94	
		Week 7 (Six days)
		TORCROSS First Western National service Plymouth -
		Kingsbridge - Dartmouth
16	10	DARTMOUTH (River Crossing)
17	11	BRIXHAM
17	11	BABBACOMBE
27	16	EXMOUTH (via Starcross/Exmouth Ferry)
21	13	SIDMOUTH
17	11	SEATON Bus services to Sidmouth, Lyme Regis, Honiton
		and Exeter
115	72	
		Week 8 (Seven days)
		SEATON Bus services from Exeter, Honiton, Lyme Regis
		and Sidmouth
23	14	SEATOWN (Dorset)
19	12	ABBOTSBURY
17	11	FERRY BRIDGE (Wyke Regis)
21	13	ISLE OF PORTLAND
23	14	LULWORTH
23	14	WORTH MATRAVERS *
22	14	SOUTH HAVEN POINT Ferry-Sandbanks, Wilts & Dorset to Poole
		or Bournemouth & Rail services Nat.
		Express coach services from Bournemouth
		to London
148	92	

* See pages 88 & 89 for opening times of Army Ranges and alternative routes.

THE SOUTH WEST COAST PATH

General

This is a series of notes on the state of the path which we hope will help you in your walking. Obviously it is very difficult to keep something as extensive as this both up-to-date and concise. Suggestions for improvement or amendments will always be welcome. We can only keep you right up-to-date with the state of the path if YOU will keep us posted about conditions as you find them on any stretch of the path. Your fellow members will be grateful, and so will we.

If you have any complaints about ordinary maintenance or signposting on the path, please write either to the Exmoor National Park Authority or the relevant County Council, Devon, Cornwall or Dorset. They should see this is done, and what is generally not realised is that any work carried out is 75% grant aided from the Countryside Agency for official National Trails such as the South West Coast Path. If you have any major problems or difficulties we would always be glad to be advised as well.

Each section has a reference to the Ordnance Survey map relevant to it - Outdoor Leisure (OS OL) and Explorer (OS E).

Towns and villages are now marked T or V respectively but the places at the end of each section appear as the first entry in the next one. We obviously stick our necks out to try and classify towns and villages. To us a town should have a reasonable range of shops, maybe even something as exotic as a laundrette. Villages should at least have a pub and a village store open all the year round, and a bus service. There are, of course, numerous other places you can get refreshment in season, but precious few out of it. Please note that all sections end at reasonable access points, usually having parking facilities.

Places which can be reached by rail are marked.

Distances

The South West Coast Path Team's 1999/2000 survey using a Global Positioning System revealed that the total length of the South West Coast Path, including the Isle of Portland, is 630 miles (1014 km).

The section distances are shown in four columns.

The first - distance of the section in kilometres
The second - cumulative distance in kilometres
The third - distance of the section in miles
The fourth - cumulative distance in miles

The distances are measured along the officially designated route of the coast path, not along any diversions we suggest offering more scenic experiences than the route installed by the authorities.

Grading

Each section is graded as Easy, Moderate, Strenuous or Severe. Please note we no longer take into consideration lack of escape routes, distances from public transport, etc; it is purely a question of physical difficulty. We will try to highlight in the sections other considerations when they apply.

We would like to underline one point; the whole of our path is certainly not easy. Some parts of it are but other parts are not. We have had a number of letters from people who have walked The Pennine Way and who have been literally amazed at the severity of some of our tougher sections. Perhaps as a further comment we may add that recently we walked two 6 mile (10 km) adjacent sections. The time taken for one was 50% more than the time taken for the other. This may give additional emphasis to the importance of studying terrain if you wish to compute time.

Section Timing

We have introduced estimated timings for those wanting to know approximately how long each section may take to walk.

We consider these times to be a fair average. There are those who will complete sections quicker or slower than our estimations. We have NOT allowed for refreshment stops or for looking at views. However, it is important to remember that many factors can influence the speed at which you walk, e.g. weather, the amount of gear carried, an unexpected diversion etc., and you should always allow adequate time for your walk, especially if you are relying on public transport at the end of your walk.

These timings relate to the official route of the South West Coast Path only, and not to any of our suggested alternatives.

WEB SITE NEWS

Any news concerning the state of the coast path received after this book is printed will be published in newsletters and on our web site www.swcp.org.uk

THE REVERSE GUIDE - POOLE TO MINEHEAD

The Association has written a description of the Trail for those walking in the Poole to Minehead direction. It deals only with the path so this Annual Guide will be necessary for all the other information. Our Reverse Guide supplement was comprehensively revised in 2002, and is available from the Administrator at £3.50 including postage.

THE TRAIL DESCRIPTION - Minehead to Poole

FOLLOW THE NATIONAL TRAIL WAYMARK (THE ACORN SYMBOL)
CAUTION

Our literature generally describes the walked and maintained route of the National Trail known as the South West Coast Path. Along its whole length the managing authorities mentioned below have a duty to maintain the path. Walkers should be warned – using out-of-date Association books could prove risky. Things change over the years including the actual route of the South West Coast Path.

Where you find we have little to say about the route we consider that it is highly unlikely that the walker will run the risk of going astray.

Those who set forth upon this beautiful trail must remember it is mainly a cliff top path - in places it can be a very high cliff top. Those who manage the coast path want to keep it safe but we remind walkers that it is unwise to leave the path at any point on the seaward side. We are not responsible for the maintenance of the cliff tops themselves which can be unstable and extremely unsafe.

Now and again we suggest an alternative path away from the officially designated route. This will be for a more scenic and enjoyable experience.

These alternative, recommended paths follow rights of way and in a few instances 'permissive routes' which are maintained by the landowner.

THIS ASSOCIATION STRESSES THAT ALL PERSONS USING THE PATH SHOULD NOT WANDER OFF IT, ESPECIALLY ON THE SEAWARD SIDE, AS TO DO SO WOULD BE PUTTING YOURSELF AND POSSIBLY OTHERS IN GRAVE DANGER OF SEVERE PERSONAL INJURY OR EVEN DEATH.

MANAGEMENT OF THE SOUTH WEST COAST PATH

The management of the 630 miles of the coast path is the responsibility of;-
The County Councils of Devon, Cornwall and Dorset
The City Council of Plymouth
The Borough of Torbay
Exmoor National Park and
The National Trust Regions of Devon/Cornwall and Wessex

The Countryside Agency has overall responsibilities and provides much of the funding.

The South West Coast Path Association has, over the past 31 years, been the premier information source for those wanting to walk the coast path. Over those years it has been the 'user' organisation and, we like to think, has been responsible, by persistent lobbying, for the enjoyable experience it is to walk it today.

IMPORTANT - PLEASE NOTE

Information included or available through the South West Coast Path Association (SWCPA) is given in good faith and is believed to be accurate and correct at the time of going to print - however it cannot be guaranteed not to include inaccuracies or typographical errors.

Advice received via the SWCPA should not be relied upon for personal decisions and you should take into account the weather and your own capabilities before following the walks set out in this Guide. It is for the individual concerned to weigh up the risks of each of the walks described in this book.

The SWCPA makes no representations about the suitability of walks to any one person and will accept no liability for any loss or damage suffered as a result of relying on this book: it should be used for guidance only.

In no event shall the SWCPA be liable for any personal injury or any loss suffered as a result of using this publication.

---

1 | Minehead to Porlock Weir (Car Park)   OS OL9 (T) Minehead

---

Grading: Official Route - Moderate   Distance -   15.3   15.3   9.5   9.5
Alternative - Strenuous

Timing: 4.5 hours

See also our Minehead to Porlock Weir Path Description.

The South West Coast Path starts from Quay Steps, 100 yards (91 m) or so beyond the Red Lion Hotel. This is opposite the celebratory marker on the sea front of a pair of hands holding a map. This was sculpted by Owen Cunningham to the design of local art student Sarah Ward, and was opened on 14th February, 2001. The construction of this striking piece of art was managed by the South West Coast Path Team and part funded by donations from our South West Coast Path Association members.

You cross the road and walk between two cottages on the sea front.

The official route, although a good moorland walk, does not follow the traditional coastal route. Strong walkers looking for something better can start at the westerly end of the sea front road, proceed via Greenaleigh Farm to Burgundy Chapel and then make a steep ascent up North Hill. An easier alternative to this first piece is at Greenaleigh Farm, immediately before the house and the signpost 'To Burgundy Chapel and Beach' to fork left and then turn back, signposted 'North Hill'. This path zigzags back to pick up the official route, so avoiding the steep climb after Burgundy Chapel.

When taking the steep ascent from Burgundy Chapel at the T-junction go left - the path to the right goes only to a view point - and at the next junction go forward.

When you have gained the summit of North Hill, there is an acorn sign pointing to Selworthy and Bossington. Follow the line of this until you come to the next coast path sign, where there is a right fork marked 'Rugged Cliff Top Path'. Ordinary walkers should proceed forward on the official route but the more adventurous can fork right and proceed, walking seaward by what is a well-defined path.

Alternative - Rugged Coast Path

Please do not be put off by the description of the path as 'Rugged' – it is a splendid alternative and not difficult, and will give you much better views than the official coast path. It is well marked, but there are signs prohibiting dogs.

At the stile with a National Trust information board, you must take the left fork towards a bench, then continue downhill to take the lower path by a 'Rugged Path' signpost, which takes you down into Grexy Combe at 937 481. From here take the well-defined diagonal path leading up the hill to the wall which is the National Trust boundary. This wall can be followed towards the sea at first and then along parallel to the sea all the way to Western Brockholes. After Western Brockholes the path bears inland, but is well signposted and rejoins the official path behind Hurlstone Point. (If you take this route you should add an extra hour plus to your walk.)

Coast path continues

Those who have taken the official route, when reaching Bossington Hill should take the definitive right of way which goes down Hurlstone Combe. There is a much more spectacular route around Hurlstone Point which can be used apart from gale force conditions. If you stay on the official path, take care to descend the path to the left of Hurlstone Point and do not be tempted to take the more obvious path to the left (no signpost) contouring round Bossington Hill.

The official path goes inland from Hurlstone Point to Bossington village and then out to sea again. The original coast path then followed the path behind the beach to Porlock Weir but this is not now possible for safety reasons as high storms have caused a wide breach in the pebble ridge and a deep and dangerous impassable gully has been formed.

Thanks to the landowners and the Exmoor National Park there are now several alternative routes to Porlock Weir. Eventually you come to a sign indicating the coast path via Porlock to Porlock Weir or direct across the Marsh to Porlock Weir. You can take your pick but beware of high tides on the marsh route – check BEFORE you make your decision, otherwise you may have to retrace your steps: for tide information, please refer to local tide tables at Minehead - the TIC is a good source (see page xx). DO NOT use the Devonport tide table published in this book.

PORLOCK ROUTE: You can turn left on the track down to Bossington beach from the village and this will take you into Porlock. If you take this path then you need to leave the village on the Toll Road past the Village Hall – do not take the road signposted Porlock Weir. Just up the Toll Road you bear right on a footpath that takes you behind West Porlock to Porlock Weir.

MARSH ROUTE: A much better route takes you down to the beach turning left as far as the lime kiln. Here you bear left across the field, over a stile and then turn right following the path across the back of the Marsh.

From April to June you will have to take a diversion to allow birds to nest in peace. After the stile you will have to continue forward to pick up a new permissive path that eventually joins up with the path described above. Maps have been provided at various points to show these paths.

| 2 | Porlock Weir to Lynmouth (Visitor Centre) | OS OL9 |

| Grading: Moderate | Distance - | 19.8 | 35.1 | 12.3 | 21.8 |

Timing: 5.5 hours

See also our Porlock Weir to Lynmouth Path Description

The official path is signposted to the left of the Anchor Hotel but you can go in front of the hotel, past the craft shops and then turn left signposted to Culbone.

This path is well marked. At Culbone turn right if you want to visit the small church. There is also a refreshment hut where you help yourself and leave your payment. From the church, retrace your steps up the path and turn right onto the coast path; in about 300 yards (275 m) turn right into Culbone and Embelle Woods and on into Yenworthy Woods. The official coast path continues to your left uphill, but the path through Culbone Woods is an excellent and less tiring route, but take note of the warnings about landslips.

BEN'S PATH DIVERSION: When you get to Yenworthy Combe there is a sign to the Pinetum, where there is a pleasant diversion. There are some unusually mature examples of trees planted between 1840 and 1860 and several are over 100 feet tall. There is also a trout pond off the stream and an icehouse which was cut into the cool, shaded bank of the stream. A tunnel leads to a deep cemented pit which was sealed by two tightly fitting doors to hold ice throughout the year for use in the kitchens before electricity.

PINETUM DIVERSION: At the end of the Pinetum is a new permissive path through woods that has been opened up called 'Ben's Path' south of Home Farm that rejoins the coast path. Before you get on to Ben's Path you may like to go to Glenthorne Beach. You will see the remains of a jetty, which was built to land heavy building materials for the estate when overland routes were impractical. There is also the remains of a boathouse, coal store and lime kiln. The limestone and coal were brought over from South Wales.

Coast path continues

Proceed to Sister's Fountain, where there is a legend that Jesus drank here with Joseph of Arimathea on his way to Glastonbury. Continue uphill through a pair of wild boar head gateposts, which was the entrance to the Victorian Woodland Lodge, which usually has barking Jack Russell dogs in its garden - take care not to miss the narrow signposted path as the drive bears left.

At Coddow Combe, the official route is again signposted inland 'Countisbury 1.5 miles'. The surefooted might prefer the right of way signposted 'Lighthouse' which proceeds out to the Foreland Point Lighthouse. Just before the entrance to the lighthouse where the wall commences on the right, the path takes off up the bank to the left. The beginning is clearly marked because the authorities tell you they no longer maintain the path. This path is more exposed than the official route and careful walking is advised. It has magnificent views if you are surefooted and the weather is calm.

The National Trust has a good path which can be taken down the seaward side of the main A39 coastal road so avoiding the upper reaches of Countisbury Hill. Lower down the hill the path joins the road but a new path on the seaward side ensures that you will not get run down.

You come out on the foreshore. Walk along into Lynmouth crossing the footbridge, and there turn right down to the sea front turning left up the steps before the cliff railway, that is assuming you are a purist and not actually going to use the railway which you can well do if you wish! If you use the railway you do suffer slightly at the top in that you will have to walk nearly into Lynton and then out again to regain the North Walk. After all, it serves you right for not having walked the whole way!

It is interesting to know that at Lynmouth you can now walk Devon's coast to coast route by using the Two Moors Way to Ivybridge then the Erme Valley Trail which links into the Erme - Plym Trail to Plymouth. Guide books to the above are available from Lynton TIC (see page ???).

---

3   Lynmouth to Combe Martin (Car Park)   OS OL9 (T) Lynton/Lynmouth

---

Grading: Strenuous   Distance -   21.4   56.5   13.3   35.1

Timing: 7 hours

See also our Lynmouth to Ilfracombe Path Description.

Please note there is a long, lonely section onward from Heddon's Mouth to Combe Martin without any chance of refreshment.

The path itself out from Lynton is a Victorian idea for a coastal footpath called the North Walk and although to our modern ideas, tarmac might not be the ideal footpath medium, it is a very fine high level walk indeed. This takes you very happily out to Castle Rock.

There are diversions which will save you some road walking. The first takes off to the right after the turning circle (roundabout) at the end of the Valley of Rocks and then goes in a loop back, to come out by the Lodge at the beginning of Lee Abbey. The second alternative is a left turn immediately opposite Lee Abbey which is labelled 'Woodland Walk' (each end) and rejoins the road about 0.75 mile (1200 m) further along.

If you do not follow the 'Woodland Walk' but follow the road past the toll house and refreshment stop (seasonal), you will climb up a hill and come across a new footpath on your right, that goes along the field edge to Crock Point and through the woods at Crock Pits. This is an excellent addition to the coast path, taking you off a busy road, with some stunning coastal walks, and we thank the Exmoor Park Authority for making this possible.

This is one of the finest pieces of coast path in North Devon and should not be missed by anyone who is reasonably surefooted, or unless weather conditions are very bad. The path takes off just before the Woody Bay Hotel opposite the Red House and the beginning of the path is marked by a signpost on the right which says 'Public Footpath to Woody Bay Beach 0.75 mile'. This path comes out on another road where you turn up left. There will be another sign 'Footpath Hunter's Inn 2.25 miles'. You will cross a stile with a sign 'Heddon Valley Hunter's Inn'. This is a superb path which is now the new official route. It is much nearer the coast giving splendid views. When the path reaches the Heddon Valley path, the official route is as follows. Continue ahead/left towards Hunter's Inn. On reaching the stone bridge over the Heddon River on your right, cross it, pass through the gate and on reaching the next path across turn hard left. Continue for 100 yards (91 m) or so to the signpost on the right to Combe Martin.

Alternative Route
For a very pleasant alternative down to the beach and restored lime kiln follow these directions. Turn hard right and walk down by the river to Heddon's Mouth, crossing the bridge by the picnic area. Carry on to the beach and the lime kiln. Return to the picnic area by the bridge and continue through the picnic area, keeping the river on your left. In a while ignore the path going down on your left. Pass through the gate and continue for 100 yards (91 m) or so to the signpost on the right to Combe Martin.

Coast path continues
Whichever route you have taken, continue as follows. Follow this path up to the right, through the gate and on up; there are seats on the way up! Continue up the path and various steps and on reaching the few steps near the top, carry on round to your right, where the path now levels off. More lovely views of the Heddon Valley open up. Carry on round the headland at Peter Rock (beware if windy) and along the coast path for a good 0.5 mile (800 m) until you start heading inland and reach the path going across you by the stone wall, with the coast path sign up to your left. Whilst in the valley of Heddon's Mouth, those requiring refreshment have easy access to the Hunter's Inn and the National Trust shop selling very good ice cream.

Just west of East Cleave you will regain the old official route passing along High Cliff and North Cleave. At map reference 628 482 take the short walk across open heathland to avoid the walk up to the old Trentishoe Down Road.

As there are many sheep tracks by Sherrycombe, we suggest you follow the grass track along the top of the combe to the inland end of it to pick up the path down.

When ascending Great Hangman from Sherrycombe you reach a seat. Keep alongside the wall on your left. There is a number of well-walked paths going out to the right but they are all wrong! From Great Hangman the path is clear to Little Hangman where more stunning views are available.

When you come to the shelter above Combe Martin, turn right on the unmarked path; this has the better views.

---

4 | Combe Martin to Ilfracombe (Harbour)   OS OL9 (T) Combe Martin

---

Grading: Moderate, Strenuous in parts   Distance-   8.6   65.1   5.3   40.4

Timing: 2.5 hours

See also our Lynmouth to Ilfracombe Path Description.

The path leaves the lime kiln car park, passing the Exmoor National Park Visitor centre; fork right and join the A399 road. Turn right (Seaside Hill Road) above the beach. Turn right onto a narrow tarmac lane, which climbs steeply to rejoin the A399 road.

Walk on the slightly raised path along the road side through two gates. Having gone along a path beside a field to the flight of steps, you should turn left up the newish slip road back to the main road and to the brow, passing the bus shelter. You then turn right to follow the road down to the old main road with a bus shelter over to the right, which is now used as an information point for the Heritage Coast. Here you turn left beside the entrance to the Sandy Cove Hotel to follow a track towards Watermouth Cove.

Watermouth Castle, built 1825, comes into view. At Watermouth it is possible to cross the foreshore at low tide to a flight of steps; take care as the rocks can be slippery. This is not possible at high tide when one has to continue along the road with no pavement for approximately 200 yards (185 m) and there is then a stile off right into the woods. Take care whilst walking this road section.

The next section of the path is very pleasant on the western side of Watermouth and continues out and around Widmouth Head. This section provides some very spectacular walking; we particularly commend the view back from Widmouth Head over Watermouth, whatever the state of the tide or sea. This will be your last good viewpoint of the dramatic setting of the Great Hangman and the Little Hangman eastwards above Combe Martin. After Widmouth Head the path continues in front of the coastguard cottages going to Rillage Point.

This fine section ends with a road walk down into Hele. Turn right and look out for some steps on the far left of the beach. The path then zigzags passing Beacon Point with a fine view of Ilfracombe, until it reaches the top of Hillsborough. There are several paths to choose from here but they all end up in Ilfracombe. We have asked for an additional waymark to route you onto the harbour road.

5 | Ilfracombe to Lee Bay   OS E139 (T) Ilfracombe

Grading: Easy to moderate   Distance-   5.3   70.4   3.3   43.7

Timing: 1.5 hours

See also our Ilfracombe to Croyde Bay Path Description.

Walk along the edge of the harbour, bear left at the slip and then right into Broad Street. At a T-junction, turn left into Capstone Road next to the Sandpiper Inn. Continue ahead along a path on the landward side of Capstone Hill so avoiding a long walk back from a path closure at Capstone Point. Then take the flight of steps that goes up the back of the Landmark Theatre. Follow this path up to the top of the gardens and the gate by a shelter. Pass through this gate and bear right to walk along Granville road, before bearing right onto an unmetalled road which takes you to the Torrs Walk: it is well waymarked.

At the top of the Torrs Walk bear right and follow the path down the field to the stile in the corner. Continue ahead around the hill and beware of the steep drop on your right, to the stile. Now cross the field to the old coach road ahead, bearing right onto it and follow it all the way to Flat Point. Along Flat Point the coast path follows the route of the old coach road. (Flat Point is National Trust land with its open access policy, and it can be roamed at your own risk and offers good sites for picnic stops.) Passing through a field gate your route is along a narrow, pleasant road down into Lee.

Refreshments are available all year round at the Grampus Inn in Lee village, which is only a minor diversion from the coast.

6 | Lee Bay to Woolacombe   OS E139 (V) Lee Bay

Grading: Strenuous, becoming easy   Distance -   6.4   76.8   4.0   47.7

Timing: 2 hours

See also our Ilfracombe to Croyde Bay Path Description.

This section will take you longer to walk than you think as it includes some up and down work but is a lovely piece of path to walk.

Proceed up the road from Lee, turn right onto a path by the National Trust sign 'Damage Cliff'. To the left of the path are the remains of a pre war golf course. Before Bull Point the path crosses two steep valleys, Hilly Mouth and Bennets Water. The lighthouse is one of the few manned stations left in the country. Rockham has a fine stretch of sand that is very popular in the summer. Morte Point is a spectacular jagged slate ridge rather like a dinosaur's back emerging from the sea. Offshore is the often submerged Morte Stone and this 'Rock of Death' was aptly named in the last century. At certain states of the tide an awesome tidal race can be seen; many ships have been wrecked off here.

7 | Woolacombe to Croyde Bay (Beach)   OS E139 (T) Woolacombe

Grading: Moderate   Distance -   10.2   87.0   6.3   54.0

Timing: 3 hours

See also our Ilfracombe to Croyde Bay Path Description.

This section starts at the Waterfall Hotel and runs parallel to the Esplanade road, then turns up Chalacombe road. This is now waymarked but a vital waymark has been removed to indicate where the route turns off the road into the warren. The path is about where the National Trust sign has been placed. The official route stays in the Warren; the alignment shown on 139 OS Explorer map is incorrect.

This section starts rather poorly along the road south from Woolacombe and the path tries hard to lose itself in the enormous dunes. Waymarking, however, has been improved and you should not go astray. A possible alternative is to walk the Marine Drive which gives fine views. If the tide is out it is easier to walk Woolacombe Beach but it should not be attempted on a flood tide as you may not be able to get off the beach at Vention.

If you have used the official path, it leaves the Warren by a set of steep steps. At the top turn right and after 500 yards (460 m) a path leaves the official route; this takes you down to a car park (refreshments and toilets). Pass to the left of the caravan site, over a stile and up the cliff slope to rejoin the official route to Baggy Point.

The high level path out to Baggy Point is pleasant. If the visibility is good you will get a good chance as you turn the corner to look at the path for a number of miles ahead across Bideford Bay. At Baggy Point itself, when you have turned the corner, do bear right on to the lower path; it is no further and provides much better sea views.

Passing the National Trust car park, there is a road walk of about 545 yards (500 m) before the turn off to the beach. Do not be tempted to use the first slipway as it would be very difficult walking over the rocks.

8 | Croyde Bay to Barnstaple (Long Bridge) OS E139 (V) Croyde

Grading: Easy   Distance -   23.1   110.1   14.4   68.4

Timing: 5.25 hours

See also our Croyde Bay to Barnstaple Path Description.

Distances are measured walking via Crow Point, and around Horsey Island, through Velator to join the disused railway track all the way to Barnstaple.

The path crosses the top of Croyde beach, and on to the low cliffs at Down End, turns left and after reaching the old coastguard lookout, one has to cross the main B3231 road. This is a very busy road so take great care as you cross over the road which has to be done at this point. Walkers are advised NOT to take dogs onto this beach between May and September.

Turn left and walk downhill a short way to reach some stone steps. After a short climb, the path contours round Saunton Down, parallel to and above the road.

From this path there are some spectacular views down the length of Saunton Sands, and if clear, across the estuary to Appledore. On the hillside to the left some ancient cultivation terraces can be seen. The path ends on the road opposite the hotel. This large flat-roofed building is the five-star Saunton Sands Hotel owned by the Brend family. Wonderful food; they welcome all, including walkers.

At this point you are confronted with three routes from which to choose:-

1. *The official route* crosses the B3231 road and passes around the hotel and descends to the large Saunton Sands car park. (The refreshment hut is open from Easter to the end of September.)

    Continue in an easterly direction across the car park and pick up a sandy lane near some holiday chalets. At the end of this lane you return to the B3231 road (some coast path!)

    Take care as there is 400 yards (365m) of that road to walk along. You pass the driveway into Saunton Golf Club then turn right at the red brick house; it is signed. From here on a new route is being installed - that too will be signed.

2. This route does not involve crossing the B3231. At the bottom of the slope, before the road, opposite the Saunton Sands Hotel, turn left onto a public footpath. You climb steeply with the path bearing right. It passes near to Saunton Court and continues on to the B3231 road opposite the red brick house. After crossing the road, you then follow the official route as described in Option 1 above.

    This diversion eliminates 400 yards (365 m) of very dangerous road walking. The Northern Devon Coast and Countryside Service suggests this route and we have asked for signs to be installed.

3. This third choice is probably the one preferred by most walkers. Cross over the B3231. Pass around the Saunton Sands Hotel and descend to the large car park. Walk south along the beach via Airy Point to Crow Point. After 3.5 miles (5.5 km) along the beach, just after the

groyne watch out for a slatted wooden catwalk on your left. This is your beach exit so walk along this to Broad Sands. As you do so you will have regained the official route.

The official route after options 1 and 2 now enters the Braunton Burrows nature reserve.

These burrows are renowned for their great wealth and diversity of their plant life, and over 400 species of flowering plants have been recorded here.

When the Burrows car park is reached (options 1 and 2) the path uses the so-called American road to Broad Sands.

Arriving at Broad Sands, either by the Burrows walk or the beach walk (Option 3), the path becomes a little vague, but keep the estuary on your right hand side and you cannot go wrong. Head for the white cottage on the estuary side.
The route now follows the estuary side on top of the Great Sea Bank. The path keeps to the top of this sea wall all the way to Velator. If you wish to visit Braunton turn left at Velator and walk along the old railway track into the village.

From Velator the route now follows the old Barnstaple to Ilfracombe railway track into Barnstaple: the railway was closed in 1970.

In the summer months, the walker will have a problem on this section of the path, as not only is it the South West Coast Path, but it is also a cycle track used by many hundreds of cyclists. Few bikes seem to have any audible means of warning you of their approach, so walking can become very hazardous. After leaving Velator you will pass the old railway station at Wrafton and after about 1 mile (1500 m) the path suddenly emerges onto the estuary side. When the tide is high it presents a very fine picture and in the winter months there are many ducks and waders to observe.

After Heanton Court, a possible stop for refreshments, continue following the old railway track which follows the banks of the estuary to Barnstaple. Cross the River Yeo bridge and continue along beside the wharf towards the old Long Bridge over the river in Barnstaple.

 9 **Barnstaple to Westward Ho! (Amusement Arcade)**
OS E139 & OS E126 (T) Barnstaple (Trains); (T) Bideford

Grading: Easy   Distance -   30.7   140.8   19.1   87.5

Timing: 7 hours

See also our Barnstaple to Westward Ho! Path Description.

Distances are measured walking through to Bideford: approximately 6 miles (10 km) can be avoided by using the Instow to Appledore Ferry, but this is seasonal and subject to the tide.

Having passed the old Barnstaple railway station, you soon pass a new recreation area with seating, a good spot for a break. Continue along beside the river to the Long Bridge and take the steps up to the left which bring you onto the bridge. Cross the bridge - there is no need to cross the road. On the other side of the bridge pass the Leaderflush/Shapland works on your right and then turn right by the roundabout. Follow this road and when it bears right, cross over to pick up the path ahead behind the houses. Follow this to where it joins the Tarka Trail by the old railway bridge, bearing right along the old railway track. There is a seasonal café at Fremington Quay in the former railway station: for further information, please see www.fremingtonquaycafe.co.uk Again be aware of cyclists as you follow this all the way to Instow where there is the option of using the ferry, tides and weather conditions permitting. However, remember the official route of the South West Coast Path is in to Bideford.

Contact Mr Ommanney   End of May to September inclusive 7 days per week - every 15 mins
The Sea Chest   Tidal - Approximately two hours each side of high water
Market Street
Appledore EX39 1PW
Tel: 01237 476191

We urge you to contact the ferry operator direct if you are relying on this service, particularly if you are anticipating a fairly late finish and need to confirm the time of its last run. It may also be possible for pre-organised parties to use the ferry out of season - please telephone for further details.

Please note, however, that absolute reliance on ferries is not advised, so if the ferry is not running, rejoin the old railway track by the old level crossing and signal box.

Continue on to Bideford under the new Bideford bridge. The old Bideford railway station is the base of the Northern Devon Coast and Countryside Service. Refreshments are available in season in the reconditioned railway carriage.

Cross the Bideford Long Bridge, turn right and walk along the quay. Continue walking by the riverside path now named Landivisau Walk (Bideford's twin town in France) keeping the car park on your left. At the end of the car park there is a waymarked lane passing the Bideford RFC stadium. Continue walking on a road to pass under the new high level road bridge, then up a rough track, turn right by the waymark, and walk down a narrow track. This rejoins the riverside by a small beach at Lower Cleave. There is some more road walking passing the Yeoldon House Hotel. Be sure to keep to the waymarked lane; do not stray up any of the many private drives. After the Second World War tank traps, fork right and the route enters the National Trust property of Burrough Farm. This is a very pleasant section through some riverside woods with fine views back up the river to Bideford.

There is now a steep descent to another small beach with a boardwalk over a marshy area. After the second National Trust sign turn right. There are now two options here. Use the low tide route except at high tide as it is the more attractive route and can be taken in all cases but high tide. These routes are both well waymarked. With the steps now provided it is not difficult to negotiate the breach in the sea wall. Having done that the path turns inland to meet up with the high tide route. Follow the waymarked route around the Appledore shipyard to reach the road, turn right and into Appledore via Myrtle Street.

At Appledore plenty of accommodation and refreshment places are available. Along the Quay you meet the ferry slipway from Instow. The route now continues into old Appledore, passing the homes of the old sailing captains to near the lifeboat house. Pass the Royal George Inn and walk along Irsha Street then, keeping in front of the lifeboat house, stay with the road until you reach a crossroads. Turn right and follow the path around the headland of Northam Burrows.

Here for some distance you are walking on the seaward side of the dunes turning to the golf links side to pass Sandy Mere, then it is a straight walk into Westward Ho!. At most states of the tide it is possible to walk the beach, but be warned, the sand can be rather soft in places. Westward Ho! has plenty of accommodation but refreshment places are limited out of season.

10   Westward Ho! to Clovelly (Mount Pleasant)   OS E126 (T) Westward Ho!

| Grading: Strenuous | Distance - | 18 | 158.8 | 11.2 | 98.7 |

Timing: 6 hours

See also our Westward Ho! to Clovelly Path Description.

After passing the last of the holiday chalets, the path follows the track of the old Bideford to Westward Ho! railway. This is a fine stretch of the coast path over Cornborough and Abbotsham cliffs. At Greencliff a very poor coal was once mined. The path now climbs steeply over Cockington cliffs only to drop again to sea level to cross a pebble beach before climbing again via a wooden staircase, to cross Babbacombe cliffs. At Peppercombe turn inland to cross the stream and then the path meanders through Sloo Woods to join the new section through Worthygate Wood.

NOTE: The route shown on OS Explorer map 126 at Gauter Pool is wrong. The path does not turn to the south but goes on through the woods dropping to Buck's Mills.

At Buck's Mills a walk down to the old Quay is worthwhile. On leaving Barton Wood, keep to the bottom edge of the field until you cross a bridge into Hobby Drive. The walk along the Hobby Drive is nearly 3 miles (5 km) long, and takes longer than you think. There is a path which takes you off the Hobby Drive down to the harbour; by walking down it and then up to the village street again, you can rejoin the coast path.

11 | Clovelly to Hartland Quay (Hotel)   OS E126 (V) Clovelly

Grading: Moderate to strenuous   Distance -   16.6   175.4   10.3   109.0

Timing: 5 hours

See also our Clovelly to Hartland Quay Path Description.

This is a very fine section indeed, what coastal walking is all about! Allow yourself plenty of time to really enjoy it. You leave Clovelly by following the coast path sign through the large gate in the wall/fence on the left of the road going down the hill - do not go down the hill. Follow the track round to the right, to the coast path signpost, where you follow the path down to the right (yellow waymark). After a while you pass through the kissing-gate and follow the fence on your right until reaching the small kissing-gate in the shrubbery. Follow this path and soon a covered seat appears on the right. Carry on through the shrubbery and through the next two kissing-gates. After a while turn right at the T-junction, following the coast path sign, and right again at the next fork.

Soon you come to an original seat called the 'Angel's Wings', with nice woodcarvings. On reaching the track, take the coast path hard to the right - do not go along the track. Follow this path to a wonderful viewpoint before it descends steeply into a valley to a track. Go right and before going immediately left and immediately right again there is an easy detour that is very worthwhile. Having turned right off the steep descent, go ahead instead of sharp left up the track beside the cliff edge. When this track levels out, look out for some indistinct steps up to the right and follow these to a cutting in the rock which take you through to a marvellous lookout platform with lovely views.

Returning back through the rock cutting, turn right and go down to the old shelter. There is a further viewpoint past the shelter but the views are quite restricted. We now recommend that you return back to the coast path sign bearing right down to the main track where you turn hard right to follow this track down the valley to the shore. Go down the narrow path, crossing the stream by the stepping stones. Pause at the shore and notice the rock formations and the waterfall along the coast to your left (at low tide). Also note the old lime kiln. Now follow the grass track inland past the lime kiln and old building. Shortly take the coast path up to your right. Half way up follow the steps to the right ignoring the path going on ahead. On reaching the top, cross the stile by the NT sign for Brownsham.

The path proceeds through one field and over another stile which is multistepped on the eastern side, then across another field to the stile in the right hand fence, and then proceed down the steps, across the bridge at the bottom, turning left, and then take the first turning on the right. This is the more seaward route and is now the official path. We asked for this path and are grateful to the National Trust for having provided it. At Becklands there is a small memorial plaque in memory of the crew of a Wellington bomber that crashed into these cliffs in April 1942.

The route now continues practically on the coast all the way to Eldern Point and then on to Shipload Bay. (Seasonal refreshment hut - Hartland Point car park.)

The path down into the Smoothlands Valley and out to Damehole Point is a wonderful part of the coast path. To cross Abbey River the path goes inland behind the cottage to a stone bridge.

On reaching the old Rocket House by the road inland to Stoke, bear right to follow the path downhill to Hartland Quay, soon picking up the small road down to the seasonal refreshments, museum, toilets and hotel.

12 | Hartland Quay to Bude (Canal Bridge)   OS E126 & E111

Grading: Severe   Distance -   24.8   200.2   15.4   124.4

Timing: 8.5 hours

See also our Hartland Quay to Bude Path Description.

This is a most rewarding but very tough section. It will almost surely take you longer than you think although the beginning is comparatively mild. Before reaching Bude you will have crossed ten river valleys. A word of caution - there are no refreshment facilities other than the seasonal opportunities at Morwenstow and Sandy Mouth, so you should consider adding to your load at Hartland Quay.

The path from Hartland Quay is largely track and becomes a grassy footpath behind St Catherine's Tor. There is then a climb up and down to the waterfall at Speke's Mill Mouth. In our opinion this is the most dramatic waterfall on the whole of the path and we do not forget Pentargon ahead.

The path keeps to the eastern side of the stream for about 150 yards (135 m) then crosses it by a new wooden footbridge. Follow the signs up the valley to the east of Swansford Hill. The path over Swansford Hill is still walkable but should not be attempted in strong wind conditions.

Take care at Sandhole Cliff after joining the metalled road to watch for the signpost after about a 0.33 mile (500 m) directing you to turn right to rejoin the coast path. If you miss this you may find yourself doing about a 2 mile (3 km) walk down the road to Welcombe Mouth. Our Association has been urging the Northern Devon Coast and Countryside Service to install a true coast path along Sandhole Cliff; those who have been this way before will notice that they have installed half of what we requested.

On the descent into Marsland Mouth, look out for a little stone building, once the seaside lookout of the author, Ronald Duncan. It will provide a shelter from the elements.

As you come across the Cornish Border you will start to find a series of extremely helpful and well-thought-out posts. You might smile at the first which says 'Cornwall' but thereafter not only do they point the way in each direction, but they also tell you where you are down the shank of the post. Our thanks and appreciation to whoever had this idea - surely the best yet!

The diversion to visit Morwenstow Church is worth consideration. In season refreshments are available at the old rectory. The eccentric Parson Hawker was vicar here in 1830; look out for his hut which he constructed out of driftwood on Vicarage Cliff, when you regain the coast path.

At Steeple Point there is a tendency to keep too far inland. The official path keeps well to seaward. To cross the stream in Coombe Valley (where there are refreshments and toilets), there is a footbridge.

At Duckpool a new path has been created which takes you slightly inland away from the original path. This is marked with a white arrow where you will soon cross a new footbridge and rejoin the original path.

At Sandy Mouth there is a National Trust café. which is usually open from April to November.

The walking now becomes easier. Soon after Northcott Mouth, Crooklets Beach is reached. Keep to the cliffs passing the cricket pitch. This is the official route and the best way into Bude.

13 | Bude to Crackington Haven (Beach)   OS E111 (T) Bude

Grading: Strenuous   Distance -   16.4   216.6   10.2   134.6

Timing: 4.75 hours

See also our Bude to Crackington Haven Path Description.

A colourful free guide to the coast is available at the Bude Tourist Information Centre.

Bude has good shops and accommodation, being a fair-sized town. Before you leave do try a short beach walk to the north on the falling tide and look at those cliffs - alternating bands of sandstone and shale in beautiful curving waves and with eroding continuations of the strata extending out across the beach. This pattern has been with you since Hartland, but as you go south there will soon be a series of changes - from tightly compressed folds to violent crumplings and igneous intrusions of a much more complex nature.

The southbound path starts from the sea lock on the historic Bude Canal, climbs to the cliff top at Compass Point and on to Efford Beacon. Looking back if the tide is out, the magnificent beach stretches before you for several miles going absolutely due north, with the dish aerials of the satellite tracking station visible beyond. To the south east if the weather is clear the high tors of Dartmoor can be seen, and to the south west the prominent outline of Cambeak on the south side of the Crackington Haven inlet.

The path over Efford Down and on to Upton is easy enough to follow, and then it is sandwiched between the cliff edge and the road to Widemouth. The beach at Widemouth is popular for swimming and surfing. Toilets, cafes and accommodation are available, but apart from the fine beach with its prominent Black Rock, an unusual stack of slump breccia, Widemouth is not attractive; but be prepared, there will be no more facilities until you reach Crackington Haven.

South of Widemouth the path follows the low cliff for a short distance and then diverts inland slightly at Wanson Mouth to join the coast road by the stream valley. Turn west and climb up to Penhalt Cliff. Major subsidence is occurring and the coast path has long gone, but don't blame the County Council, you will see that the road is going as well! At the southern end of the cliff top car park the coast path proper recommences through a field and then descends steeply into Millook Haven.

Those with a geological interest should go on to the stony beach to view the remarkable chevron folded rock strata in the cliff on the north side - a classic textbook photograph and in sharp contrast to the curving folds to the north beyond Widemouth.

Follow the steep road beyond the stream crossing in Millook for a short distance, then branch right on to the cliff top path at Raven's Beak. From here the path climbs steadily but is fairly easy going all the way to Chipman Point. Note the ancient stunted oak wood in the area of Dizzard Point. The stream valley at Chipman Point is steep and deep, one of a series ahead, some with spectacular waterfalls cascading over into the rocky beach below. A tough ascent, then a further drop into the valley at Cleave Strand followed by a ridge walk at Castle Point giving tremendous views. The descent to the Coxford Water stream is severe and the climb onwards to Pencannow Point will certainly exercise the heart/lung system. Pause to recover and enjoy the views before the descent into Crackington Haven.

14 | Crackington Haven to Boscastle (Footbridge) OS E111 (V) Crackington Haven

Grading: Strenuous   Distance -   10.9   227.5   6.8   141.4

Timing: 3.75 hours

See also our Crackington Haven to Tintagel Path Description.

At Crackington Haven it is usually safe for a swim, but never go out of your depth on Cornwall's north coast. There are toilets and a seasonal shop, pub and café, and a long, tough, remote stretch ahead. The folds in the rock strata are remarkable, with interesting patterns down on the beach at Tremoutha Haven. Take particular care to the west of the Cambeak headland - keep away from the cliff edges and just admire the views - Hartland and Lundy Island to the north; Tintagel and Rumps Point to the south.

The path is now relatively level and generally stays above the massive landslip zone at Strangles Beach. There is a good path down through the landslip to the beach, which is interesting and pleasant at low tide, but it is an arduous climb back. At the northern end of the beach is the conspicuous Northern Door rock arch. There is access to the road and car parking at the National Trust Trevigue Farm (Coast Information Centre).

Ahead looms High Cliff, the highest point on the coast path in Cornwall and best avoided when a gale is blowing. Just before High Cliff the path goes round the back of a small stream valley where there is a diversity of minor paths, but then just aim for the top. The southbound descent from High Cliff is precipitously steep so take it slowly, then the path up through the massive landfall at Rusey Cliff twists and turns through the brambles and gorse. This is a major geological fault zone. The path is easier to follow than it used to be, but the ground here is soily and the vegetation grows rampantly in summer which presents a continuing problem to the County Council which has difficulty keeping it cleared back.

Once at the top of Rusey Cliff there follows an easier stretch through grassy sheep fields, with the approach to Buckator now being more coastal than shown in earlier guides.

The sheer black cliff of Buckator hangs over the sea inlet, with impressive white bands of quartz running through, quite different from the brown and grey cliffs of predominantly sandstone to the north. The path dips slightly to cross a bridge then onto some stepping stones which provide firm footing, then continues on at high level to Fire Beacon Point. Here the descent is steep but there are attractive slate steps on the most precipitous part. The path then keeps close to the cliff edge and into the Pentagon inlet where an impressive waterfall cascades down to the sea. The best view of this is now from the southern side, cliff falls having caused the path on the north side to be diverted and the old viewpoint has been lost. You are advised NOT to leave the official coast path to attempt a better view of this waterfall. It is a long way down.

Further cliff falls seem imminent on the south side of Pentargon, but from here on it is easy going into Boscastle. Aim for the white mast atop Penally Hill, then follow the path to the beautiful harbour inlet and past the Youth Hostel into the village of Boscastle. Penally Point is well worth the detour, an exciting viewpoint, but the slate rock is dangerously slippery when wet. Note the extraordinary small scale distortions in the strata alongside the path.

15 | Boscastle to Tintagel (Haven)

OS E109 (V) Boscastle

Grading: Moderate

Distance -   7.4   234.9   4.6   146.0

Timing: 2.25 hours

See also our Crackington Haven to Tintagel Path Description.

There are shops, pubs, toilets, accommodation and an excellent Heritage Coast Centre in Boscastle, and the old village up the lane by the Wellington Hotel is well worth exploring.

The next section on to Tintagel is shorter and easier then the two previous sections. The path leaves from the south side of the harbour and climbs steeply past the gully to Eastern Blackapit to the Willapark headland with its prominent white watch tower. Go up to the watch tower, or take the short cut across the back of the headland past the ancient Forrabury strip field system now preserved by the National Trust. The path soon descends into the stream valley of Grower Gut - there is a bridge to help you if the water is in flood. Further on the path turns sharp right to keep to the seaward side of the Manor House and onto a prominent headland which overlooks Short Island. If you are a birdwatcher, here is a good place to stop, picnic and observe through binoculars. Both Short Island and its neighbour Long Island are densely populated with breeding seabirds during the early summer, including guillemots, razorbills and a few puffins. Always look down on the water; they tend to float around in groups when off duty.

As you go on past Firebeacon Hill look for the Ladies Window rock arch in the gully to the right - walking west it is easy to miss this attractive photo opportunity. From here to Rocky Valley the going is level, but do look back to the dramatic pinnacles below Trevalga Cliff. On your left you are soon confronted by a conspicuous cliff top caravan/camp site - the path runs seaward of it. Trewethet Gut is a dangerous and eroding inlet that has necessitated a slight diversion of the path, and then you descend into the exquisite Rocky Valley. Look for seals in the surging sea as you cross the footbridge, and for the dippers that feed in the water of the stream. There is a path through Rocky Valley to the coast road, where cars may be parked.

From the footbridge a steep climb to high level again, and you find yourself overlooking Bossiney Haven. There is a crossroad of paths giving access to the beach from Bossinney village, and indeed this is an excellent place for a swim just after low tide. But the coast path goes on straight ahead and bears right to another prominent headland called Willapark, the second in just 2 miles. Again birdwatchers should go to the end and scan The Sisters and the ocean through binoculars. There are often terns, gannets and even shearwaters further out, but beware the precipitous cliff edge as you return to the path. Then on to Barras Nose headland, dominated by that awful hotel eyesore, and down to Tintagel Haven below the Castle ruins. Here there are toilets and a café.

16 | Tintagel to Port Isaac (Beach)

OS E9 & E106 (T) Tintagel

Grading: Severe

Distance -   14.7   249.6   9.1   155.1

Timing: 4.75 hours

See also our Tintagel to Port Isaac Path Description.

Tintagel has many shops, cafés and guest houses. The Old Post Office, owned and restored by the National Trust, dates back to the fourteenth century when it was no doubt a house of some importance.

Around The Island and down in Tintagel Haven there is some interesting and complex geology with older rocks (Devonian) overthrust on top of more recent rocks (carboniferous), and bands of lava and tuff. The severe erosion, which is no doubt compounded by these faults and thrusts, is making access to The Island increasingly difficult to maintain. In the shelter of Tintagel Haven sailing ships used to be loaded with the high quality slate that is still extracted from several quarries inland away from this highly disturbed coastal zone.

The path to Trebarwith Strand climbs up from Tintagel Haven below and to the left of the Castle entrance and gives an excellent view of the rocks on the south face of The Island. From here on and past St Materiana's Church it is easy going. The Youth Hostel at Dunderhole Point was once a quarry office building. The best route, for glorious views, is the National Trust path out around the headlands of Penhallic Point, rather than the boring official route across three fields. There are further old quarries ahead as you approach Hole Beach and Trebarwith Strand, and surprisingly sailing ships were loaded under the cliffs at Penhallic Point, where the remains of the wharf can still be seen. The path drops down by the toilets in Trebarwith Strand, and opposite is a welcome pub serving hot food. The beach is worth exploring at low tide, but watch that you don't get cut off, and do be warned that swimming can be dangerous here.

From here to Port Isaac the path is long and very tough in parts. The descents to the valley streams and up again on the other side are about the steepest on the whole of the coast path. Do not leave Trebarwith Strand unless you have food, energy and plenty of time in hand. The climb up out of Trebarwith Strand, which is stepped almost all the way, will give you a foretaste of what lies ahead. And having reached the top, you must go all the way down again into Backways Cove, then up again to a more restful level stretch for about 1 mile (1500 m) to the stream valley behind Tregardock Beach, where you are confronted by a detached and eroding piece of the cliff known as The Mountain. As you descend on the inland side of The Mountain you will meet a crossroad of paths from Tregardock village to the beach. The beach is worth a visit at low tide but your route lies straight ahead and you have quite a long way to go.

From here the stretch marked on the maps as Tregardock Cliff is easy enough, but at Jacket's Point the deepest and steepest valley of all lies before you - the commencement of the National Trust Dannonchapel property. An excellent job has been done on the path, the stream crossing and the staircase of steps on the ascent on the south side. However having reached the top, you drop down again into yet another deep valley. There are more steps up on the south side of the valley, then you go over to the Barrett's Zawn stream valley where another mineworking adit faces you. This gave donkeys burdened with slate access to Barrett's Zawn beach - don't even think about it as this tunnel is collapsing.

On the climb up round the Barrett's Zawn cliffs you will certainly see that there have been massive rock falls and that another will occur any time. You then descend very steeply on the south side into the next stream valley at Ranie Point, and as you slide down the stony slope you may well feel that the path here could be improved. Some walkers evidently complain about the staircases of steps on these valley sides, but they are so exceptionally steep we believe that steps are the best option and we have been urging the hard-pressed County Council to put some here.

Now at last the path levels out through the sheep meadows with just a small valley to cross at St Illickswell Gug where a boardwalk takes you across the marsh. When you reach the road at Cartway Cove the official path is directly opposite and drops down by the side of the hotel at Portgaverne. But, for the best views, take the path to the right and go round the headland and if the tide is out walk along the old harbour quay, where sailing ships were once loaded with slate. Either way there is then a short road walk up to the cliff car park at Port Isaac. Go through this past the public toilets and follow the well-signed path round to overlook the attractive inlet and thence the village street.

| 17 | Port Isaac to Polzeath (Beach) | | | | OS E106 (V) Port Isaac |

| Grading: Strenuous | Distance - | 14.2 | 263.8 | 8.8 | 163.9 |

Timing: 4.25 hours

See also our Port Isaac to Padstow Path Description.

Port Isaac is a gem, with narrow streets and tiny cottages which are no doubt easier to look at than to live in. There are two excellent pubs and one of the cafés is in an extremely old and crooked little building. Do take time to explore the back streets and the small fish market, and see if you can find Squeeze-ee-belly Alley!

Another tough walk lies ahead and there are no facilities until you reach Polzeath, but the scenery is superb. Take the road to the right behind the fish market and past more toilets. The path bears right along the cliff in front of two prominent guest houses and takes you on past Lobber Point then down into Pine Haven. From here on the path is magnificent, and keeps close to the cliff edge all the way to Port Quin. The fence stays on your left for over a mile of steep ups and downs, but it does protect you from the enormous herd of beef cattle that generally roams the meadows during the summer. Watch out for the peregrines that hunt along this stretch, the occasional adder basking in the sun, and seals on the rocks below.

At Kellan Head The Rumps promontory faces you at the far end of Portquin Bay. Then as you turn the corner the path overlooks the beautiful Port Quin inlet and descends to the village, once a busy little pilchard port, but there are no facilities here now although there is a tap marked drinking water on the wall in front of you as you descend the steps into the harbour. Follow the road westbound until half way up the steep hill where a new slate stile gives access to the south side of the inlet. You are on National Trust land and free to explore Doyden Point, formed from rocks of greenstone. The path follows the stream valley some distance in front of the old Prison Governor's House, and soon passes two fenced mineshafts where you might still find interesting mineral samples amongst the loose spoil material nearby - but keep away from the dangerous cliff edge.

At Trevan Point there is a sharp descent to Epphaven Cove which, with its neighbour Lundy Bay, has a beautiful beach at low tide. You then enter a surprisingly wooded valley where in late spring you will hear the delightful call of the willow warbler. As you climb up out of the bay look out for the startling Lundy Hole behind a protective fence on your right. On the cliff top again as you approach The Rumps you will see the earth ramparts of an Iron Age Fort in the lower ground in front of the headland. When you get there the detour through the entrance and on round the rocks overlooking The Mouls island is well worthwhile and can give good seabird watching; puffins nest on The Mouls most years.

It is then quite easy going on to Pentire Point, another headland formed from pillow lava. A perfect cross-section can be seen in the small vertical rock face on your left as you leave The Rumps headland, the rounded hollow shapes having been formed of molten lava under the sea. The walling stone alongside the path reveals the structure of small holes in the rock caused by gases and steam, but do not remove pieces as samples; the National Trust spends much time and money maintaining these walls and they provide wind shelter for the sheep. Look out for a plaque just before you get to Pentire Point in memory of the Fallen.

There are many good viewpoints on the coast path, but that from Pentire Point is one of the best. In clear conditions south to Trevose Head and beyond, and north to Bude, the satellite tracking station and even Hartland Quay and Lundy Island are visible, but you will need binoculars! Then follows an easy descent into Polzeath with the Camel Estuary before you and Stepper Point with its Daymark Tower on the opposite side. In contrast to the last 20 miles of perfection, the cliff top housing and car parking in New and Old Polzeath are unfortunate, but the sea, the sand and the surf are magnificent. There are toilets on the left as you reach the road beyond Pentireglaze Haven. The path continues along the cliff edge to the village centre and gives access to the beach on the way.

18	Polzeath to Padstow (Harbour)	OS E106 (V) Polzeath; (V) Rock

Grading: Easy

Distance -	4.7	268.5	2.9	166.8

Timing: 1.25 hours

See also our Port Isaac to Padstow Path Description.

Polzeath is a surfers' paradise with several shops, cafés, accommodation and campsites. On the left by the park is a small Tourist Information Centre and there are toilets opposite.

Follow the road past the beach car park and take the path right by the cottages where the road bends sharp left on the steep hill. The path follows the edge of Tristram Cliff where you can watch the expertise of the surfers. From here to Daymer Bay the path along The Greenaway is intensively walked throughout the year, and measures have had to be taken to discourage people from wandering off the route and scarring the fragile turf with alternative tracks. In fact this path is so good it is now classed as suitable for wheelchair users, which is almost unique on the coast path. There are houses on your left, but the coastal scene is beautiful with a rocky sea-washed platform below - the haunt of curlews, redshanks, grey plover and oystercatchers, with the headlands of Stepper Point and Pentire Point in the background. Many fishing and pleasure boats can be observed entering and leaving from Padstow, some 2 miles (3 km) up the Camel Estuary.

Just off Trebetherick Point is the Doom Bar, noticeable only at low tide when the waves are breaking over the sand; there were many wrecks here during the days of sail when ships were largely at the mercy of wind and tide. There are toilets and a cafe in Daymer Bay car park and the beach is one of the safest for a swim - but keep out of the estuary channel at low tide.

The coast path goes down the steps on to the beach and then through the dunes and over a footbridge just below Brea Hill. To visit little St Enodoc Church, which was once buried beneath the blown sand, turn left midway along the dunes and follow the white markers across the golf course. You must then retrace your route back to the dunes, or you can go on through the golf course to rejoin the coast path in the dunes on the far side of Brea Hill, but this is a busy golf course and you may wish you had a protective helmet and visor. Your route through the golf course is marked by large white painted rocks. From the footbridge you can go either way round Brea Hill, or straight over the top! Alternatively, if the tide is out you can walk along the beach to Rock and the Padstow ferry. All routes are pleasant and the sheltered estuary surroundings make quite a change from the exposed cliffs that you have been used to. The official path goes through a hollow just behind the dunes on the south side of Brea Hill, a Site of Special Scientific Interest for the rare plant life that thrives on the calcium-rich sand. At the southern end the path branches left to a higher level and on to Rock car park, but you can continue on along the beach, except at very high tide. There are toilets in the car park and the ferry landing is on the shore below. Be warned however that at exceptionally low tides the ferry may sail from quite some distance downstream in front of the dunes, so keep a lookout as you walk.

Rock/Padstow (River Camel)
Black Tor Ferry
Padstow Harbour Commissioners,
Harbour Office, West Quay,
Padstow, Cornwall PL28 8AQ.
Tel: Padstow 01841 532239
Fax: 01841 533346
www.padstow/harbour.co.uk
e.mail: info@padstowharbour.fsnet.co.uk

Ferry operates all year at 20 min intervals
No Sunday service from last
Sunday in October to
1st Sunday in April
(or Easter if earlier)

A water taxi also operates between Rock and Padstow between 1900 and 2300, 1st March to 31st October, weather and tides permitting.
Contact: GB Smith and Son, 01208 862815 (day): 01208 862217 (evening): 01208 863090 (fax), or contact the boat direct on 07778 105297.

We urge you to contact the ferry operators direct if you are relying on this service, particularly if you are anticipating a fairly late finish and need to confirm the time of its last run.

The Saints' Way, Cornwall's coast to coast path from Padstow to Fowey starts here. A guide book is available from Padstow TIC (see page 150).

19   Padstow to Trevone (Car Park)   OS E106 (T) Padstow

Grading: Easy   Distance -   9.1   277.6   5.7   172.5

Timing: 2.5 hours

See also our Padstow to Porthcothan Path Description.

Normally the Padstow ferry will take you into the harbour, but at low tide it will deposit you a short distance downstream at St Saviour's Point, just below the path to Stepper Point. Do not take this as an opportunity to cut out Padstow; you should go into the town and explore. The harbour area, the narrow lanes in the old town and up to St Petroc's Church are attractive and fairly traffic free. A glass of beer and a genuine Cornish steak pasty make an excellent traditional lunch. A visit to the Tourist Information Centre on the harbour is recommended, and on your way it is interesting to look at the places of origin of the many fishing boats - all ports from the Hebrides to the Channel Islands!

The coast path starts on your left at the north end of the harbour and is wide and well trodden. In the early summer blackcaps and warblers sing in the wooded stream valley at St George's Cove. From Gun Point you can, if the tide is out, take a short cut across the beach to Hawker's Cove by the prominent old Lifeboat House. If the tide is in you can enjoy a quiet swim; this is a very pleasant and usually wind sheltered beach. Go round the back of the old pilots' houses from Hawker's Cove and then climb up to Stepper Point, with its stone-built Daymark Tower.

From this high ground there is a remarkable panorama behind you and on a clear day you will see the granite tors of Bodmin Moor in the distance.

So now you are back on the exposed Atlantic Coast. Approaching the precipitous inlet of Butter Hole Cove, look out for the small Pepper Hole a few yards to the right of the path. There follows a long easy stretch to Gunver Head, followed by a steep descent to the small stream valley. The rocky pinnacles of the Merope Islands just behind you are spectacular. After a short climb up again you will see the Marble Cliff and Porthmissen Bridge ahead. The cliff comprises many bands of hard limestone and softer shale on which razorbills, guillemots and kittiwakes nest in the summer. At Roundhole Point the path skirts the impressive Round Hole collapsed cave which should be approached with caution, and then descends to the car park at Trevone.

20 | Trevone to Porthcothan (Footbridge)   OS E106

Grading: Easy   Distance -   12.7   290.3   7.9   180.4

Timing: 3.5 hours

See also our Padstow to Porthcothan Path Description.

There are toilets, a café, pub and a good beach in Trevone, plus some bed and breakfast accommodation. The path passes behind the little headland on the south side of the bay and follows the cliff edge round rocky Newtrain Bay. There are refreshments, toilets and a beautiful beach at Harlyn.

The stream generally has to be crossed via the road bridge, and then the path follows the beach for about 330 yards (300 m) before climbing slightly into the dunes and so on past the end of the bay to Cataclews Point. The hard erosion-resistant dolerite rock here was used to make the polished font in Padstow Church. In Mother Ivey's Bay there are some unpleasant man-made features which mar the coastal scene, including an often foul smelling sewage discharge which frequently contaminates the nearby beaches. There is a huge and conspicuous caravan site near Trevose Farm, and access to the headland by the new Padstow Lifeboat Station is barred by an ugly concrete and mesh fence, reminiscent of prison camps which is in sharp contrast to the old tamarisk hedges nearby. How sadly all this compares with the painstaking remedial and conservation work that has been carried out by the National Trust on long stretches of the coast to the north of the Camel Estuary.

At Trevose Head you can generally visit the immaculately kept lighthouse, but keep away when the fog horn is blowing. On a clear day you will see the granite hills of West Penwith behind St Ives to the south and the satellite tracking dish aerials beyond Bude to the north. Turning south, the path passes yet another large Round Hole as it descends to Booby's Bay. There is something of a rocky scramble to get through to Constantine Bay, but it is beautiful here with a particularly attractive beach at low tide - not really safe for swimming unfortunately. Beyond the dunes the path leaves the beach to go round Treyarnon Point, revealing another attractive beach at Treyarnon Bay. The Youth Hostel is on the left, and in the car park area there are toilets and refreshments. If you are intent on swimming, observe the safety notices which will certainly tell you not to do so at low tide.

An unusually indented coastline follows beyond Trethias Island, but the path cuts across the narrower headlands. Between Pepper Cove and Warren Cove are the ramparts of an Iron Age Fort, and in Fox Cove you may see the remains of a ship which ran aground in 1969. Minnows Islands and the cove beyond are quite spectacular. The path turns into Porthcothan Bay, descending through the protected National Trust strip which contrasts with the housing development on the opposite side. To reach Porthcothan's pub, the Tredrea Inn, take the road before the bridge and go uphill for approximately 500 yards (458 m).

21 | Porthcothan to Newquay (Harbour)   OS E106

Grading: Moderate   Distance -   17.9   308.2   11.1   191.5

Timing: 5 hours

See also our Porthcothan to Newquay Path Description.

Porthcothan has toilets, a shop, limited accommodation and a pub. The path leaves past the shop and keeps in front of the houses and on round the headland overlooking Trescore Islands.

There is a short steep descent into Porth Mear valley, a popular spot for birdwatchers, and an equally short steep climb up again, then it is an easy walk to Park Head, another spectacular viewpoint. As you approach Park Head you will come across a National Trust landmark stone - keep to the path to the left of the landmark as there are numerous landslips here and signs warn to keep well inland of the white posts because of cliff falls. Ahead lies the famous Carnewas property of the National Trust, with a beautiful beach at low tide. As you leave Park Head you will see that the cliff is slowly sliding down, although it has been like this for many years. Bedruthan beach itself has a recurring accessibility problem due to the dangerous condition of the cliffs, but a great deal of money is being spent on the long flight of steps down. If the tide is on its way out, it is worth going down to explore the pools, caves and the rock stacks, Bedruthan Steps, but don't get cut off and don't even think about swimming. The National Trust café and Information Centre in the car park are open throughout the summer.

Bedruthan Steps can be busy, but you will soon find yourself on a quieter stretch of path to Trenance Point. A steady descent into Mawgan Porth follows where the coast path crosses the beach. This is one of the few beaches in North Cornwall where dogs are permitted in the summer. At Mawgan Porth there are toilets, shops, cafés, and a pub. The road must be used here for a very short distance in order to cross the stream. The westbound path leaves to the right on the sharp road bend on the hill out of Mawgan Porth. Then follows a long high level stretch to Watergate Bay, with minor descents at Beacon Cove and Stem Cove, between which across Griffin's Point headland are the ramparts of another Iron Age Fort. Just inland is the airport and RAF station at St Mawgan, and you may find yourself being targeted by high-powered military jet aircraft as they come in to land. Ahead lies the magnificent Watergate Beach, but the path remains at high level until it crosses to the road behind the Watergate Bay Hotel into Watergate itself, where there are toilets, cafés and a pub.

After crossing the stream bridge by the car park, where there are toilets, the path leaves to the right from the road to Newquay and again climbs to the high cliff top where it remains all the way to Whipsiderry. Here some ugly cliff top development has been permitted, but the coastal scene is great, with Newquay and Towan Head in the background. The cliffs at Whipsiderry are high and precipitous, but there are steps down to the beach and some caves to explore. There are new coast path signs here which take you along the pavement down the hill to Porth Beach. However you might prefer to take the original route that starts with a narrow path between a hotel and the cliff edge, and then leads you on to Trevelgue Head. You might then choose to cross the footbridge onto the island where a rough sea can be most spectacular.

You must now return to Porth Beach where there are toilets, cafés, beach shops and pubs. You may then walk along the beach which is signposted from the Mermaid Inn, rather than taking the official route, joining the path opposite the Porth Beach Hotel at the Porth Beach car park - from here it crosses the headland between Porth and Lusty Glaze. This short cut avoids the road and takes you round the cliff edge at Lusty Glaze and into the Barrowfields Park. You are then on the road into Newquay town centre, but if the tide is out, you can walk along the magnificent beach from Lusty Glaze or from Barrowfields all the way to the harbour.

22 | Newquay to Holywell (Beach)   OS E104 (T) Newquay (Trains); (V) Crantock

Grading: Moderate   **Distance -**   10.2   318.4   6.3   197.8

Timing: 4.5 hours (Official Route)

See also our Newquay to Perranporth Path Description.

Newquay is the biggest town on the north coast and the pedestrianised shopping centre is quite attractive. There is no shortage of restaurants, pubs and accommodation here, and there is even a railway station! But do explore the beaches and the harbour before you leave, and if the tide is out you can gain access to the coast path by the steps at the back of the harbour.

The coast path leaves just above the harbour and climbs past the old Huer's Hut to Towan Head. In the cliffs below the Hut is a noisy kittiwake colony and this is a very good spot to observe the differences between kittiwakes, fulmars, black-headed gulls and the rest. Towan Head is particularly good for seabird watching; with binoculars you may spot gannets, petrels and shearwaters further out.

From Towan Head the path follows along the back of Fistral Beach. This is probably the most popular surfing beach in the British Isles and international competitions are held here. The path climbs to the cliffs at the southern end, passing in front of the housing development at Pentire, then across the headland at The Warren over to The Gannel river estuary.

There are four ways that you can cross the River Gannel, three of which are available, tide permitting, throughout the year. The distances via the Penpol crossing assume that you have walked via Fern Pit; the same applies to the other two crossings of Trenance Footbridge and the A3075 main road route. However, it is possible to reach the Trenance and Trevemper crossings from the town itself.

1. Newquay to Crantock via Penpol

This is now the official crossing of the River Gannel. Up river there is ferry and a tidal footbridge off Trevean Lane which crosses over to Penpol Creek. If you are at Fern Pit and need to go upstream, go east (inland) along Riverside Crescent, Riverside Avenue, Fistral Crescent, turn right into Pentire Crescent, continue along Penmere Drive and turn right into Trevean Way, then turn right at the coast path sign. Be warned; there is an earlier footpath sign to Crantock - DO NOT take it because you may find it is under water. Having crossed the Gannel, turn right to follow an estuary side path. Presently it becomes a track and you pass a house on the right, then some bungalows and can soon turn right down into the National Trust car park at Rushey Green. Take the exit practically opposite where you came in. There is a seasonal café close to the car park. (Note that the NTG refers to this crossing as being at the bottom of Trethellan Hill.)

2. Newquay to Crantock via Fern Pit Ferry Crossing (summer only); (deduct approx. 2 miles / 3 km)

Newquay/Crantock (River Gannel)	Spring Bank Holiday
Fern Pit Café and Ferry	End of May to mid-September
Proprietor - G A Northey	continuous 7 days a week
Fern Pit, Riverside Crescent, Newquay. TR7 1PJ.	1000-1800 hrs
Tel: 01637 873181	

We urge you to contact the ferry operator direct if you are relying on this service, particularly if you are anticipating a fairly late finish and need to confirm the time of its last run.

You have to pass Fern Pit to reach the official crossing of the Gannel. If the ferry is running, it is a comfortable and scenic way to cross; there is even a café on the Newquay side so that you can while away your waiting time with refreshment. However, neither the ferry nor the footbridge, which is used at low tide instead of the ferry, is available when the café is closed.

3. Newquay to Crantock via Trenance Footbridge (add approx. 3 miles / 4.8 km)

Further up stream again, just before the estuary becomes a river, there is another footbridge which we call 'Trenance'. It is beside the new A3075 Gannel Road just before the boating lake on the left and its junction with Trevemper Road. If you are in Newquay and know the tides are against you, the quickest way to get here is to walk down the new Gannel Road (A3075). On the other side of the footbridge, walk forward for about 165 yards (150 m) keeping the hawthorn hedge on your left, until you come to a clearing on your left, offering various routes for you to choose. You can either turn right through the pedestrian gate that is a permissive path (this path is dependent on the tide, and should be navigable for two hours either side of low tide) or, if you have any doubts about the tide, you are advised to take the old bridleway through the big gate going towards Trevemper. Proceed forwards uphill and having gone over the brow, turn right before you get to the tarmac. You walk via Treringey coming to Penpol Creek and so on, to Rushey Green as described above.

4. Newquay to Crantock via the A3075 (add approx. 4.5 miles / 7.2 km)

However if all these crossings fail there is the A3075 main road itself, which is the only all-states-of- the-tide and all-seasons route. Those taking the A3075 should proceed along it until just after the roundabout where the A392 branches off. In about 100 yards (90 m) take the little unsigned lane on the right. You immediately pass a partly ruined barn on your right and soon you pass a house on the outskirts of Trevemper. Then as the road bears left, go forward and right. Pass through a gate and turn left to go via Treringey to Penpol Creek and so on to Rushey Green. Needless to say the A3075, although the one route that is always certain is quite the longest and certainly the most uninteresting.

Coast path continues

Crantock Beach is attractive at low tide and can give good views of terns fishing in the Gannel below the cliffs of Pentire Point East. The path passes behind the dunes to the National Trust car park at Rushey Green, then westwards through the dunes to the cliffs of Pentire Point West. Alternatively you may walk along the beach to gain access to the path by scrambling up at the western end of the dunes.

Porth Joke is a sheltered sandy inlet, then follows a climb to Kelsey Head, another Iron Age site.

From here in the distance can be seen St Agnes Head with Bawden Rocks offshore. Holywell Beach lies before you and the path descends to the dunes and then into Holywell. Those continuing onwards can take advantage of the splendid new National Trust footbridge across the river seaward of the village.

23 | Holywell to Perranporth (Beach car park)   OS E104

Grading: Moderate. Sand dune route - Strenuous.   Distances -   7.3   325.7   4.5   202.3

Timing: 2 hours

See also our Newquay to Perranporth Path Description.

The path cuts across Penhale Point headland and then skirts the seaward edge of the rather ugly Penhale Camp, where there is a short fenced section. The army presence here has however served to preserve the beautiful wild dunes area inland from being overrun by campsites and chalets, and it now deserves to be protected as a nature reserve. The path goes out to Ligger Point and you get the first good view of the long Perran Beach.

The easiest path, if the tide permits, is now along the great stretch of firm beach to Perranporth rather than over the dunes. Even if, as is sometimes the case, you can only walk part-way along the beach it is worth going down to do this, there being a number of 'escape routes' up from the beach going west. The important point to watch if you want an easy descent to the beach is to fork left along the sandy path after the old wooden stile; the right fork is quicker but much steeper. It is essential that you stay on the marked route through the dunes as there is recent news of collapsing mine shafts.

The official path takes you towards the dunes where you will see the rusty coloured Perran Iron Lode in the cliff quarry. The path descends behind this and follows the back of the beach for almost a mile then climbs up through the dunes behind the rock cliff at Cotty's Point. The incoming tide will reach the foot of the cliff here but there are escape steps to the dunes at each side, and if the tide is out you can continue on along the beach rather than going over the top. The path descends to the back of the beach just south of Cotty's Point, crosses the stream by a footbridge and so takes you into the town or the car park where there are toilets.

24 | Perranporth to St Agnes (Trevaunance Cove)   OS E104 (T) Perranporth

Grading: Moderate   Distance -   6.0   331.7   3.7   206.0

Timing: 2 hours

See also our Perranporth to Portreath Path Description.

Perranporth is a busy holiday centre during the summer and has good shops and accommodation. The eroding rock stacks at the western end of the beach are interesting, and may be explored using the beach access at the far end of the car park in front of the hotel terrace. Round the corner you will find a staircase from the beach up to the cliff car park at Droskyn Point. The official route leaves west from the town car park and follows the hill up Cliff Road, but just to the left of the Atlantic House Hotel there are some steps up and a footpath which takes you past the Droskyn Point car park. Whichever way you have chosen, keep inland of the prominent castellated building and on along Tregundy Lane to the end of the houses. The westbound coast path is signposted half left at the entrance drive to the Youth Hostel and the South West Water sewage pumping station. It then descends slightly to the right before climbing to the cliffs overlooking Shag Rock.

From here on you will see increasing evidence of mining activity. The path is fairly level going, passing the small outcrop of granite at Cligga Head which has been quarried and displays conspicuous stripes of greisen (for the chemistry of which you must consult the textbooks!). The mineralisation along the coast here and to the west is attributable to the intrusion of the granite which extends over a considerable area below the surface. Walking westbound through the quarry and mineworkings, you are unlikely to lose the path. Hanover Cove is named after a shipwreck. The Hanover was lost in a storm in December 1763 on route from Lisbon to Falmouth: all hands were lost plus a cargo of gold. It is rumoured that £50m of gold still onboard. The rock formations around the cove are dramatic and green copper stains the cliffs. There are many mineshafts in this area capped with conical steel mesh which allows access for bats.

45

The long stretch to Trevellas Porth is level easy going alongside the airfield perimeter; you will progress much faster here than you did further east. There is a sharp descent into Trevellas Coombe where there are many mine workings with their decaying buildings. Go upstream to the bridge which crosses the stream in front of the Blue Hills engine house and then right over the top to Trevaunance Cove. The western path is the recommended route here, as the current official path passes close to the cliff edge. Cross over the road and turn right behind the four storey grey rendered housing block to pick up the official path. If you go down into the cove, where there is a seasonal café and toilets, a footpath behind the Jubilee Terrace and steps take you back up to the coast path.

It is possible to cross the beach from Trevellas Porth to Trevaunance Cove at low tide, but be warned that the boulders are dangerously slippery. Surprisingly there was once a harbour under the cliff on the west side of Trevaunance Cove, but all you will find now is a tumbled mass of granite blocks.

25 | St Agnes to Porthtowan (The Unicorn pub)   OS E104 (V) St Agnes

Grading: Moderate   Distance -   7.4   339.1   4.6   210.6

Timing: 2 hours

See also our Perranporth to Portreath Path Description.

From the top the coast path stays at high level out to St Agnes Head, passing many mineshafts and waste tips on the way. Here you are circumnavigating St Agnes Beacon, a small outcrop of granite 0.5 mile (800 m) back from the coast. As the path turns west, you will see Godrevy Lighthouse across the bay, with St Ives and the massive granite of Penwith beyond. The going is relatively easy and soon you will pass the much-photographed Towanroath Engine House, part of the Wheal Coates tin and copper mine and now preserved by the National Trust. The path then descends into Chapel Porth where there is a car park, toilets and a seasonal café. At low tide, if you walk some distance east along the beach, you will see a streak of copper ore in the cliff beneath the Towanroath shaft.

The westbound path leaves The National Trust car park, travelling inland for 200 yards (185 m) on the right of the small stream, before joining the wide rough track to Mulgram Hill, then there is a good cliff top walk to Porthtowan. The path descends to the back of the beach and on past the car park where there are toilets. The transition from mining to tourism here has produced some unattractive features, but the beach is beautiful and extensive at low tide, from Tobban Horse in the east to Chapel Porth in the west.

26 | Porthtowan to Portreath (Harbour)   OS E104 (V) Porthtowan

Grading: Strenuous   Distance -   6.3   345.4   3.9   214.5

Timing: 1.75 hours

See also our Perranporth to Portreath Path Description.

Porthtowan is popular for surfing and has accommodation, a pub, a few shops and seasonal cafés. To find the westbound path turn right along West Beach Road then left up the narrow road to the cliff top. On the headland the path turns west, passing many mineworkings, and keeps some distance back from the crumbling and dangerous cliff edge. At the steep valley drop to Sally's Bottom, where steps have been installed on either side, then on reaching high level again you find yourself walking alongside the unattractive Nancekuke fence which encloses the large military establishment just inland. It stays with us for over a mile and almost to Portreath, where the Daymark above the harbour entrance can be seen ahead. The path turns west just before you reach the Daymark, avoiding another dangerous cliff edge, and joins the road down to the harbour. The long narrow inlet is unusual, but the protective pier which extends over the rocks on the west side is now out of bounds; too many people have been swept off by waves breaking over.

27 | Portreath to Hayle (White Hart Hotel)　　　OS E104 & E102 (V) Portreath

Grading: Moderate　　　　　　　　　　　Distance -　　19.9　　365.3　　12.4　　226.9

Timing: 5.5 hours

See also our Portreath to Hayle Path Description.

There are shops, cafés and bed and breakfast accommodation in Portreath, but the beach is small in comparison to most on this coast. To gain the southbound path go round the harbour to the beach car park, then to the right up Battery Hill. Where this road drops to the beach again at the western end the coast path branches left up the valley. In approximately 10 yards (10 m) there is a low National Trust sign marking Western Hill. The official coast path begins with a right turn up well made steps and carries on up Western Hill; you have views from here after your initial effort to gain the cliff top.

At Basset's Cove you go through a big car park and start several miles of easy cliff top walking. There are practically no signs but you are unlikely to go astray. After 1.5 miles (2.5 km) you get closer to the road between two car parks and then start to get away from it again.

You pass Hell's Mouth which has a seasonal café just across the road. The path strikes up to the north-west and becomes narrow. From the highest point you may just see the top of St Michael's Mount to the south-west. Be careful to avoid a path to the right which eventually drops steeply to the beach. Pass through stone posts onto a farm track which soon bears left towards a house and other buildings; here you take the stone stile into the field on your right. Keep to the seaward field boundary and cross another stone stile. Almost immediately cross a wooden stile placed to keep in the Shetland ponies used to maintain the habitat of the Knavocks.

There is then a very pleasant walk round Navax and Godrevy Points; there are good views out to sea and ahead to St Ives. You then have to negotiate a big car park but by keeping well to seaward you can miss most of it and the road that leads to it.

You will find Godrevy Café, which is open all year round. To find the Red River footbridge leave the car park's south-western corner along a board walk. You will see the bridge to your left. After crossing it walk seaward along the bank of the river.

You can walk along the beach after crossing the Red River but beware the tide which can come in behind you and then cut you off near Black Cliff, some 3 miles (4.5 km) away. The walking is easier on top of the shingle bank. From here you will see a lifeguard hut, slightly to your right. You then begin a stretch through the dunes following way-posts which are well sited and lead you accurately.

If you have come along the beach leave it at the lifeguard hut near the foot of Black Cliff to rejoin the dunes path. If you come through the dunes avoid turning left (up a very narrow passage between houses) at the confusing waymark just above the lifeguard hut, but carry on (in front of the convenient pub garden) to turn left up some steep steps just before two holiday chalets. Turn right and walk towards a house called Silver Spray. Leave this house to your right and walk along a line of chalets on your left. Keep straight on. Part of the path is slightly overgrown here but it soon opens out to become a track and heads towards a car park.

There is no ferry and the river cannot be forded so you have to follow the estuary inland. Walk along the old quay until you cross the swing bridge. Then turn right on the main road and follow it to the railway viaduct by the White Hart Hotel.

28 | Hayle to St Ives (Western Pier)　OS E102 (T) Hayle (Trains); (V) Lelant (Trains)

Grading: Moderate　　　　　　　　　　　Distance -　　9.0　　374.3　　5.6　　232.5

Timing: 2.5 hours

See also our Hayle to Pendeen Watch Path Description.

Distance is measured from the railway viaduct/the White Hart Hotel at Hayle, around the estuary to Lelant then along the coast road to St Ives.

At Hayle, double back under the railway viaduct and continue along Carnsew Road. You can either walk all the way to Griggs Quay along the road or take a detour around a lagoon in the estuary which offers more opportunities for bird-watching. To detour take the footpath to the right, signposted 'The Weir 0.5 mile'. Walk round the embankment and, when you come out again on the main road, turn right.

At Griggs Quay bear right off the Causeway on the A3074, passing the Old Quay House. The official route continues along the A3074 through Lelant. A quieter alternative of the same length is described below.

After passing under the railway bridge, turn right - it is signed St Ives Park and Ride. When you come to a toilet block cut through to the road on your left in front of the board showing car park charges. Follow the road, passing Lelant railway station, all the way to Lelant Church.

At the church continue ahead on the same line to go across a golf course and under the railway again. Here turn left along the seaward side of the railway. The path narrows and becomes winding but stay with it.

Just before Carrack Gladden where you are close to the sea there are several paths going down to the beach. If the tide is well out you can go down and save yourself several ups and downs by walking along the beach to Carbis Bay. If you stay on the path you come up alongside a pedestrian railway crossing and then bear right. On the descent avoid the two beach paths on your right.

At Carbis Bay circle round the inland side of the café complex and leave on a tarmac path above the beach but to seaward of the hotel. Climb up, crossing a railway footbridge, then keep ahead avoiding the path on the left, which is where St Michael's Way leaves the coast path. Continue along ignoring the 'Private road - pedestrians only' sign on the right. The path becomes a minor road and, where there is another private road on your right, go straight ahead. Cross the railway again on a more substantial old fashioned bridge to bear right and downhill. This brings you to Porthminster Café and then out below the railway station in St Ives.

For those interested, there is a cross-peninsula path, St Michael's Way between St Ives and Marazion. The waymark is a cockleshell and the path can be picked up at St Uny Church in Lelant. There is a guide leaflet to the St Michael's Way available from St Ives TIC (see page 150).

29 | St Ives to Pendeen Watch (Lighthouse)   OS E102 (T) St Ives (Trains)

Grading: Severe

Timing: 7 hours

Distance -	22.3	396.6	13.9	246.4

See also our Hayle to Pendeen Watch Path Description.

You are now starting the longest and most deserted stretch of coast on the whole South West Coast Path, so think about refreshments and accommodation. You will have to walk for some 22 miles (35 km) before finding refreshment (at Sennen Cove) actually on the path. You can divert inland as listed below but all suggestions are subject to some seasonal closing and opening hours. There is not even a telephone box on the path. It is magnificent walking, but do not start out unprepared.

Refreshment possibilities are Zennor (0.5 mile/0.8 km off the path, inland), Gurnard's Head (0.6 mile/1 km inland) Pendeen (1 mile/1.6 km inland), Botallack (0.4 mile/0.6 km inland) and St Just (1.5 miles/2.4 km inland). In summer there is a mobile snack wagon in Cape Cornwall car park (on the path).

One other warning, the path is often rough and rocky, the terrain is severe and in places after rain surprisingly boggy; few will average 2 miles (3 km) an hour; in other words it may take you longer than you expect.

Many use St Ives as a staging post; if however you should just want to walk through continue along the path below the railway station by which you enter. This becomes a tarmac lane which proves to be called The Warren at its end. Keep as close as you can to the harbour, until you reach its north-west corner. Here you have a choice; the purists will stay with the harbour and walk out round what is called The Island or St Ives Head; it is a pleasant walk. The less pure or perhaps those with lots of miles to cover can cut the corner by following signs to the Tate St Ives - this will bring you out behind Porthmeor Beach. Those going out to The Island can walk right round the harbour to turn left signposted The Museum.

You can walk round The Island but the interesting little St Nicholas Chapel is on the high point in the middle. When you have completed your circuit you turn right to pass along in front of the Tate St Ives.

Go along behind Porthmeor Beach ignoring the ramp going down to it. The road starts to rise - there is a car park on your right and the path you want starts to bear off right by some public conveniences. You pass a putting green and continue along the tarmac path which becomes the true coast path.

Shortly after the National Trust Hellesveor Cliff sign turn right on the track rather than going inland. At Pen Enys Point the coast path cuts behind the National Trust property. If you have time it is a pleasant extension out to the headland.

If the weather is clear Carn Naun Point (where there is a trig point) is the place to look back and gloat at what you have done. On a clear day you can see St Agnes Beacon and sometimes Trevose Head. Be careful though a little later, just before the stream, where there is a path down to the beach which you should avoid and shortly after the stream a path running inland which you should also ignore. Look out for seals on the Carracks; you may even hear them 'singing'.

Just before you reach Zennor Head a coast path sign takes you down to the right, then shortly the path divides. At this point take the lower, seaward path to go out round Zennor Head, or take the upward path to avoid eroded cliffs and miss out on the headland. As you come inland again the coast path soon turns right to descend steeply down steps. Zennor itself is ahead along the track, so the miles you have planned ahead will no doubt help you decide whether to make a diversion in search of refreshment.

Back on the path you pass some of the most beautiful coastal scenery of this section with plenty of ups and downs before Treen Cove and Gurnard's Head. If you have time it is a splendid diversion out onto the latter, once an Iron Age settlement.

Bosigran is difficult to negotiate but there is now better signing. As you drop off Carn Veslan look ahead to the ridge of Bosigran cliff and aim for the high point on the cliff. Follow the path to its highest point and just after passing through a gap in a low wall turn right up to top of the ridge. From here descend to the stream by the obvious path with good views of the coast path continuing ahead. Cross a small bridge just inland of a ruined building and follow the path uphill, just to the seaward side of the furthest field boundary. If you turn and look back you may see (and hear) the rock climbers on the cliff.

As you descend from Chypraze Cliff you see the lighthouse of Pendeen Watch ahead. You can take the inland path to your left to Rose Valley for accommodation at Morvah, Bojewyan and Pendeen, or continue on round Portheras Cove to the lighthouse and a road walk back into Pendeen.

30 | Pendeen Watch to Cape Cornwall (Car Park)   OS E102 Inland (V) Pendeen; Inland (V) St Just

Grading: Moderate	Distance -	6.5	403.1	4.0	250.4

Timing: 1.75 hours

See also our Pendeen Watch to Porthcurno Path Description.

Remember what was said about refreshment in Section 29.

The official path from Pendeen Watch starts at the car park and goes along the road to the far end of the row of white ex-coastguard cottages on your right. Here you turn right, off the road. A granite marker tells you it is 3.5 miles (5.25 km) to Cape Cornwall.

The route is well-defined and brings you to the old Levant Mine dressing floors. A minor inland diversion is recommended to Geevor Tin Mine (closed Saturdays) where you will find a museum, underground tour, refreshments and toilets. If you can find time for a visit you should - the glittering displays of minerals are breathtaking.

Refreshments may also be obtained a pleasant 0.75 mile (1200m) walk away by turning left at the Levant Beam Engine up a track that becomes Levant Road, into Trewellard where there is a pub and a seasonal tea-room.

From the Beam Engine House the path is a broad gravel-type that goes straight on to

Roscommon and stays well inland of many interesting diversions. With care you can take paths closer to the cliff edge, and see the remains of old mine workings and the spectacular Stamps and Jowl Zawn, but be prepared to retrace your steps and turn inland again to the main path. As you approach Botallack look for the famous Crowns mine engine houses down below.

About 300 yards (275 m) past Wheal Edward keep a sharp lookout for a sign directing you to the right off the granite-set driveway. Your route now leads you towards the sea and the ancient settlement at Kenidjack Castle.

Proceeding on round the headland you descend into the Kenidjack valley. The path drops to a broad gravel track where it turns left, upstream. Continue until you reach a cottage and then turn right over a footbridge. The path then bears right to a junction by a ditch. The official path bears left and zigzags uphill, then goes right at the top. An alternative route continues right at the junction (and is not recommended in summer or early autumn when it can be very overgrown). If you take this proceed along the path and, as you near the sea, scramble up a few yards to turn right on a similar path above, which leads to the road.

In either case you will reach the road (from St Just to Cape Cornwall) and should turn right down it to the National Trust car park near the cove. Turn left if you want to go to St Just. In season you will find a mobile snack wagon in the car park.

If you have time go out on the Cape; it is a wonderful spot owned by the National Trust for 57 good reasons and open to all. It is a good place to watch for dolphins, sharks, seals, and of course to see the Scilly Isles on a clear day.

31 | Cape Cornwall to Sennen Cove (Beach Car Park) OS E102

Grading: Moderate Distance - 8.1 411.2 5.0 255.4

Timing: 2.5 hours

See also our Pendeen Watch to Porthcurno Path Description.

From the car park descend into a small field where, at the bottom, you turn left, and descend granite steps then turn sharp left up a concrete-covered drive, then take a right turn onto a granite gravel covered path. The steep climb ends at Carn Gloose where the road bears off left to Ballowall Barrow and St Just but the path bears right down to Cot Valley. Half way down a new waymarked path will take you straight down to the Porth Nanven beach.

Following the coast path, in Cot Valley turn right down the road and head towards the beach at Porth Nanven then cross the stream and climb up on the path. There are several zigzag paths to make the climbs easier as you proceed around Gribba Point towards Nanquidno.

From here to Gwynver Beach the path is fairly level and the walking is moderate (with one difficult step) but the coast path is everything a coast path should be - we predict that everyone will enjoy this section! Look out for rare flowers in early summer in fields near to Nanquidno.

Below Escalls cliff between Gwynver Beach and the sands of Sennen Cove the path runs along the edge of fast-eroding low cliffs. It is suggested you might consider walking the firm sands of Sennen Cove, at any time but very high tide, rather than the official soft sand route in the dunes at the back of the beach.

32 | Sennen Cove to Porthcurno (Beach) OS E102 (V) Sennen Cove

Grading: Moderate Distance - 10.6 421.8 6.6 262.0

Timing: 3.25 hours

See also our Pendeen Watch to Porthcurno Path Description.

We recommend that during your planning of this section, you should allow a good hour for a visit to and exploration of the scenic Minack Theatre. Entry can be gained when there is no performance. Please remember that any visit you make to the theatre is not included in our estimated timing for this section. However, we need to warn you about your accommodation requirements to Penzance. From mid May to mid September there are performances at the theatre, and theatregoers take up many B & Bs so bear this in mind and perhaps book ahead.

Leaving Sennen Cove you pass the Round House; go on into the car park area and turn left at the public toilets. Proceed ahead shortly to turn right and then head for the battlemented lookout post. From the lookout there are many well-worn paths to Land's End - needless to say, the best is the most seaward - just keep heading on towards the hotel block at Land's End. The coast path provides free access to the Land's End complex, indeed the route passes through it. By keeping to the seaward paths you may avoid some of the crowds, although you may want to use the cafés and other facilities.

Proceeding on, be careful to watch for path rerouting. The proprietors of Land's End are trying to encourage the growth of grasses on areas badly affected by foot erosion. The path leads to Greeb Cottage which now houses an animal collection.

From Land's End to Porthcurno is one of the finest sections of the path, and effects of the sun on the water make you conscious of having turned to walk in a southerly direction. As you approach Nanjizal Beach look across to see where the coast path turns right and uphill after the small stream. Once across the stream by a small wooden bridge proceed ahead for 40 yards (36 m) and then turn right to go steeply uphill on a stepped path.

Care should be taken to keep to the seaward path out to Gwennap Head. It is the official route but it can be tempting to keep to the easier, wider, inland path and you will miss many grand sights. Tol-Pedn-Penwith means the 'holed headland of Penwith' and that hole is easy to miss. From the Coastwatch hut walk on a bearing of 140 degrees for 153 yards (140 m) then walk along a path which bears 190 degrees. It is up to you but if you do go to walk across the natural arch then take GREAT care and, having crossed over, bear left along a path to rejoin the higher coast path.

The path drops into Porthgwarra where, if tide permits, a walk down the granite slipway towards the beach is rewarding. From the beach you can walk up through a fisherman's pasage, out the other end then return to the refreshment hut (open early April - October).

The path leaves Porthgwarra along a track in front of cottages, then turns slightly inland to go behind another. The path is now easy to follow and is well-marked along Carn Barges. As you descend towards Porth Chapel beach take a short excursion out to a granite point for glorious views of the beach. The path descends to the back of the beach passing by St Levan's Holy Well. You can descend to the beach for a swim or bear off left within 10 yards (9 m) of the bridge. The path traverses cliffs behind the beach then climbs towards the headland of Pedn-mên-an-mere. Another rewarding diversion is to go out and round the headland.

You come out into the car park behind the Minack Theatre through a kissing gate. Go through the car park to leave at the other end on a path parallel to and behind the Theatre entrance. The path drops very steeply, with steps, to Porthcurno Beach. A notice warns 'A difficult descent not recommended for young children or elderly persons', and we could add that if one suffers badly from vertigo then go, have a look and make up your own mind. An alternative path around by the road can be used.

At the bottom turn left and unless you want a swim do not go onto the beach but keep along the path contouring above the beach. Drop down to the path from the car park to the beach. You may detour left for transport or refreshments, or to visit the museum at Porthcurno that celebrates the history of submarine telegraphy.

33 | Porthcurno to Lamorna Cove (Harbour) — OS E102

Grading: Strenuous		Distance -	8.8	430.6	5.5	267.5

Timing: 3.25 hours

See also our Porthcurno to Penzance Path Description.

There is again fine walking in this section and some of it easy going; however parts of it are not easy and it may well take you longer than you expect.

The path starts at the back of Porthcurno beach. You join a steep track, overlooking the beach to Percella Point.

Just beyond the Telegraph Cable sign the National Trust has put in a short path which loops round the next headland and keeps you nearer to the sea. Along this path there is a very steep path to Pednvounder beach which many use for swimming.

The path then crosses behind the earthworks of Treryn Dinas (fortress settlement) with an Iron Age cliff castle. A diversion can be made to see the Logan Rock on the headland but you have to return to the path where you left it.

At Penberth Cove cross the slipway, pass the old capstan and go up the other side outside the house to climb a cove-side path.

As you progress east along Trevedran Cliff the path veers away from the cliff top and you cross a heathlike stretch of cliff top and then come upon a well-marked turn right, with a white painted sign on a granite boulder directing you to 'Lamorna'. Turn down here and follow the waymarks.

Nearing St Loy the path gradually moves inland. You will pass a house seaward and below you - after passing it watch out for a sign and stile. You will descend steeply through woodlands. You will find a B&B and refreshment available here in this tranquil spot at Cove Cottage. The path continues on to the bouldered beach. There are only 55 yards (50 m) of boulders to cross before you leave them to regain the coast path. Watch carefully for the beach exit: in the past several have missed it and continued walking on the boulders to have to return.

After you pass the path down to the lighthouse at Tater-du you cross a tumbled granite landscape to Lamorna. You will pass the entrance to the Oliver Land Reserve, 'a place of solitude', purchased by Derek and Jeannie Tangye to create a wildlife sanctuary and now protected by the Minack Chronicles Nature Trust.

Be careful on Carn Barges not to be diverted on to the inland path to Lamorna - the better and official route is round the coast.

34 | Lamorna Cove to Penzance (Railway Station)   OS E102 (V) Mousehole; (V) Newlyn

| Grading: Strenuous and then easy | Distance - | 9.7 | 440.3 | 6.0 | 273.5 |

Timing: 2.5 hours

See also our Porthcurno to Penzance Path Description.

After the café at Lamorna you bear right behind the harbour and cross the bridge. You go up past a complicated waymark which, unless you look at it carefully, almost sends you the wrong way. However, keep right with only one house still on your right.

Few find the correct route into Mousehole. When you have passed the Bird Hospital on your left there is a post box on your right with a coast path sign pointing the way you have come, but not the way you are going! Turn right opposite 'Lowena', and at the sign for Merlin Place head towards the rocks (St Clement's Isle) which you can see out to sea.

Just before the foreshore bear left along a terrace and fork right into a car park. Go to the bottom right end of the car park to continue briefly along the harbour side. You then have to turn in again left and first right. However, those with an interest in history should go past the house with the pillars, the Keigwin, the oldest and most attractive house in the village. It has a large porch with granite columns. The turn brings you out on to a busier street; bear right along it to come behind the harbour again.

The official coast path leaving Mousehole goes up a narrow road. We suggest you pass through the car park at the other end of the harbour, near some toilets, and along a concrete path. Go round the corner and up steps into a small car park with a café. At the top turn right along a pavement.

A new cycle/walkway has been opened seaward of the road to Newlyn. Follow the signs and when you reach Newlyn go round the back of the harbour passing the War Memorial. Then bear right over the little bridge; the Seaman's Mission is on the right. Over the bridge bear right to come out once more behind the beach. Walk along the promenade into Penzance.

Pass the open air Jubilee swimming pool and continue round to pass Penzance Harbour and on to the railway station.

35 | Penzance to Marazion (Market Place)   OS E102 (T) Penzance (Trains)

Grading: Easy   Distance -   5.4   445.7   3.4   276.9

Timing: 1 hour

See also our Penzance to Porthleven Path Description

Leave Penzance from the Tourist Information Centre, seaward of the railway station, and walk towards the sea, picking the new waterfront walkway past a footbridge over the railway tracks. This is a cycle route but a vast improvement on the old route along a dangerous road. The route follows the top of the sea wall to Marazion.

If the tide is right it is possible to walk all the way from Penzance to Marazion along the beach, though you will have to ford some small streams on the way.

Further along where the railway veers away from the beach you will come upon Marazion Bridge, which has a large car park. As you pass the café known as The Station you emerge onto the road and head for Marazion.

You will have to cross the Red River either by the road bridge or a footbridge to bring you to a grass car park known locally as Folly Field. Follow the edge of the field past the sailing dinghy compound, across a car park and into historic Marazion, behind the new sea defence wall.

Between Marazion and Lelant there is a cross-peninsula path, St Michael's Way. This could be used to make a circular trip round Penwith by walking round the coast path and coming back inland from Marazion to Carbis Bay, Lelant or St Ives. There is a guide leaflet to the St Michael's Way available from St Ives TIC (see page 150).

36 | Marazion to Prussia Cove (Bessy's Cove)   OS E102 (V) Marazion

Grading: Moderate   Distance -   6.8   452.5   4.2   281.1

Timing: 1.75 hours

See also our Penzance to Porthleven Path Description.

Walkers are treated badly at the beginning of this section, as there is no path at all for a while and then the first coastal length is on a beach.

You go up the road in Marazion for some way and pass the 40 speed restriction sign. Shortly after this you see the sign which thanks drivers for driving carefully and turn right into a driveway. As the driveway bears right into a private house you go left down a little concrete staircase and then follow the path down to the shoreline. Walk along the beach (but not when the tide is very high) and ascend some hideous metal steps. There is a marked diversion at Trenow Cove. Follow the diverted track for 274 yards (250 m) and look out for a yellow arrow pointing you back to the coast.

After that you will have no trouble getting to Perranuthnoe where there are refreshments in season. The path comes out onto a tarmac road by a car park. Walk on into the tarmac lane immediately opposite and to seaward of the car park. Go right at the fork by Blue Burrow Cottage and bear right. Just before you get to the beach the path turns left into a field.

At Cudden Point the path cuts slightly inland but then the true coast path goes seaward again towards Little Cudden. The view from Cudden Point takes in the whole of Mount's Bay from Lizard Point to Tater-du. Notice particularly the unusual view of Mousehole.

At Bessy's Cove the path goes up to join a track by a letter box. Continue ahead bearing right beside a pair of granite gate posts.

| 37 | Prussia Cove to Porthleven (Harbour) | OS E102 & E103 |

Grading: Strenuous Distance - 10.3 462.8 6.4 287.5

Timing: 3 hours

See also our Penzance to Porthleven Path Description.

The path at Prussia Cove is quite a surprise, a sunken lane between two large stone buildings. You continue along a lane with the old coastguard row up on your left to pass through a gate, after which the track becomes a path and you should fork right at the first junction.

The path later becomes a green track down to Praa Sands where there are plenty of refreshments in season.

The official route is along the road but it is preferable to continue on near the sea, so turn right down onto the beach onto a slipway between the Welloe Rock public house and the car park. Walk along the front of the pub and the beach shop, then take the steps off the beach beside the shop/café. Turn right across the top of the sand dunes going left when signed, into a small estate of houses. As you come out of the estate bear right and pick up the path in the dunes once more.

The path now takes you across Rinsey Head, with a diversion sign taking you inland to cut off the point. Go through the National Trust car park. As you drop down to the restored engine house you will see two paths ahead, one going uphill, which you do not want, the other going down, which you do. When you reach the engine house pick up the path below it on the other side.

At Trewavas head the path bears inland of the old mine ruins and is well marked. Between Trewavas Head and Bullion Cliff the coastal route changes often due to constant erosion. It is well to be cautious and always take the newest track even if the old does appear to be intact. You will see evidence of recent landslides. The advice is keep well away from the edge.

As you approach Porthleven you pass a cross erected in memory of drowned sailors buried in unconsecrated ground.

On entering Porthleven you join a lane and then take the first road down to the right which will lead you down into the town and harbour.

| 38 | Porthleven to Mullion Cove (Harbour) | OS E103 (V) Porthleven |

Grading: Moderate Distance - 11.4 474.2 7.1 294.6

Timing: 3.25 hours

See also our Porthleven to The Lizard Path Description.

At Porthleven as so often you have to walk right round the back of the harbour and out the other side. You go beyond the battlemented tower-like building to keep up the coastal road, using Mounts Road although it says it is a cul-de-sac.

Shortly after the last building on the right, a hotel, turn left off the track into the National Trust property Parc-an-als Cliff to avoid a landfall. Over the top you pick up the track again to proceed on and down to the beach.

If you have plenty of time there is a walking route right around Loe Pool, the biggest natural lake in Cornwall.

As you cross Loe Bar look for the path going up just to the right of the field but divert to see the white cross on your right. You pick up the path you want on 126 degrees from the cross. After the path levels out you pass a wooden seat and about 100 yards (90 m) after this, fork right to pick up the old route.

At Gunwalloe Fishing Cove you come out onto a gravelly road; do not take the first right which goes down to the beach but bear right on the second turning to pass inland of a house. At the top of the hill there is a stile where walking gardeners should look left.

Above Halzephron Cove you join the road and walk along the verge until bearing right through a small car park to gain the cliff top once again. Continue to just before a field gate where you turn right to follow the cliffs along to Dollar Cove.

At Gunwalloe Church Cove there is an alternative. If you want to see the church, and it is interesting, when you join the road go right and after you have seen the church you can usually cross the beach and its stream.
If a church visit is not for you, the correct route bears left aiming for buildings which prove to be public conveniences and a very seasonal cafe. There is a sign where you join the road but it is badly sited so is not obvious. Proceed down the road with the National Trust Gunwalloe Towans sign on your right. Bear left off the road just before a turning space. Cross a bridge over a stream and turn right round the back of the beach. The path is narrow until you come to a track where you turn left uphill.

At the top there is a small car park; as soon as you have gone through this you can bear right to walk along the cliff tops and so miss a length of tarmac road.

There is a seasonal café at Poldhu Cove. You walk round the back of the beach on the road and go up the drive of the residential care home. Turn right off the driveway shortly before you get to the big house.

Skirt around the back of Polurrian Cove to go up the steps, then take a track to turn right on a road. Where the road bears left proceed ahead on a path. If you are a purist the coast path goes in front of the old coastguard lookout, but this bit of path is seldom cleared.

Just past the Mullion Cove Hotel the path veers right, through the car parking spaces opposite starting by an old cannon. At the bottom turn left.

39 | Mullion Cove to The Lizard (Lighthouse)   OS E103

Grading: Moderate	Distance -	10.9	485.1	6.8	301.4

Timing: 3.25 hours

See also our Porthleven to The Lizard Path Description.

This is a wonderful, spectacular section with lots of interest, and it can be accomplished without great effort. Unless the weather is inclement you will certainly enjoy this stretch. If you can arrange the transport it makes a spectacular long half day excursion.

You go up the road; a very little way turn right and then right again.

After Mullion Cove in several places there are alternative paths but usually it makes little difference which you take, except as mentioned below.

After Parc Bean Cove going up Lower Predannock Cliff you want the higher path not the lower and at the top bear right.

After Vellan Cliff just before Gew-Graze, the path veers slightly inland for a stile.

Taking the path down to Kynance Cove, as you go down aim for the further headland you can see which is Lizard Point. Later you will see a sign close to the sea where you have to turn left; go down further to cross a wide concrete bridge by a house.

There is a good, long season café at Kynance Cove. Unless the tide is right in, the quickest route is to cross the few yards at the back of the beach and go up the steps the other side. If the tide is right in you have to go up the drive before the cafe and bear right at the top.

Leave the car park just to the right of the public toilets.

Lizard Town is exceptionally well footpathed so if you are lodging there you have a great many options.

Turn left above the Most Southerly Café and go along in front of the lighthouse.

Grading: Moderate but strenuous in parts   Distance -   **17.1   502.2   10.6   312.0**

Timing: 5.75 hours

See also our The Lizard to Coverack Path Description.

A word of warning; old stone stiles are made of the local serpentine which can prove very slippery when wet, so take care on wet polished rock.

Unless you suffer from vertigo, do not miss diverting right shortly after the lighthouse to see the spectacular Lion's Den, which although is only about 20 yards (18 m) off the path, is still missed by many.

You pass the Housel Bay Hotel (open all year) then cross the top edge of a field to a stile where the path returns to the seaward edge again.

You pass the old Lloyd's Signal Station and come out on a drive by a house. You go along this only a short way and the coast path then takes off right.

At Kilcobben Cove you come just inland of the top building of the lifeboat station, walk round it and go down the first little flight of steps but then go forward and not down the long flight of steps to the lifeboat.

At Church Cove go across diagonally behind one building to go through beside a big gate. Avoid the next four right turns to go uphill and over a stile.

After Polgwidden watch for a sharp right turn going along in front of an isolated house; the wrong path goes forward and looks more impressive.

You pass the National Trust Devil's Frying Pan sign and the true coast path is diagonally ahead, down steps into the car park and out the other end to turn right. In fact it has lately been signposted avoiding the car park; the choice is yours. Whichever way you went you drop down a lovely path through a garden. Watch for the right turn just after you have gone over a stone stile next to a metal gate.

You drop into Cadgwith behind the beach where there is a chance of refreshment, and then start up the hill staying with the road to turn first right just past Veneth Cottage.

After Enys Head there is a poorly marked section: you come to a fork where you go left, soon there is another right turn which you ignore, then you come down to a gate where you turn right. Go down until you see the National Trust Poltesco sign on the left. Here turn right going down steps and over a bridge. Avoid both the next right turns unless you wish to see the old Poltesco serpentine works. At the next junction, as you go up, bear right and again at the next junction. Later you go through a golf course area at the end of which you bear right. You come out on a road where you turn right.

At Kennack Sands (refreshments in season) the path is behind the beach towards the toilets and then is well marked behind the two beaches. If the tide is well out you can walk along both beaches to the far end but as the proper path, at the time of writing, is well maintained there is little gained. What you do need to watch for at the far end of the second beach is that you take the coast path which looks fairly insignificant starting up nearly on the cliff edge; there is a bigger, wide path going inland but do not take it. There is another minor junction shortly where you keep right again.

Care should be taken in front of Borgwitha and behind the cliff castle Carrick Luz, because you cut across the neck of the peninsula and do not go inland or seaward. Improved waymarking should mean that you do not now go astray.

There is a very steep if scenic drop to Downas Cove and up the other side. After Beagles Point there is another smaller drop; cross a bridge and go up what is almost a stone chute the other side. At the top turn right.

After Black Head there is a very fine viewpoint looking ahead along the South Cornish Coast. The path has been much improved and now goes along the top of the cliffs before dropping down at Chynalls Cliff to pass seaward of what was the Headland Hotel to Chynalls Point. For more scenic views go out onto Chynalls Point and look back along the coast path which you have just walked and look ahead to the delights in front of you. In any case the walk to the point is part of the

National Trail. Follow the seaward path until it becomes tarmac; turn right and drop down to join a road. If you wish to do all the coast path, there is then a little loop that many miss. 20 yards (18 m) down the road the path goes away right above a children's playground. The path then looks as though it is going to end, but press on over a slight rise to go down steps and turn left in front of a house.

Keep right of the back of a pub into the car park, turn left and left again to pass the front of the same pub.

41 | Coverack to Helford (Ferry)　　　　　　　　　OS E103 (V) Coverack

Grading: Moderate　　　　　　　　　　Distance -　　21.1　　523.3　　13.1　　325.1

Timing: 5.75 hours

See also our Coverack to Helford Path Description.

This distance includes the walk around Gillan Creek. If you arrive there at low tide and paddle across, deduct 2 miles (3.2 km).

Note: Evening meals can present a problem in Helford. At busy periods the Shipwright's Arms (01326 231235) will only serve pre-booked meals. There is also the Rose Tea Gardens which serves meals but shuts earlier. Think about this before leaving Coverack or you may go to bed hungry.

In Coverack the coast path continues behind the harbour and the beach and where the main road bears inland, go ahead up the small tarmac road. The tarmac ends just before a small rise; go over this and start to drop down and look for a path turning off right just before a gate across the road.

The path out to Lowland Point is improved, but the further you go the less evidence of path there is. However the basic ploy is to keep close to the shore, going east until you have to turn north at the point.

After Lowland Point the coast path goes through Dean Quarry. This Association fought hard to get the path on the coast here rather than a long diversion inland. Heed the notice for times of blasting; at these times the path will be closed but you can use the diversion if travelling north.

Most of the quarry area is well signposted, but it is important that when you come up level with the first building, you start down the steep ramp to the beach - the footpath goes left off this. Towards the end of the quarry area, signs are more scarce but keep with the track close above the sea to go down on to the beach at Godrevy Cove.

Walk just over half way along the beach, crossing the stream bed which sometimes has water but is often dry, then turn half left to circumvent a marshy area and pick up the path at the back of the beach. Here turn left until you can turn inland through fields up a gravel track and sunken lane to Rosenithon.

At the T-junction in Rosenithon turn right and go up the hill. The road bears right and just after this the footpath takes off left into a field. Cross one field and a traditional Cornish stile, surely the forerunner of the modern cattle grid. Cross two more fields in the same direction and surprisingly, the stile is just below the gate you come to.

Turn left on the road then first right down into Porthoustock. From Porthoustock to Porthallow the official route again goes inland to avoid the now unused quarries around Pencra Head and Porthkerris Point. However, there is a coast path.

Coastal Route
In Porthoustock, keep right of the telephone box and pass the entrance to the beach, forking left up a bank passing in front of a thatched cottage. You soon come to a big metal gate; the pedestrian access is just to the right round the wall.

Continue along the track and take the left fork approximately 150 yards (137 m) beyond the northern end of a disused quarry, which leads to a steep uphill slope. 20 yards (18 m) beyond the top of the slope, fork right for the shorter route to Porthkerris beach, except around high water spring tides. The simpler route for any state of the tide is to proceed up along the track for a further 450 yards (410 m), and turn right onto another track through a field which leads down to behind Porthkerris beach. Walk straight up the hill opposite, passing the way up to a restaurant on the left. (Should this latter track not be open, continue on to the MOD building and turn right along the road.)

Where the road bears left, carry straight on through two fields parallel to the coast to a kissing gate. Proceed ahead up the path and then steeply down to the beach at Porthallow.

Official Route
You leave Porthoustock going up the hill, but soon, where the road bears right, go ahead on a track. You pass houses on your right, the track ends and you keep ahead into a field. Here turn steeply up the field 302 degrees joining the right hand field bank at the top. Keep close to the bank to a sunken stile in the corner then slightly more right 338 degrees to another sunken stile just left of the gate.

Bear left on the road which later bears left to Trenance; here turn right. At the next T junction look for the footpath ahead and a few yards to your right. Go down alongside a vineyard to join the road where you turn right down to Porthallow. There is a café at Porthallow which is open from Easter to October, Wednesday to Sunday, 1030 – 1700.

For those interested in their progress along the South West Coast Path, you will pass the halfway point on reaching Porthallow.

You leave Porthallow by taking the second turning on to the beach and immediately turning left to go along the back of the foreshore and up steps, bearing right at the first junction.

As you approach Nare Point, ignore a stile on your right but turn left along a one-time track which served the lookout. You go through a gateway and when the track bears uphill, proceed ahead across a footbridge.

After the second National Trust property 'The Herra', you come to a small beach where you go across the back. You come to a second beach, Flushing Cove, where you turn right on a path behind the beach.

A very short distance beyond the beach, a footpath takes off left and it is decision time. If you know the tide is in and you want to walk round, turn left.

Gillan Creek - Walking Round
Go up the grass-centred concrete track to and along a made-up road. At a left bend the coast path is signed to the right of a pebbledashed house. Proceed along a short stretch of a narrow, possibly overgrown, path into a field. Keep to the hedge on the left to a six bar gate, then go diagonally across the next field over another stile just left of another gate. Turn up the field to locate a ladder stile well to the right of a bungalow to the road and turn right down to Carne and right again beyond the creek head to St Anthony.

If time is of the essence, you could go via Manaccan and be in Helford in 3 miles (5 km), but that is of course not walking the coast path.

Gillan Creek Crossing (Deduct 2 miles / 3.2 km)
No ferry but it can usually be forded from one hour before Low Tide to one hour after. Predicted low water is 15 minutes earlier than shown in the Tide Tables. But do proceed with care.

There are two possible crossing places. Proceed until you can go no further along the path by the river, descend steps to the beach and wade across towards two caravans on the far shore.

A little further upstream you can cross part way on stepping stones in two sections: however this is not the easy option it sounds because they are extremely slippery and do not go across the whole river. It is advisable to carry handfuls of sand to scatter onto the stepping stones and even then be careful. If you do not use the stepping stones, it is possible to paddle across.

Once across turn right to pass in front of the church. Turn left up the hill. About 10 yards (9 m) past a mounting block on the left, look for a path going off at an angle right, take this and turn first right. You may then see the sign which should be at the bottom.

Coast path continues
For the short route you need to turn left just after the house on your right beyond the kissing gate. If you have time the circular route out around Dennis Head is rewarding. To walk this, proceed ahead into the open field along a vestigial track towards a wood, keep to the left of the wood but close to it. Pass round the back of it where you will find a stile on your left; you can complete the circuit of the head returning to the stile and then back along the right hand hedge. You pass through several fields but then watch out for the sharp and partially concealed right turn into the wood. (Dogs must be kept under strict control.)

You come out by an old railed hound enclosure to bear slightly right and then go up a tarmac drive with grass in the centre. At the top turn right down the road, turn left up steps just as you get to the drive of a house called Traeth Cottage; it is easy to miss; if you get to the shore you have missed it!

Go along the back of the car park, down the road, crossing the first bridge over the creek. Turn right and go along past The Shipwright's Arms to the ferry point.

42 | Helford to Falmouth (Ferry Terminal)   OS E103 (V) Helford

Grading: Moderate   Distance -   16.1   539.4   10.0   335.1

Timing: 4.5 hours

See also our Helford to Falmouth Path Description.

Helford to Helford Passage - use ferry, see details below. If the ferry is not running your alternatives are probably a taxi or a walk of 13 miles (21 km). This is mostly road but you can incorporate Frenchman's Creek. (Local taxis service - Autocabs 01326 573773 or Cove Cars 07980 - 814058).

Helford Passage (Helford River). Seasonal. April 1st to October 31st. Departs hourly - Helford River Boats, Helford Passage, Helford Passage on the hour and Helford 10 mins. Nr Falmouth Tel Mawnan Smith past the hour. 9am to 5pm daily. Summer months 01326 250770 only (July and August) runs on demand from e.mail: enquiries@helfordferry.com 9am to 9.00pm. All crossings subject to tide and www.helford-river-boats.co.uk weather conditions.

We urge you to contact the ferry operator direct if you are relying on this service, particularly if you are anticipating a fairly late finish and need to confirm the time of its last run.

Helford to Helford Passage (Walking route) approx. 13 miles (21 km).

This moderate to easy route, on footpaths and minor roads, is as close to the Helford River as possible.

Take the path up the hill in front of the Shipwright's Arms; you will pass houses on your right and come down to Penarvon Cove. Back at the west side of the cove you will need to turn inland. Follow this track up a road where you turn right then left onto a farm track. This will lead you to the permissive path above Frenchman's Creek, eventually descending to continue alongside it through the woods. At the head of the creek you come to a definitive footpath. This is at the sign of the permissive path to Frenchman's Creek. Take the path on the right to Withan and Mudgeon past Frenchman's Pill cottage on the left, and across a footbridge over the river. Follow the waymarked route through the woods. When you get out of the woods, aim for the far left corner of the field and take the stile with the iron wheel gate on the left. Follow the boundary on the left and over the stiles past Withan Farm, from where you head in a westerly direction, until you reach a concrete-block stile to a farm lane where you turn left. Pass Mudgeon Farm on your right. When you reach a crossroads, turn right towards Mawgan. After a short distance, the path goes downhill.

Proceed uphill and you will join the road from St Martin where you turn right, passing the ancient settlement at Gear. Going downhill, you soon reach the narrow bridge over Mawgan Creek and on the next bend, you come to Bridge Farm. Turn left and proceed up the road. When you reach the main road, turn right. Just before the church turn left at the Gwarth-an-drea sign and left at the back of the bungalow called The Oaks. When you reach the road, turn right along Gweek Drive and follow this road until you meet a road on the left with a ford, and cross the bridge and follow the road to Gweek.

From Gweek, take the road opposite the Gweek Inn past the post office and take the footpath on the right through a wooden gate, just before light industrial units. The path runs parallel to a stream and it is not very clear. You join a bridleway at the ruins of a building and need to turn right, passing Kestle Dee farm. You will meet the road at Carwythenack Chase and need to take the Constantine/Port Navas road. Follow the field edge and cross the corner of the field to the stile by the signpost. Follow the road, crossing a stream and take the footpath on the left after the stream. Follow the field edge and go over the stile in the corner of the field behind the hut. Follow the road to Nancenoy and Polwheveral. You will now have to climb uphill.

Descend from the footpath junction towards Polwheveral. At the crossroads, turn right into the Port Navas road. After about 140 yards (128 m), take the left footpath into the corner of a field and cross the field to a stile left of the gate. Follow the field edge and cross the corner of the field to the stile by the signpost. Follow the road to Port Navas. We suggest you walk through

Port Navas, exploring the creek and the quay. At Trenarth Bridge, by the post box, follow the Mawnan/Falmouth sign.

At the head of Port Navas Creek is a footpath on the left to Lower Penpol. Take the next footpath on the right, just past a turning to some houses. Cross the field to a stile left of a house. Continue right up the road past Budock Vean Golf and Country Club. Turn right at the road for Helford Passage. Turn right past Dring House. At the end of the road turn left onto a new definitive footpath before 'Ridifarne' and walk down to The Bar and turn left, following the coastal path to Helford Passage. You now reach the Ferry Boat Inn at Helford Passage, where the ferry from Helford would have put you down had it been operating.

Coast path continues
At Helford Passage go along the beach eastwards to go up the steps at the end. At Durgan bear sharp right, when you reach the track, then bear left by the old school. Go up the road past a little grassy area with a seat on the right then DO NOT turn first right; it is the second turning you want.

At the next beach you come to Porth Saxon; you go in front of the boathouse, and the path is then at the back of the shore. At the following beach, Porthallack, the path in contrast stays in the fields to go on to the beach beyond a building.

The true coast path goes out round Rosemullion Head with its fine views, but there is a short cut across its neck. You come to the National Trust Nansidwell property and shortly into a big field; go downwards and across to join the bottom hedge. The exit is in the corner. There is another path better walked going ahead but it is the wrong path. The path does not go on the beach but bears left at the last moment.

You come out onto the road at Maenporth (refreshments in season). Turn right along the road, turning right again at the other end of the beach.

There follows a 1.5 mile (2.25 km) stretch past a golf course and around Pennance Point to the outskirts of Falmouth.

On reaching the road turn right for Swanpool, there walk across the back of the beach to continue on the coast path turning right at the first junction. At Gyllyngvase Beach turn right along the road; it will not be most people's favourite walking but it is quite rewarding looking back to where you have previously been.

When you get towards the end of the sea front passing the last big hotel, The Falmouth Hotel, do not go down right but continue on the pavement beside the road until you have passed the cul-de-sac notice, then you can bear right if you wish, away from the road. However presently you will need to cross the road for the safety of the pavement around Pendennis Point.

There is a path on the right from Pendennis Head towards the docks which you can take if you wish.

You come to a T junction where you turn right, there is then a town centre sign pointing left but that is the long way round for traffic so stay with us. Go ahead under the railway bridge. The road shortly bears left and there is a pub on the right which still proclaims it has hotel stables and a motor garage.

The road bears right passing a big car park and the new National Maritime Museum and soon becomes a shopping street. Continue until Marks & Spencers, and the next turning on the right takes you to the ferry.

| 43 | Falmouth to Place House | OS E105 (T) Falmouth (Trains); (V) St Mawes |

| No Grading | | Distance - | 0 | 539.4 | 0 | 335.1 |

See also our Falmouth to Portloe Path Description.

In season you can cross by using two ferries, see details below. The only point to watch is that depending on conditions, the first ferry takes 20 to 30 minutes for the passage.

The ferry from Falmouth to St Mawes runs the whole year round except for winter Sundays. The scarcity of public transport in winter on Sundays combined with the fact that it is a long hike, makes us advise anyone arriving in Falmouth in winter on a Sunday to take it as a day off!

The ferry from St Mawes to Place only runs in season. If you are a purist there is a reasonable walking route round of 8-9 miles (13-14 km), two sections of which are very good walking indeed, see below for details. There are about a couple of buses a day from St Mawes to Gerrans, except on Sundays, or you could consider a taxi. If the ferry is not in service you can always ask. We have heard from walkers who have been lucky enough to get a lift from local boat owners.

Falmouth/St Mawes   All year round. Weather permitting.
St Mawes Ferry Co   Summer service every 1/2 hour, Winter service
106 Acacia Road, Falmouth, TR11 2LA   every hour.
01326 313201 - Office   Summer Sundays departs Falmouth on the hour,
01872 862312   departs St Mawes 1/2 past the hour.

Winter service every hour but no sailings at 0915 and 1215 from Falmouth, and 0945, 1245 and 1545 from St Mawes. No Sunday service.

The St Mawes Ferry Co. is prepared to land pre-organized parties of 20 or more at Place House. To do this they would need prior knowledge to lay on an extra boat. This is also dependent on the state of the tide and weather.

St Mawes/Place House (St Anthony)   Seasonal
For information please contact: Daily 1st April - 31st October.
Gary S Cairns   0930 - 1630
6 Cogos Park, Mylor Bridge
Falmouth TR11 5SF
Tel: 01326 372703
Mobile: 07790 647169   group bookings/parties accepted
or: 07791 283884

We urge you to contact the ferry operator direct if you are relying on this service, particularly if you are anticipating a fairly late finish and need to confirm the time of its last run.

Ocean Aqua Cab
A new service has been launched and will be operational all year round, weather permitting, between 1000 and 0100. The service will carry you from Falmouth to St Mawes or to Place direct and vice versa. We have been told it would be best if you could telephone the day before you require the crossing. Telephone: Alec Jordan on 07970 242258 www.aquacab.co.uk

Walking route around the Percuil River (approx. 9 miles / 14 km)
At St Mawes, on leaving the ferry from Falmouth turn left along the road. As you approach the castle, take a minor road going left, the most prominent sign being 'St Mawes Castle car park'. If you look carefully there is a small footpath sign amongst the clutter. Follow this minor road until you come to the National Trust's Newton Cliff, which you enter. The route follows a very scenic path along the Carrick Roads with superb views across to Falmouth and the far shore. Ignore two minor stiles on the left which lead down to small coves. You come out on a minor tarmac road to turn right. Continue along this road bearing left at the junction to pass in front of a boatyard. Immediately after passing the boatyard buildings the path bears a few yards to the right to proceed along the bank above the shore.

You come to the gate leading to the churchyard with a large sign 'Dogs on Leads Please Consecrated Ground'. Go through this gate keeping left all the way to pass the church on your right. Ignore the turning right marked 'way out' but instead keep left through a lych-gate and pass a house called Lanzeague. After its second gate the path bears right up the hill. You go through a metal gate where there is a public footpath sign 'St Just Lane' and continue uphill with views of the creek to your left. You go through another gate into a lane, in parts muddy in parts green, to finally exit onto the road.

Turn left and walk along the road for about 150 yards (135 m), ignore the first footpath on the right immediately past a house, but take the second on the right shortly afterwards. For the first field you have the hedge on the right. For the second and third it is on your left, then for the fourth it is again on your right. Take care in this fourth field, as there is a temptation as you enter to turn right; do not do this but go straight ahead to continue with the hedge on the right. Look for the sharp right turn through the hedge a little before you come to the end of the field. Descend the bank to the road, where you turn right and proceed down to meet the main A3078 at Trethem Mill.

Turn left - this is on a bridge crossing the creek - and immediately turn right up some stone steps and ascend the footpath through a wood. Coming out of the wood, cross the field on a bearing of 110. In the next field bear right on 140 and leave by a wooded track. At the top there is a stile; cross it and bear 137 diagonally across the field to a hedge and follow this to the road. Turn right down the road.

At the next junction follow the road curving round to the right past Polhendra Cottage. Here almost immediately turn left through the second gate, a metal one. There is a footpath sign if you look for it, but it is not readily apparent. Aim across on 123 to descend to the bottom of the hedge which you can see on the opposite side of the valley. Here you will find a bridge, cross it and proceed up, with the hedge on your left. At the top ascend some stone steps and cross the next two fields on 125. On reaching the road turn right into Gerrans and walk down to the church.

At the church take the left fork (not left turn) into Treloan Lane. You walk via Treloan and Rosteague, at each junction keeping straight ahead. At the house just beyond Rosteague you pass through a pedestrian gate and the path unexpectedly goes right, through a hedge gap, before continuing in the same direction but with the hedge on your left. You cross an open field to enter an enclosed lane eventually coming to the road at Porth Farm about 1.5 miles (2.4 km) from Gerrans.

The slightly quicker way is then to turn right along the road and left where there is a sign 'Footpath to Place by Percuil River' to cross a wooden bridge. The pleasanter alternative, a few yards longer, is to go ahead on the road to turn right through the gates of the Trust's Porth Farm then turn right to come to the same bridge.

Over the bridge the path turns right to follow Porth Creek and then the Percuil River, down to the low tide landing point for the ferry and soon on to Place itself. This last stretch of walking is very scenic.

44 | Place House to Portscatho (The Quay)   OS E105

Grading: Easy   Distance -   10.0   549.4   6.2   341.3

Timing: 2.75 hours

See also our Falmouth to Portloe Path Description.

The St Anthony Peninsula, thanks to the National Trust, offers a very good half-day circular walk. Most people will start at Porth Farm, walk to Place as already described, and then follow the coast path round St Anthony's Head and on to Towan Beach, here turning back inland to Porth Farm.

Some maps show a definitive right of way across the front of Place House; this route however is not really practical except at very low tides.

The coast path continues up the road at Place passing the gates of the house and shortly turn right to go behind the church. You get back to the creekside, soon to leave it again to go over behind Amsterdam Point. The path then is superb with wonderful views across the Carrick Roads. After the footbridge across the top of a one-time dam turn sharp right. Shortly even sharper left to go up steps and turn right again at the top. Look for the very little path forking right up to the topograph for the best viewpoint.

The path then proceeds forwards without problems to Portscatho; however, owing to the lie of the land you do not see the village until the very last moment and it always seems to take longer than you think it should.

45 | Portscatho to Portloe (Post Office)   OS E105 (V) Portscatho

Grading: Strenuous   Distance -   12.0   561.4   7.5   348.8

Timing: 3.75 hours

See also our Falmouth to Portloe Path Description.

You leave Portscatho going through a couple of small fields; if the tide is out you have a choice. You can start down the steps then turn right and go down to cross Porthcurnick Beach - this is slightly shorter. The reward for not turning for the beach but going up the steps opposite is that you then pass a seasonal refreshment hut.

If the tide is out it is easier to walk along Pendower Beach to Carne Beach. You can look forward to see if this is feasible as you walk down by the car park before Pendower Beach. Those who have walked this section over the past few years will notice that the coast path has been reinstated to seaward of the Nare Hotel. Thanks are due to Cornwall County Council and everyone else involved.

Having ascended Nare Head, it is possible to short cut it by veering left but, unless the weather is poor, do not do this or you will miss out on the rewarding views. Study the way the first arrow is pointing and follow its direction along the edge of the gorse. There is an unmarked path going right to the head itself. Shortly afterwards there is a post with an arrow pointing left here on a bearing of 120 degrees; if you look carefully you will see a small path going forward into the gorse - take this. This path gives the best views of Gull Rock offshore. It winds back to join the main track, where you turn right.

At the other end of the track about 200 yards (185 m) on, where it opens up, there are little ventilators; bear across right to pick up the coast again; do not stay on the track.

Another place you can go wrong is after the very steep descent off The Blouth where the path bears left and then right over a stile. There is a sign but it is badly sited so it is easy to miss and as a result a lot of people go wrong here.

At The Straythe there is a pleasant surprise for those who walked this way some years ago. A well engineered path zigzags up to replace the old uncomfortable and nearly vertical flight of steps. At the top the route is well signposted through the gardens, but you do need to turn right in the field when you get there.

There is a long descent into Portloe but at least you can see it, unlike Portscatho. Watch for the sharp left turn just as you draw nearly level with a green seat on your right. Then you want the second turning on the left to pass in front of the public toilets and so down to Portloe.

46   Portloe to East Portholland (Car Park)   OS E105

Grading: Strenuous   Distance -   3.8   565.2   2.4   351.2

Timing: 1.25 hours

See also our Portloe to Mevagissey Path Description.

From the quay the coast path goes up the road near a post office which serves teas. It turns right then shortly leaves the road down some wide steps past some houses. Go left at the sign for the NT Flagstaff to go behind the old coastguard lookout.

Do not be tempted to use the sea wall to walk between West and East Portholland – it is very slippery and dangerous.

47   East Portholland to Gorran Haven (Beach)   OS E105

Grading: Strenuous   Distance -   10.3   575.5   6.4   357.6

Timing: 3 hours

See also our Portloe to Mevagissey Path Description.

The path starts along a one time tarmac lane from East Portholland. Turn right at the end of this lane to descend a field and continue alongside the coast. There is a path forward but if you use it, you simply get a longer stretch of road to walk to get to Porthluney Cove.

There is a seasonal cafe behind the beach in front of Caerhays Castle. Note one point, on leaving the road you cross half the first field joining a rough track close to a projecting corner of waste land. The path does not stay on the track here but turns sharp right along the fence; the badly sited marker post is usually invisible in the long grass.

From Hemmick Beach via The Dodman to Gorran Haven, it is all good walking; there are wonderful views from The Dodman in the right conditions. You can look back on triumphs past and challenges still long to come! Just north of The Dodman Cross is an 18th century coastguard watch-house which does prove useful shelter in heavy rain.

At Little Sand Cove there is an old path cutting the corner off Pen-a-Maen Point. We do not recommend it - you climb higher and will not have such good views.

You come into Gorran Haven on Foxhole Lane. Turn right towards the beach, but just before it turn left into Church Street. Proceed up this – there is a footpath loop to the right if you want a brief and better look at the beach, then turn right into Cliff Road.

48 | Gorran Haven to Mevagissey (Harbour)   OS E105 (V) Gorran Haven

Grading: Easy   Distance -   **5.7   581.2   3.5   361.1**

Timing: 1.5 hours

See also our Portloe to Mevagissey Path Description.

You go up past the old coastguard row and turn right again at the top, still Cliff Road. At its end Cliff Road turns left and you go over a stile into a field.

From Turbot Point you descend to Colona Beach passing the National Trust Bodrugan's Leap sign. Turn right to pass behind the beach, do not go left when the track bears left, but proceed ahead very shortly to cross the tarmac drive to continue ahead on a footpath across the grass. At its start you are heading in a straight line for Mevagissey harbour; later it veers a little left and you pick up a hedge on your right. Continue along this hedge until it goes up to join the road where you turn right.

At the end you will find the road is called Chapel Point Lane; turn right, bear left at the sea and follow the road round past the Rising Sun.

You bear right on entering Mevagissey on Polkirt Hill. You pass buildings on your right and then enter a park; proceed through this to the other end. Turn right down the first flight of public stone steps on the right to come out on the quay close to some public toilets.

49 | Mevagissey to Charlestown (Harbour)   OS E105 & E107 (V) Mevagissey; (V) Pentewan

Grading: Strenuous   Distance -   **11.6   592.8   7.2   368.3**

Timing: 4 hours

See also our Mevagissey to Fowey Path Description.

(It may be of interest to know that there is now a ferry service between Mevagissey and Fowey which runs from May until mid October, weather and sea conditions permitting. Timetables are available from Fowey TIC (see page 150) and information is usually available on 07977 203394.)

In Mevagissey walk along the back of the harbour to turn right and then very shortly bear up left veering away from, and up above, the quayside. You come out into open playing fields, go across but aim for the extreme right end of the terrace of buildings you see opposite.

Continue along, avoiding the right turn down some steps. The path comes out again into a field and there is a descent to cross a bridge. Here, turn left. You descend from Penare Point to walk behind the ruins of Portgiskey. Ignore the next stile on the right but proceed, curving right up the hill, following the signs to join the road, where you turn right.

You come out on to the road close to the entrance of a massive caravan park. Here you have the choice of:

1.   turning left to the main road B3273, then right towards St Austell and first right again signposted Pentewan and called West End, which is the official route, or;

2.   turning right towards the sea, then left after the public toilets along the front, then go over a bridge across the St Austell River. You then make for a stone arch ahead, and turn right to go over a narrow wooden bridge.

This route avoids the shops at Pentewan, although there is a seasonal café on the campsite.

Do not leave Pentewan unrefreshed as you have a long tough section ahead.

You are then faced with another choice. You can either:

A. continue on the road through Pentewan, and take the road to the left to follow the official path (you will need to walk back from the harbour if you followed option 2 above).

B. take the Association's preferred route by turning right off the road into the harbour area just after the public toilets, and walking along the harbour to the end of the cottages where you will see a path on your left going up through gardens to link up with the coast path behind the cottages. (If you followed option 2 above, simply pass the winding gear, turn right immediately in front of the Pentewan Beach sign to join the path going up through the gardens.) The path through the gardens is signed as a public footpath and does not look like a public right of way, but it is!

Back on the coast path put this book away; you will need your energies for other things! However take it out again when you have crossed a wooden bridge in a sizeable wood.

Having crossed the bridge, you soon cross another small stream and come to a T-junction. The right turn will take you down to Hallane Mill Beach, a lovely spot for a picnic with a waterfall. The coast path turns left soon to turn right again to start ascending to Black Head, a superb diversionary viewpoint on a clear day. It was once a rifle range but was purchased by the National Trust, helped in a small way with a donation from this Association. If you wish to visit Black Head, turn right at the memorial stone to A L Rowse, the Cornish poet and historian: to continue, turn left.

The passage of the wood behind Ropehaven can give trouble if signing is not maintained. On entering the wood you turn right taking care on this rocky path which can be slippery when damp, then left at the seat. Avoid the right fork down to a cottage and turn sharp left at the top into a narrow walled lane. Turn right on to the narrow road. The path leaves it to go into a field just beyond the little car park/lay by. After the stile which follows the long climb to Silvermine Point, keep to the fence, and don't be tempted to follow the better defined track inland.

At Porthpean Beach the sign forward can be misleading - you do in fact go down on to the promenade to walk along past toilets and a seasonal café. Continue to the end; it does not look likely, but there is a steep set of steps at the end to get you back on track.

50 Charlestown to Par (Polmear)   OS E107 (V) Charlestown

Grading: Easy   Distance -   7.0   599.8   4.3   372.6

Timing: 1.5 hours

See also our Mevagissey to Fowey Path Description.

The official path does not go across the dock gate at the mouth of the harbour, but provided the gate is closed most people will go that way.

You come up from the harbour keeping to the right of a house called Salamander. The path is tarmac and fenced in order to prevent erosion, but the views are wonderful. Later you come out beside a road, walk a few yards along it to turn right and then fork left.

You may like to divert right to visit the new National Coastwatch station, which was opened in October 2003 by its patron, author E V Thompson.

After passing the Carlyon Bay Hotel you come out by a car park area; keep to the right of this to cross the road and continue alongside a golf course.

The clay processing industrial complex gets nearer, and you turn left just before a wall/wire netting fence. The path continues through the complex itself, giving you a detailed look at one of Cornwall's major industries. When you reach the road, turn right to go past the entrance to the clay works.

Continue north on the road and go under a railway viaduct to turn first right signposted A3082 Fowey, cross a level crossing and under another railway bridge. The road forks, and you should keep right to enter Par Green, which is a one-way system, and brings you into the town of Par. You pass The Good Shepherd Church on your right and Welcome Home Inn on your left. (If your journey ends at Par and you need the railway station, keep walking along Par Green until the turn on your left for Eastcliffe Road, which you follow until you reach the station.)

When you reach the National Trail waymark just past 52, Par Green (Sandroy), the official route continues along the road to the interesting almshouses at Polmear, but there is a better, more seaward alternative.

Alternative route to Polmear

Turn right up the alley just past 52, Par Green. You walk alongside a tidal stream then cross the road leading to Par Docks to come out into Par Sands Caravan Park. Keep down to the right hand side to turn left and seaward of a blue-roofed building. You pass a café, toilets and a lake after which you bear right by the Ship Inn to rejoin the official path.

51 | Par (Polmear) to Fowey (Town Quay Ferry)   OS E107 (T) Par (Trains)

Grading: Moderate   Distance -   9.6   609.4   6.0   378.6

Timing: 2.5 hours

See also our Mevagissey to Fowey Path Description.

It is a fine walk out from Polmear via Polkerris around Gribbin Head to Menabilly and so on to Fowey. The availability of public transport from Par to Fowey makes this a very practical half day excursion with lovely views nearly all the way.

The path leaves the main road at Polmear just beside the eye-catching Rashleigh Cottages. At the first junction keep right and at the second turn right.

As you enter Polkerris you turn right. Go down to the beach and turn left, currently no sign, to proceed up the ramp and join a zigzag path to the top.

You should have no problem then until you enter the National Trust The Gribbin property through a field gateway. At the fork, bear right and you come to a pedestrian gate. The official route goes to the Daymark and then sets off downhill inland. (There is a better alternative seaward; bear right along the fence from the pedestrian gate to presently go through a second pedestrian gate and the way forward is then obvious passing through a little wood; when you come out proceed downhill to join the official route. If you want the best route but also wish to make a closer examination of the Daymark itself bear left and go and find out. When you have satisfied your curiosity, proceed due south and you will come to the second gate already mentioned.)

The Daymark is owned by the National Trust and will be open from the beginning of July to mid September on each Sunday from 11-5, and entry is free. For more information, contact S & E Cornwall countryside office on 01208 265211. The views from the top are memorable. The Trust provides torches, and there are guides at the bottom and the top of the tower, so it is thoroughly recommended, provided you are not anxious or do not have a head for heights.

You come down towards Polridmouth Beach and walk around close behind it; the path becomes concrete and there are even concrete stepping stones. This does not sound delightful but this is a lovely little stretch by the house and lake. The path goes steeply up bearing right through woods at the other side.

Again there should be no navigational problems until you reach Allday's Fields (memorial stone on your left). You enter Covington wood; first right is a loop path out towards the castle and there is a steep path dropping to the beach which can be used as a short cut when the tide is out. On entering the wood the more direct route is to go ahead at the first junction and to turn left at the next. This takes you down an increasingly rock cut lane which has a very sharp elbow about two thirds of the way down.

The path comes out at Readymoney Cove and it is then all road to Fowey. However if you are continuing along the coast path, watch for the ferry point on your right before you get into the town. It is down steps just after Fowey Hotel's tea garden (although if you are walking in low season, you may find that the ferry is operating from the Town Quay in Fowey itself). (**BUS USERS, PLEASE NOTE:** you will pass a bus stop on your left as you leave the Esplanade. If you need a bus, it is imperative that you check the displayed timetable at this bus stop, as the regular 24 service no longer leaves from this stop – it is only the off peak 24B which stops here. Both services do stop in Lostwithiel Street which is uphill from Town Quay, where this section ends – the stop is almost opposite the turn off for Hanson Drive.)

A guide book to the Saints' Way is available from Fowey TIC (see page 150).

52 | Fowey to Polperro (Harbour)   OS E107 (T) Fowey; (V) Polruan

Grading: Strenuous

Distance -   **11.5**   **620.9**   **7.1**   **385.7**

Timing: 3.5 hours

See also our Fowey to Polperro Path Description.

This section is very good value for money in two senses of the word. Firstly there is a fine path all the way from Polruan to Polperro with magnificent sea views. Secondly, it is probably the toughest stretch of walking on the South Cornwall coast. (Leaving Fowey, if you have time on your side, you can go via the higher vehicular ferry to Bodinnick and walk The Hall Walk to Polruan [4 miles / 6 km].)

Fowey/Polruan (River Fowey)	All year round at 5-10 min intervals.
Polruan Ferry Co. Ltd	1st May - 30th Sept. Daily 0715 - 2300 hrs
Toms Yard	except Saturday 0730 start, Sunday 0900 start.
East Street	1st Oct - 30th Apr. Daily 0715 - 1900 hrs.
Polruan-by-Fowey	except Saturday 0730 start, Sunday
Cornwall	1000 - 1700hrs. Closed Xmas Day
PL23 1PB	
Tel: 01726 870232	

We urge you to contact the ferry operator direct if you are relying on this service, particularly if you are anticipating a fairly late finish and need to confirm the time of its last run.

In winter months when the weather deteriorates you will find that the ferry operates to and from the Town Quay at Fowey rather than from Whitehouse Quay lower down the harbour; there should be a sign up to this effect.

Landing from the ferry in Polruan, go along the quay and up Garrett Steps just beside The Lugger and at the top turn right along West Street and then left when you get to Battery Lane. The path comes out in a grassy area; keep with the wall on your left going round the corner. The path goes right, just after an earth bank and then you proceed ahead across another open area with a small ruin up on your left. It joins the road beside a school; continue ahead to turn sharp right just before the notice saying 'Furze Park'.

When you reach the National Trust money box on the path, take the right, downward path.

About 2 miles (3 km) after leaving Polruan there is a considerable hill behind Great Lantic Beach. You can go all the way to the top and turn right there. The route we recommend turns right about 30 yards (28 m) before the top, goes over a stile and drops down again. Ignore the first two turnings right as these are beach paths. Presently a wide path, the other route, joins from the left (there is a gate on your right).

Although a definitive right of way is shown below the Watch House, at the moment the practical route is the broad path above it. Assuming you are on this path, ignore the stile on your right which goes directly to the house. Just after this is another loop path right but it has little in views to compensate for the extra effort. After this you can either take the right turn, or keep to the upper path and then join the lower one to follow the path around the back of a cove. When you come to Lansallos Cove, turn inland for the coast path.

Later, as the first houses in Polperro come into view, there is a series of parallel paths all going to Polperro. You should take the rocky path on your right by an outcrop on your left, as you get a glimpse of some houses on the opposite cliff. This is the most seaward path and passes several seats and shelters to arrive at a rocky area overlooking the mouth of the harbour. From the rocky area turn left and the official route into Polperro is the first set of steps on the right. (When you arrive, you will notice a marker which indicates that you have walked the wrong path – ignore it.)

53 | Polperro to Looe (Bridge)

OS E107 (V) Polperro

Grading: Moderate

Distance - 8.0 628.9 5.0 390.7

Timing: 2.25 hours

See also our Polperro to Looe Path Description.

This next section is particularly well walked and the local bus company is sufficiently commercially minded to put up bus times for cliff walkers between Polperro and Looe actually on the path!

In Polperro you have to walk behind the harbour crossing the Roman Bridge to turn right. Leaving Polperro there is a loop path right called Reuben's Walk. If you take this turn left again just before the miniature lighthouse.

Just before the top of the hill, take the right fork at the junction of two well-defined paths; thanks to the National Trust, a wonderful new stone sign has replaced the former wooden signs which were previously vandalised.

Note the spectacularly sited War Memorial on Downend Point. A little way past this is another beach path right which you ignore.

There are seasonal refreshments at Talland.

After the beach café go up the tarmac track, turn left to pass the toilets, and then right. Turn right at the Smugglers Rest café into a small car park to rejoin the path.

The walk to West Looe is pleasant and quite easy.

On entering Looe at Hannafore, you have a choice. You can either follow the official path along the road, passing flower beds and a seasonal café, or you can take the first right to walk alongside the beach, ascending the steps in front of a black barrier and turn right. Either route will bring you to a stretch of road with no pavement. This drops into a dip and watch for a battlemented look-out platform on your right. Just past this are steps down to the harbour area of the river; that is the best way to go. This has a double advantage; it keeps you away from the traffic and takes you past the seasonal ferry to East Looe: certainly if you are walking straight through, this is the best way to go.

The ferry runs between West and East Looe and is dependent on both the weather and the tide. During 2002/03, the ferry ran all year, and you may find that it does so in future years.

If you are walking, simply keep to the quayside in West Looe, cross the bridge, and turn right into the main street, Fore Street, in East Looe.

54 | Looe to Portwrinkle (Quay)

OS E107 & E108 (T) Looe (Trains); (V) Downderry

Grading: Strenuous, moderate in parts

Distance - 12.2 641.1 7.6 398.3

Timing: 5 hours

See also our Looe to Portwrinkle Path Description.

You leave East Looe by turning up Castle Street, cross a minor crossroads and continue up the hill. The road peters out becoming a pleasant high level path above the sea.

The path becomes a road again and at the first junction bear right into Plaidy Lane. Pass Plaidy Beach on your right, and continue on the road until just after it has veered left. Here a steep tarmac path takes off right just beyond a big electric cable post.

At the top of the path you come to a road again to continue ahead for a while until the road bears left but the path goes forward again between houses. Go down steps, do not turn left or right but continue nearly opposite to go ahead.

The path comes down to Millendreath (seasonal refreshments): pass behind the beach to go up the cul-de-sac road the other side. The road becomes a path in a sunken lane, but 150 yards (135 m) after you reach the road again, turn right into the National Trust's Bodigga Cliff property, keeping to the left of the picnic tables. This beautiful place is now accessible for people of varying abilities, including wheelchair users.

The path comes out on the road above Seaton, and you turn right down what is Looe Hill. Go down to the bottom and turn right into Bridge Road. The coast path continues along the road through Downberry.

Beach Route
There is however an alternative which is a low tide route only – the decision is yours. Where the road starts to go uphill opposite the post office and general store, there is a wall on the seaward side. Behind this wall is the beginning of coastal defence works with a path on top. After a while you have to go down to the beach and make a choice. The first left turn by a stream will bring you into the centre of Downderry for shops, toilets and seasonal refreshments. The next will bring you to the Inn on the Shore. If you don't need any facilities, you should continue on to the next stream and turn left up some concrete steps; this latter option will lessen the amount of road walking, and there is a lot to come in the next section. You come up beside a school to turn right along a road, and to rejoin the official route.

Coast path continues
Continue with the road as it bears sharply inland at a hairpin bend. Take the waymarked turn off right, next to a house called Downderry Lodge, ignoring the right turn immediately after you have taken this path. The path zigzags uphill to come eventually into a field.

The long-awaited coast path was officially opened in May, 2002: this Association lobbied for over 15 years for its installation. The Association thanks those responsible, particularly Cornwall County Council and the Port Eliot Estate. This wonderful path is easy to follow, so enjoy your walk.

(If you wish to use the First Bus service number 81a which runs between Plymouth, Portwrinkle and Polperro, please note that not all services stop in Portwrinkle. However, it is possible to walk up the road from Portwrinkle (a 10 minute walk) and catch the bus in Crafthole.)

55 | Portwrinkle to Cremyll (for Plymouth) OS E108 (V) Cawsand/Kingsand

Grading: Moderate   Distance -   21.4   662.5   13.3   411.6

Timing: 5.75 hours

See also our Portwrinkle to Plymouth Path Description.

The coast path takes the second path on the right, opposite the entrance to the golf club. It is currently well marked except right at the end of the course, where you need to aim for the pedestrian gate seen on top of a rise.

PERMISSIVE PATH THROUGH THE TREGANTLE RANGES

We are delighted to be able to advise you that you can now take a fascinating walk through the Tregantle Ranges, thanks to the work of the Ministry of Defence (MOD).

We have to inform you that the latest news is that the MOD is unable to supply a firing schedule for 2004. However, you will be able to obtain information from the Range Office on 01752 822516 (Fax: 01752 823875). It seems that shooting at Tregantle is more flexible than Lulworth. As you draw near to the ranges you will hear firing, see red flags and the gate will be locked, and sadly you will have to resign yourself to the rotten walk-around route below.

Having passed a navigational beacon, you will see a new gate on your right, which you take if the gate is unlocked. The path is well marked and omits 1.5 miles (2.4 km) of road walking. When you leave the Range path through a high gate, turn right to walk along the road to rejoin the official coast path; take care of traffic.

OFFICIAL COAST PATH (when permissive path is closed)

You come out to the road but the path for a while is just inside the hedge. This travesty of a path ends by the road junction to Torpoint where you have to come down to the road and turn right along it. This is an awful path all the way along until you regain a true coast path on the National Trust land on top of the cliffs. You pass the Tregantle Fort entrance, then the road bears left and shortly you turn right, signposted Whitsand Bay etc.

Coast path continues

The road shortly bears left to lead you to a National Trust path. There is then another long stretch of road, until you see notices for Whitsand Bay Holiday Park on the left and the coast path starts again on the right; at this point even sharper left is a seasonal café. The coast path is now well marked and a great improvement over the road, but it does involve two steep climbs.

The path continues to be well marked, and now includes four brand new gates donated by the South East Cornwall Tourism Association to commemorate the 25th anniversary of the coast path. Another piece of furniture of note is a memorial bench with the sentiment 'gone fishing' on it. If time allows, you should take the diversion onto the lovely Rame Head.

Continue along the tarmac avoiding the path turn off on the right. The road turns left with intermittent views ahead to Plymouth Sound Breakwater and presently, over a 0.25 mile (400 m) later, takes off into the wood right.

Traversing Cawsand/Kingsand the official and in fact easiest way is not straightforward and only some of it is signposted, so read the next paragraph carefully.

You enter Cawsand from Pier Lane, go across the square to pick up Garrett Street. As you come towards the end of this street look for the old Devon/Corn boundary mark on a house on your right. Then turn right in front of the post office. Soon you will approach a street called The Cleave. Just before you reach it, turn left. Then turn first right up what is Heavitree Road but you will not know this until you are a few yards up it. As you ascend you will presently see Lower Row on your left; here turn right and enter Mount Edgcumbe Country Park.

When you come out on to a road at Hooe Lodge turn right, but look in 20 yards (18 m) for the path leaving the road on the left. You continue along a section of the Earl's Drive. There was a major landslip here in 2001 and a new path has been installed. It is quite well signposted, although steep in places, and will return you quickly to the original path. Follow the signs which direct you down to the foreshore: the Country Park Rangers have improved this area beyond recognition, and it is a shame to ascend once more.

You continue through a high deer gate; you come out by a classical summer house and you should keep along right to pick up a concrete driveway, and later right again when the drive goes left to walk inside of a hedge. You pass an old blockhouse on your left.

If you are not too pushed for time, a visit around the gardens of Mount Edgcumbe is worthwhile, and free. A charge will be made if you wish to visit the House.

The path comes out by The Orangery; go through an arch then go forward to turn right through the park gates to the ferry point for Plymouth.

(At Plymouth you can take the coast to coast walk to Lynmouth by using the Erme - Plym Trail, the Erme Valley Trail and the Two Moors Way. Guide books to all three routes are available from Ivybridge TIC (see page 150).)

56 | Cremyll (for Plymouth) to Mountbatten Point   OS E108 (T) Plymouth (Trains)

Grading: Easy | Distance - | 12.0 | 674.5 | 7.5 | 419.1

Timing: 3 hours

See also our Plymouth to Wembury Path Description.

The distance includes the signed coast path route around to Mountbatten Point via Cattedown, Oreston, Hooe and Turnchapel. If you use the Mountbatten Ferry service, then deduct approximately 5 miles (8 km).

Cremyll/Plymouth	All year round at 30 minute intervals, but no sailings at 0930, 1230 and 1530 from Mount Edgcumbe, and 0945, 1245 and 1545 from Plymouth.
Cremyll Ferry,	**Summer service** from 1st May to 18th Sept.
Cremyll Quay,	From Mt Edgcumbe Weekdays 0650 to 2015
Cremyll,	Saturdays 0815 to 2100, Sundays 0900 to 2100
Torpoint,	From Plymouth Weekdays 0715 to 2030

Cornwall. PL10 1HX
Tel: 01752 822105.
(Full timetable available - phone above no.)
www.tamarcruising.com
info@tamarcruising.com

Saturdays 0845 to 2115, Sundays 0915 to 2115
Winter service from 19th September to 30th April
From Mt Edgcumbe Weekdays 0650 to 1815,
Saturdays 0815 to 1830, Sundays 1000 to 1700
From Plymouth Weekdays 0715 to 1830,
Saturdays 0845 to 1845, Sundays 1015 to 1715
Closed Xmas, Boxing & New Year's Days

We urge you to contact the ferry operator direct if you are relying on this service, particularly if you are anticipating a fairly late finish and need to confirm the time of its last run.

Plymouth's new Waterfront Walk has been installed. From stepping ashore at Admirals Hard, watch out for a variety of information plaques and pieces of artwork all relating to Plymouth's history.

On landing at Admirals Hard, walk up the road and turn second right into Cremyll Street, and continue to the massive gates of the Royal William Yard. Pass them on your right and continue on out to Firestone Bay. At the sea wall you have a fine view to Drake's Island and beyond towards Wembury. A slight excursion could be made by turning right to walk out to Western King's Point and Devil's Point, for River Tamar views, but you will have to return.

From the sea wall turn inland to walk into Durnford Street, continue along it and walk past the Royal Marine Barracks, turning right immediately after them. This will bring you into Millbay Road where you continue, passing the Dock Gates (east). Then you turn right into West Hoe Road. Keep to this road. You are now in the West Hoe area and the streets surrounding you have numerous B & B establishments. Fork right into Great Western Road.

As you approach a terrace of three storey small hotels, watch out for a path on your right known as Rusty Anchor. This is a slight diversion from the main road and provides a shore line walk.

On regaining the main road, turn right and continue along the Hoe foreshore. You stay on this promenade all the way around to The Barbican and Sutton Harbour. However, you could achieve grand views over Plymouth Sound by climbing steps opposite the swimming pool up to the lighthouse, Smeaton's Tower, and passing that to cross The Hoe to have a look at Sir Francis Drake, still scanning the English Channel for the Armada.

Retrace your steps and continue your shore line walk to The Barbican. A small jetty on your right is of historic significance in that it is the site of the Mayflower Steps; of great interest to our US members.

Whatever you decide upon, ferry or the walking route, it is well worth exploring the ancient Barbican area before carrying on.

Sutton Harbour / Mountbatten
Mountbatten Ferry
07930 838614
www.mbwt.co.uk

All year round. Runs 15 and 45 minutes past the hour from Sutton Harbour, and on the hour and 30 minutes past from Mountbatten Point. Ferry starts at 0745 from Commercial Wharf Pontoon, Barbican on weekdays, and from 0900 at weekends. Last ferry departs Mountbatten at 1830 in winter, and 2300 in summer.

We urge you to contact the ferry operator direct if you are relying on this service, particularly if you are anticipating a fairly late finish and need to confirm the time of its last run.

In the unlikely event of the ferry not operating to Mountbatten Point, this is your walking Route from Sutton Harbour to Mountbatten Point. It is well marked with Plymouth's innovative signs and symbols and is officially signed 'Coast Path'.

Lock gates have now been installed at Sutton Harbour, so walk on across them into Teat's Hill Road. As you progress along Teat's Hill Road you will arrive at Breakwater Hill. Turn right here, but do not walk into the scrap yard unless you want to view vehicles being broken up. Carry on up the hill for a limestone, cliff top walk with views over the Cattewater. At a fork in the lane bear left and you will descend to the area of Cattedown Wharf. We will now just supply directions - continue on past warehouses into Maxwell Road, a road will take you direct to Laira Bridge which you take to cross the River Plym. You now have pavements to walk upon. At the first roundabout turn right into Oreston Road.

After a small roundabout, keep on to the top of the road, bear right, then when you reach Rollis Park Road, turn right to descend to Oreston Quay. You are beside the water only for a couple of hundred yards. At the far end enter Park Road and stay with it to the top of the hill. Tucked away in the left hand corner is the entrance to a path. Climb the ancient stone stile and continue along. You will cross Broad Park and into another footpath which leads down to Radford Lake.

The 'castle' through which you walk was once the lodge to a large house, now no more. Turning right after the causeway brings you to a path alongside the southern shore of Hooe Lake. You will join a narrow road which leads to Hooe Lake Road.

Walk straight across the grassy area keeping to the shore and turn right along Barton Road, and by staying with this road you will come into Turnchapel. Continue on up St. John's Road to a car park on your right. In the corner is a signed route to Mountbatten Point.

57 | Mountbatten Point to Wembury (Warren Point Ferry)   OS E108 & OL20

Grading: Easy   Distance -   11.8   686.3   7.3   426.4

Timing: 3 hours

See also our Plymouth to Wembury Path Description.

Due to the praiseworthy activities of Plymouth City Council you are about to step out onto welcome coast path realignments. Those who have walked this section before will be amazed at the difference and those who have been Association members for a while will realise that our efforts have been successful.

The path goes around Mountbatten Point then runs south climbing to Jennycliff.

Keep to the cliff edge and continue south, that is to the end of the grassy area where you will find a signed path entering woodlands.

This up and down new path is a delight and well below the dangerous road that we once had to walk. Within a 0.25 mile (400 m) this new path links in with the original coast path. Turn right for a scenic uncomplicated path to Fort Bovisand, one of the great forts that once defended Plymouth.

Those who have been this way before should now pause to reflect. Since Mountbatten Point you have not had to set foot upon a vehicular road! We congratulate all responsible for this improvement.

On the descent to a road the path can be seen ahead between hundreds of chalet/huts and the sea. At Heybrook Bay when you reach the road, turn right.

The path passes in front of HMS Cambridge, the one-time gunnery school.

Now follows a low cliff top walk to Wembury Beach. The path passes seaward of the church and climbs to a level path that leads into the estuary of the River Yealm. At a small house, The Rocket House, once used for the storage of life saving apparatus, the official path takes off downhill diagonally towards the river and the ferry point. We suggest you walk down to the ferry point, even if the ferry is not running or you do not intend to use it, because you can take advantage of a scenic short circular walk back to the Rocket House. Once the ferry steps have been reached, carry on for a few yards then take a wooden stepped path on the left that climbs to good views over Newton Ferrers and Noss Mayo.

58 | Wembury (Warren Point) to Bigbury-on-Sea (Car Park)   OS OL20

Grading: Starts easy then strenuous   Distance -   21.8   708.1   13.5   439.9

Timing: 5.75 hours

See also our Wembury (Warren Point) to Bigbury-on-Sea Path Description.

The first obstacle is crossing the River Yealm

Wembury (Warren Point) to Noss Mayo Ferry.
River Yealm
Bill Gregor,   Seasonal all week, on demand.
1 Underhaye,   Easter until end September
Yealmpton   1000 - 1200 and 1500 - 1600 hrs.
PL8 2JR.
Tel: 01752 880079

We urge you to contact the ferry operator direct if you are relying on this service, particularly if you are anticipating a fairly late finish and need to confirm the time of its last run.

During fine weather and school holidays the ferry is operational between 1000 and 1600 daily - but please phone first. Mr Gregor is often there outside normal operating hours. There is a signal board to summon the ferryman by the steps at Warren Point or at the slipway at Noss Mayo. We suggest you might also telephone ahead to Mr Gregor to give him an idea of your estimated time of arrival.

If there is no ferry then this means a walk back to the Rocket House to follow the path described below into Knighton. There is an hourly bus service (number 48) to Plymstock and Plymouth where there is available an infrequent service to Noss Mayo (number 94). For a quicker conveyance around the estuary there are reasonably priced taxis available:-

Wembury Cabs - John Pitcher 01752 862151 and

Tim's Taxis - Tim Craig 01752 830225

Walking route around the River Yealm.
From the Rocket House the track leads into a road. At Wembury House a stile leads to a field and to the footpath junction. The path you want is the one to the right which runs alongside a high wall. Follow it to the end of the wall where it goes through two successive kissing gates. It then bears left approximately 330° across fields towards Knighton. As you leave the fields it goes down a few steps. Turn left and then first right. This will bring you out onto the road. Turn left and the bus stop is a little further along on the other side of the road just before the pub. The distance from ferry point to bus stop is 1.5 miles (2.5 km). Before reaching the bus stop you will pass a telephone box where you can call a taxi if you want.

Go across to a minor road opposite to descend and turn left and then right at the next road junction. Continue along the road for about 0.5 mile (800 m) ignoring all turnings and footpaths. At a major road turn left for a few yards to turn right on a footpath just by a bus stop. This is now a waymarked route, the Erme-Plym Trail. Stay with it down to Cofflete Creek and up the other side until you reach the main A379 road. Turn right and a mile of main road walking follows, the best pavement is at first on the left, then switches to the right leaving Brixton, then for a long stretch there is none at all but it restarts on the left. (There is a safer but longer alternative starting at Brixton Church, see below.) Turn right down the road signed Newton Ferrers 3 miles. Go down to Puslinch Bridge and bear right up the hill. Nearly at the top, a footpath goes right cutting the corner to Wrescombe. Emerging onto the road turn right to continue along to The Butts and down the main road to Newton Ferrers. If you arrive within approximately two hours of low tide you can bear right down Yealm Road and turn down Newton Hill, to cross a tidal causeway to Noss Mayo and another across the inlet at Noss. If you are not so fortunate turn left down the road to Bridgend and Noss Mayo, being sure to turn first right as you enter Noss. Here those who have come around will have a picturesque riverside walk out to where those who have been fortunate enough with the ferry will disembark.

Alternative route - Brixton to Puslinch Bridge
At Brixton Church go up Old Road and follow the waymarked Erme-Plym Trail signs until you arrive on a minor road in the outskirts of Yealmpton. Here turn right and continue down the road ignoring the footpath left turn of the Erme-Plym Trail. At the main A379 road, cross over turning left and immediately right into Stray Park. At the bottom bear right along a tarmac footpath. This comes to a road; turn left along a stony track. At the footpath sign continue ahead to pass the entrance to Kitley Caves. The path eventually emerges in a car park. Leave this and turn left on the road to reach Puslinch Bridge. From here on the route is as described above.

Coast path continues
From the ferry, the Erme Estuary is about 9 miles (14 km) ahead. You are the best judge of how long that will take you to get there for low tide, so plan your Noss Mayo departure accordingly. The well-marked path climbs through woodlands to pick up Lord Revelstoke's nine- mile drive, made for the carriages of his guests at Membland Hall, since demolished.

At Battery Cottage, just as you are leaving the woodlands, look out for a path going off to the right. You can take this down to Cellars Beach, for a swim maybe. It continues on around the back of the beach then climbs to rejoin the coast path at Brakehill Plantation where you turn right onto Lord Revelstoke's drive.

There is a definitive seaward path at Stoke Down at 560460 just after passing a single stone gate post on the left. Use this if you wish to visit the historic Church of St Peter the Poor Fisherman; this will mean an uphill road walk to regain the coast path. If you do not divert then the path crosses the Stoke Beach road to continue along, passing the ruined 'Tea House'.

You are now in for a very steep descent and further on a steep climb up to St Anchorite's Rock and you pass Bugle Hole. The section then to Mothecombe Beach provides superb views to the Erme estuary. It has been fairly described as England's most unspoilt river estuary: we certainly believe it to be the most attractive. At the beach do not turn inland but take the seaward path in the woods at Owen's Hill.

River Erme   No ferry

Low water here is at about the same time as the Devonport Tide Table shown on pages 19 & 20.

It is usually possible to paddle across the river 1 hour each side of low water along the old ford and under normal conditions, at low tide the water is about knee deep. Great care should be taken because heavy rains or seas can make the crossing dangerous. On modern maps the old ford is not shown but this in fact ran from Ordnance map ref. 614 476 to map ref. 620 478. In other words, the old ford connected the road by the row of coastguard cottages with the end of the inland road to Wonwell Beach from Kingston.

Should you arrive at the River Erme at a time that promises a very long wait for low tide to enable you to wade across then there is an inland alternative. This alternative is of about 7 miles (11 km) with fairly steep up and down country lanes. You are the best judge of your rate of travel so the decision to wait for the tide or continue walking is yours. (There is a taxi service which operates in this area - please contact John Edwards on telephone 01548 830859 or mobile 24 hrs 07967 374502.)

Walking route around the River Erme
If you follow the riverside paths shown on OS map OL20 you will be trespassing on a private estate so follow the narrow country lanes to Holbeton village. Then continue on a northerly route to Ford and Hole Farm. Soon after passing Hole Farm take off on a public footpath on your right. From here to the main A379 road is about 0.75 mile (1.2 km). Turn right to cross the River Erme at Sequer's Bridge. Stay on the A379 for about 0.5 mile (0.75 km) but take care as this is an extremely busy road. You will see a road on your right signposted to Orcheton. Follow this road south towards the village of Kingston but before you reach that village you will see road signs to Wonwell Beach. Just before the slipway on to the sands you have a choice. If the tide now permits you can continue south along the beach or take to the waymarked coast path in the woodlands on your left.

Coast path continues
Beyond the Erme the walking becomes tougher but the all round views will compensate for the effort. The path passes Challaborough with its café and caravans to Bigbury-on-Sea, where the Bay Café is open all day and the only establishment for evening meals.

Burgh Island can be visited by walking across the sands or by a 'sea tractor' if the tide is in. The pub is very old, the hotel is fascinating art deco modern and the hut at the top of the island stands on the site of a chapel. This hut was used by the 'huers' - pilchard fishermen on the lookout for shoals of fish.

---

59 | Bigbury-on-Sea to Hope Cove, Inner Hope (Lifeboat Station)   OS OL20 (V) Bantham; (V) Thurlestone

Grading: Moderate		Distance -	9.2	717.3	5.7	445.6

Timing: 2.75 hours

See also our Bigbury-on-Sea to Salcombe Path Description.

There are riverside footpaths along both west and east banks of the River Avon to Aveton Gifford. This makes the inland walking route from Bigbury-on-Sea to Bantham and vice versa about 9 miles (14.5 km) in total. The OS OL20 map shows the riverside paths. What you have to watch is that the road between the two words 'Ford' is tidal and therefore is at times submerged. This route is described below.

Coast path continues
The official route turns right at the bottom of the road on to what is called Clematon Hill at the western side of the mouth of the River Avon. There are good views here across the estuary but unfortunately you have to walk up the busy road to Mount Folly Farm afterwards. However, again there is compensation because the views southward across the estuary just after the farm are particularly spectacular.

Bigbury/Bantham (River Avon)	Seasonal - Monday to Saturday.
Neill Schroeter, Harbourmaster	from 5th April - 4th Sept.
Marsh Cottage, Fore Street,	1000 - 1100 hrs and 1500 - 1600 hrs.
Aveton Gifford, Devon TQ7 4LR	
Tel: 01548 561196	

We urge you to contact the ferry operator direct if you are relying on this service, particularly if you are anticipating a fairly late finish and need to confirm the time of its last run.

The ferryman is generally around, and can be called by waving. Low water is about the same time as the Devonport Tide Table. It is possible at low tide, when not rough, or the river is not in flood, to wade the river. However, we strongly stress we are not advising this as a cheap method of avoiding the ferry crossing. When the ferry is working, you are strongly advised to use it because wading is not easy and you may get a lot wetter than you expect. You will most likely be up to your thighs in water and in no circumstances should the crossing be attempted if conditions are wrong. The two guide points are just below the ferry crossing. On the true right bank - the western side - there is a line of Christmas trees on a bank running north and south with a pine tree on the edge of the river bank. On the left bank - the eastern side - there is a castellated building with battlements and a little flag pole in the middle. However, if crossing from the true right to the left - in other words from west to east - take off at the hedge and wade towards the castle-like building. If going the other way, vice versa. Please note it is important that you do wade at this point. The river looks shallow in a number of other places but there are deeper channels and indeed soft sand patches which can make it extremely difficult. Further towards the sea, there is a considerable tidal ebb which can be exceedingly dangerous.

PLEASE NOTE WHEN THE FERRY IS NOT OPERATING A RECOMMENDED WAY TO REACH BANTHAM IS BY REASONABLY PRICED TAXIS:

Acorn Taxis - Telephone: 01548 531010 : Mobile: 07967 023336 / 7

Arrow Cars - Mr Kemp - Telephone: 01548 856120

John Edwards - Telephone: 01548 830859. Mobile 24 hrs 07967 374502

Phoenix Taxis - Telephone: 01548 852906

It should always be borne in mind that the depth of water at low tide and consequently safe passage across is affected by natural conditions inasmuch that strong south west or westerly winds tend to bank up water in the English Channel and, therefore, there will be a greater depth of water than expected. This will also happen if there is a lot of rain in the catchment areas of the rivers, with consequently more water coming down. Caution: although we know several who have waded the River Avon we do not recommend it; great care is required, especially by those with backpacks.

VERY IMPORTANT - PLEASE TAKE NOTE

EVEN AT LOW WATER WE STRESS THAT YOU MUST SERIOUSLY CONSIDER, EVEN AT LOW TIDES, WHETHER YOU SHOULD WADE THIS RIVER. IT IS VERY DIFFICULT AND CAN BE DANGEROUS EVEN FOR TALL AND STRONG ADULTS. MANY OF OUR MEMBERS, INCLUDING YOUR SECRETARY WILL NOT VENTURE ACROSS. THEIR OPINION BEING - 'WHEN THE FERRY IS NOT RUNNING THEN THE *ONLY ALTERNATIVE IS TO GO ROUND'.*

Inland Walking Route - approx. 7 miles (12 km)

Much of this route has been waymarked 'Avon Estuary Walk' with a heron motif in blue and white.

When the tide is not low (and we urge you to read again our advice about wading) and the ferry is not available, the only way to the other side is an inland walk to Aveton Gifford and around.

This is a pleasant 7 mile (12 km) diversion as it is mostly along country paths. Walking through agricultural land in deep country makes a change from the coast. The paths are shown on OS OL20 and are quite well marked but they are little used and are not always easy to follow. Allow plenty of time for some heavy walking, for straying off route or for a possible delay at the tidal road near Aveton Gifford.

Disregard the coast path where it turns right through Mount Folly Farm and descends to the ferry point, but proceed towards Bigbury for 60 yards (55 m) to the next footpath sign. Turn right into the field over a stone stile and walk along the field edge. Over a wooden stile will bring you onto the golf course where, after a short distance, you meet a surfaced track. Go northwards along the track towards the clubhouse for 200 yards (185 m), turning right at an entrance between two huts going down a track to Hexdown Farm. Pass left of the farmhouse to bear immediately right and then left. Bear right before the next gate to continue downhill with the boundary on your left. Proceed along a track through a timber gate. Follow the footpath sign slightly left along a tarmac drive, into woodland, then through Lincombe and on to the B3392 on a corner. Proceed northwards towards Bigbury for 350 yards (320 m) (be careful of the traffic) and turn right at the footpath sign to Aveton Gifford (via tidal road). Cross the field to a post and wire fence and enter the top of Doctor's Wood. Re-emerge into a field and cross due east to a wooden stile. Proceed along a high level path (beautiful views) then walk downhill to the tidal road which will bring you to Aveton Gifford. There is a viable alternative if the tide is over the road by walking north-westward to Foxhole then north-eastward to Waterhead and Aveton Gifford. The whole path is adequately waymarked.

Cross the Avon on the roadbridge (A379) towards Kingsbridge, and turn right at the end of the bridge into a cul-de-sac named Bridge End. Continue to a gate at a signpost, and straight on to a metalled road, where you turn right at a signpost.

Bear left at the road fork, following the footpath sign to a gate; turn right here and follow a fence on the right, and through another gate into a field.

Turn half right down to the bottom of the valley, and bear right to a gate with a waymark 'to Stiddicombe Creek'. Cross this and enter the wood on the right. Work steadily uphill to the top corner and follow the waymark signs along the top of the field with a hedge on the left (watch for herons by the river) to a stile by a gate; over another stile and continue. Bear right and cross a farm track to a gate between walls. Cross the stream ahead with stepping stones, and along to a stile and waymark signs, where you turn right and go straight on to Bantham, where you turn right and go through the village where you will see the ferry sign; here you would have stepped ashore had it been operating. The coast path is straight on towards the sea. Some of this walk is shown in the National Trail Guide.

Coast path continues
You should take great care where the path proceeds along the seaward boundary of the Thurlestone Golf Course; watch out for golfers and where they hit the ball. We have had a report of a walker on this section who was hit in the mouth by a golf ball at close range, with resulting horrific damage to teeth and lips.

60 | Hope Cove, Inner Hope to Salcombe (Ferry)   OS OL20 (V) Hope Cove

Grading: Strenuous   Distance -   12.9   730.2   8.0   453.6

Timing: 4 hours

See also our Bigbury-on-Sea to Salcombe Path Description.

Excellent coastal walking, some of the finest in South Devon. Before leaving Inner Hope you ought to walk along the inland road to look at The Square and its attractive thatched cottages. It is well marked out to Bolt Tail where the remains of an Iron Age fort are marked by a dry stone wall and the remains of a ditch.

The path is obvious to Bolberry Down (refreshments available - Port Light Hotel) and on to a viewpoint overlooking Soar Mill Cove. There is a steep descent to the cove but the climb out is easier. We have heard of walkers going wrong as they near the splendid rocky Bolt Head. The correct route is the coast route; do not divert inland anywhere until the headland is reached. The path then runs due north into and around Starehole Bay.

From the bay the path joins the Courtenay Way which was cut out under rocky pinnacles. The way ahead is through woodlands to the roadway below the National Trust's Overbecks House and Youth Hostel. Follow the road to South Sands where, in season, a ferry can be taken to the main ferry point in Salcombe. If it is not running or you are a purist, the way ahead to the town and ferry for East Portlemouth is along the most seaward roads ahead.

OS - Outdoor Leisure Map 20. The coast path runs out onto Bolt Head. This is not shown on the map.

61 | Salcombe to Torcross (Car Park)   OS OL20 (T) Salcombe; (V) Beesands

Grading: Strenuous   Distance -   20.8   751.0   12.9   466.5

Timing: 6.75 hours

See also our Salcombe to Torcross Path Description.

This is first class walking, some of the best of the whole coast path.

Salcombe to East Portlemouth Ferry   All year round.
The Salcombe Ferry,   Winter - $^1/_2$ hourly between 0800 - 1730 hrs.
Somerset House,   Summer - Continuous service 0800 - 1900 hrs.
Devon Road,   (July & August)
Salcombe   0830 hrs start weekends and bank holidays.
Devon TQ8 8HQ   Check times before travelling.
Tel: 01548 842061/842364

We urge you to contact the ferry operator direct if you are relying on this service, particularly if you are anticipating a fairly late finish and need to confirm the time of its last run.

Having crossed the estuary the path goes off to the right along the narrow road. Just after the National Trust car park at Mill Bay the path now goes uphill on the left through the trees. Refreshments are available at the Gara Rock Hotel if you want to climb the hill from the path.

The official route is to the very end of Prawle Point, to the Coastguard lookout. It is hoped that the National Trust will mark a path out to the point along the western side of the headland. The path is there and it is a better route than the one on the top. The official route is back inland again but near to the lookout on the east side of the point is a path descending a valley; this is the better one. Prawle Point is National Trust property and there is a true coast path along the top of low cliffs around Copstone Cove to link in with the official route at Western Cove.

It is easy walking for a while along the edges of fields on what is a 'raised' beach. The path then becomes rocky and up and down prior to Lannacombe Beach. About 0.5 mile (800 m) before Lannacombe, try to find time to take the new path that the National Trust has cut to the right, signposted to the previously hidden Woodcombe Sand beach. Until now the beach, a peaceful isolated spot, could only be reached through the grounds of Woodcombe House, and many people didn't even know it was there. The path twists and drops, and you have to come back the same way, but it is only about 100 yards (90 m) and well worth the effort.

The path is straightforward to Start Point and on to Torcross and has recently been rerouted following the purchase of land between Hallsands and Beesands by the National Trust - this is a distinct improvement. It is not currently possible to visit the old deserted village at Hallsands, and the latest news is that it is deemed to be unsafe. You can, however, get a glimpse of the ruins by taking the path to the village as far as the closure notice, which will not take long and is a very moving experience.

62 | Torcross to Dartmouth (Lower Ferry)   OS OL20 (V) Torcross; (V) Strete; (V) Stoke Fleming

Grading: Moderate   Distance -   16.4   767.4   10.2   476.7

Timing: 4.75 hours

See also our Torcross to Dartmouth Path Description.

The coast path runs along the length of the shingle bank. You can walk either side of the road; the top of the beach for sea views or alongside the Ley for bird watching.

There is no true coast path from Strete Gate to Warren Point and virtually the whole route is inland and some on a busy main road. This is reckoned to be the worst section of the whole of the South West Coast Path and the Association continues its efforts to obtain an enormous improvement. WE CANNOT OVEREMPHASISE THE NEED FOR EXTREME CAUTION ON THIS SECTION, SOME OF WHICH IS ON DANGEROUS, BUSY ROADS.

If you intend to avoid the busy main road through Strete, then as you approach the village, look for Hynetown Road on your left and turn into this road to follow the official path to rejoin the main road on the other side of the village. After this follow the main road for about 200 yards (185 m) and then take care to fork left, signposted 'Southwood' - there is no coast path sign here. Immediately before the entrance to Blackpool Sands you must turn left by the cottages.

Follow the inland signed route to Stoke Fleming and the rest of the signs along this poor route. You have about another 2.5 miles (4 km) to go before you regain the coast path proper.

As you stand on the National Trust's Warren Point this is another occasion to pause and reflect. The beautiful path you see ahead of you towards the River Dart estuary could easily be continued behind you nearly all the way back to Slapton Sands, if it were not for landowners who do not like you.

However, we are a step nearer to achieving the installation of a true coast path along the lines of the route this Association has been lobbying for many years. The Countryside Agency Board has accepted the review by the South West Coast Path Team. By the time you read this there could be some improved realignments – watch out for signs.

Dartmouth Castle commands the mouth of the River Dart and should be visited, time permitting. In season there is a regular ferry from the castle to Dartmouth and this can be utilised for a pleasant river trip, instead of walking down the road.

63 | Dartmouth to Brixham   OS OL20 (T) Dartmouth; (V) Kingswear (Trains)
(King William of Orange Statue)

Grading: Strenuous   Distance -   17.3   784.7   10.8   487.5

Timing: 5.75 hours

See also our Dartmouth to Brixham Path Description.

Walkers will probably use the lower ferry to cross the River Dart but there are two other regular ferries which also run all year round. Nearby is the passenger ferry, which lands by the steam railway station, and which gives a more comfortable crossing, and if these two are not running then further up the river is the higher ferry taking pedestrians and vehicles. If you use the higher ferry you will then need to turn right along the railway line to the road, then turn right again and descend the hill to join the coast path by the lower ferry slipway.

Dartmouth/Kingswear   All year round, continuous
South Hams District Council, Lower Ferry,   between 0700 and 2300 hrs.
Lower Ferry Office, The Square,   Sundays start 0800 hrs. (Not Christmas Day)
Kingswear TQ6 OAA
Tel: 01803 752342
Fax: 01803 752227

We urge you to contact the ferry operator direct if you are relying on this service, particularly if you are anticipating a fairly late finish and need to confirm the time of its last run.

On landing at Kingswear, by the lower ferry, pass through an arch on the right. Ascend Alma Steps then turn right along Beacon Road. In 1.25 miles (2 km) turn right down steps at Warren Woods.

When you reach the old Battery Buildings at Froward Point do divert inland to see The Daymark navigation tower nearby if time permits but then return to the coast path to continue. The sign here is 8.75 miles (14 km) to Brixham and the path descends steeply going right from the back corner of the derelict look out building and then passes through the World War II gun and searchlight positions. Next at Pudcombe Cove you can obtain access to the National Trust gardens at Coleton Fishacre if they are open.

Walking on above Pudcombe Cove and Ivy Cove to Scabbacombe Head, you will see the Scabbacombe Sands, Long Sands, Man Sands, Southdown Cliff and Sharkham Point before reaching St Mary's Bay. Taken together, the strenuous grading of this section is well justified.

Now you have a pleasant walk to Berry Head Country Park, a Nature Reserve with much of interest - do spend time there if you can. The Northern Fort, one of the two Napoleonic Forts, contains the Berry Head lighthouse; next to it, the old Artillery Store houses an exhibition centre explaining 400 million years of Berry Head history, and the old guardhouse is now a café, open in the season and sometimes out of season as well.

When you leave Berry Head and go past the Berry Head Hotel, turn right through the public car park and follow the path past Shoalstone Beach and along the new promenade. (In wild weather it may be better to continue along the road until you are level with the breakwater, and then take the steps down to the promenade.) This follows the water's edge past the marina to the inner harbour.

64 Brixham to Torquay Harbour   OS OL20 (T) Brixham; (T) Paignton (Trains)

Grading: Moderate   Distance -   13.5   798.2   8.4   495.9

Timing: 4 hours

See also our Brixham to Shaldon Path Description.

The path goes along the back of Broadsands, along the back of Goodrington Sands beach, around Roundham Head, along Paignton and Preston sea fronts and along the promenade at Torquay.

From Brixham to Elbury Cove the path is fair though not as scenic as one might hope. Thereafter it becomes more urbanised with the poorest section from Hollicombe to Torquay Harbour where you usually have quite heavy traffic nearby. Remember, in case of need, there is a very frequent bus service from Brixham to Torquay via Paignton! There is also a regular Brixham/Torquay seasonal ferry service.

When departing from Brixham leave by the new path running along the harbour, signposted Coastal Footpath to Oxen Cove and Freshwater Car Park. At the car park continue on past the Zeneca Brixham Environmental Laboratory and on to the Battery Gardens where you follow the lower path to Fishcombe Cove. Ascend from the cove and at the road junction turn right, signpost Public Footpath to Churston Ferrers. (By the road junction, the Battery Heritage Centre, illustrating the importance of the site from the Napoleonic Wars to D-Day, is well worth a visit if it is open.)

At the far end of Elbury Cove ignore the more obvious path going inland and leave the beach by ascending the steps. Take care at Broadsands beach that you do not follow the path up the cliff at the eastern end, but turn left up the minor road, pass under the railway viaduct and then turn immediately right where the coast path is signposted.

At Goodrington turn right under a railway bridge, follow the promenade round and just before the end a zigzag path takes you up, through ornamental gardens on to Roundham Head.

At Hollicombe Head you can turn right and go through the delightful park that was once the gas works. Bear left to emerge through the main gate onto the road. Then turn right for Torquay and continue along its sea front.

65 Torquay Harbour to Shaldon (Ferry)   OS E110 (T) Torquay (Trains)

Grading: Strenuous   Distance -   17.3   815.5   10.8   506.7

Timing: 5.75 hours

See also our Brixham to Shaldon Path Description.

At Torquay harbour go across the new pedestrian bridge between the inner and outer harbours. Go up Beacon Hill, passing the Living Coasts Centre (with penguins and puffins visible under a vast netting tent – well worth a visit if you have time) until you reach the Imperial Hotel. Turn in right here to pass in front of the main entrance to the hotel and then follow the scenic path to the grassy plateau of Daddyhole Plain, which you cross to find the path descending to Meadfoot Beach.

At the far end of Meadfoot Beach turn right through a small car park and ascend to Marine Drive where you turn right. There is some subsidence on this road but it does not affect pedestrians. Shortly, turn right at a signpost for the coast path, going towards Thatcher Point. However, at present, you will have to return on the same path as the footpath is closed between Thatcher Point and Thatcher Pines; this is because of a cliff fall which the path managers have yet to resolve. At the road turn right and shortly find a path above the left hand side of the road, and at the end of this cross the road and take the Bishop's Walk path signposted to Anstey's Cove.

As you join the road by the car park above Anstey's Cove you can, time and energy permitting, take the steep path down to the picturesque cove; however, you'll have to return the same way, as following repeated rock falls the adjacent Redgate Beach has been sealed off indefinitely by Torbay Borough Council, and it's no longer possible to cross the two beaches and regain the official route by the path up the cliffs. Instead, about 50 yards (46 m) beyond the turning down to Anstey's, take the path through the woods to the right signposted 'To Babbacombe & St Marychurch over the Downs', which takes you up to Walls Hill.

From Walls Hill the path will take you to the road descending to Babbacombe Beach, at the far end of which you traverse a wooden bridge structure to Oddicombe beach, where the path bears upwards just before the lower station of the Babbacombe Cliff Railway. Shortly you pass under the railway and then take care to turn right downwards at the start of a pleasant path leading to a grassy picnic area where you bear left uphill. Because of a landslip, the official path is now closed and you will have to make an inland diversion here. Keep to the right hand side of the grassy area and you will see a clear diversion notice, with a map, directing you up to the road. Turn right along the road, go down Petitor Road and turn left at the end to rejoin the track to Watcombe.

At the valley road linking the main Torquay/Teignmouth Road to Watcombe Beach, turn left and immediately right, signposted Maidencombe 0.75 mile (1 km) and follow a wooded path. There are two places along this route where 'alternative inland' routes are signed, but you are recommended to keep to the lower, more coastal routes. From the car park at Maidencombe, go a few yards up the road and turn right.

From here there are some quite stiff gradients until you reach the road at Labrador where you turn right and in a few yards leave the pavement to take a sunken path on your right and shortly enter a field on your right via a stile by a field gate.

You will get superb views now as you descend along the coastal side of the field system, then take the path round The Ness to Shaldon.

66 | Shaldon to Exmouth (Ferry)   OS E110 (V) Shaldon;
(T) Teignmouth (Trains); (T) Dawlish (Trains); (V) Dawlish Warren (Trains); (V) Starcross (Trains)

Grading: Easy   Distance -   12.7   828.2   7.9 514.6

Timing: 3 hours

See also our Shaldon to Sidmouth Path Description.

The above figures relate to the distance involved when the Starcross ferry is operating. If not, the walking route around the Exe is described below, and you should add approximately 10.6 miles (17 km).

This is a section where you may have problems depending on the time of year and state of the tide. If the ferry is not working for some reason, your walking route around is to continue along riverside roads from the ferry point and cross Shaldon Bridge. Immediately after crossing the railway line, exit from the bridge into Milford Park. Walk beside the railway line, through Bitton Sports Ground into Park Hill, cross into Bitton Avenue at Clay Lane then turn right into Willow Street. At the end bear left then right which will bring you into Quay Road, into Osmond Street and then straight on to Harbour Beach and the ferry. Keep going on out onto 'The Point', turn north east and once more you are upon the coast path.

Shaldon/Teignmouth (River Teign)   All year round. (except Xmas Day)
The Teign Ferry Ltd.   20 minute intervals.
38 Dunmore Court, Dunmore Drive, Shaldon, Summer 0800 - dusk
Teignmouth. TQ14 0BS
Tel: 01626 873060 Fax: 01626 872996   Winter Weekdays 0800 - dusk
Mobile: 07880 713 420 (for daily updates) Winter Weekends 1000 - dusk
E-mail: teignferry@eclipse.co.uk
www.teignferry.eclipse.co.uk

We urge you to contact the ferry operator direct if you are relying on this service, particularly if you are anticipating a fairly late finish and need to confirm the time of its last run.

Coast path continues
After crossing from Shaldon by ferry, follow the promenade past the pier and shortly you reach Eastcliff Walk forking up on your left and there you must make your first decision. The true route

is ahead along the sea wall but at certain states of the high tide and particularly in bad weather it may be impossible after a 2 mile (3.2 km) walk to pass under the railway line at the end of the wall, and if this appears likely a detour is needed. You should ascend Eastcliff Walk which soon becomes a track and will eventually lead you to the A379 where you turn right and rejoin the coast path at the top of Smugglers Lane.

If conditions look right, enjoy the walk along the sea wall and at the end pass under the railway line and ascend Smugglers Lane to the A379. Now you have a short walk on this busy main road, although there is a footpath on the left hand side, and after about 150 yards (135 m) turn right into Windward Lane, then immediately left and take the path over a stile on your left. After a field section you are back on the road but immediately follow the Old Teignmouth Road on your right, until you reach the main road yet again, turn right and shortly by some railings turn right and follow the path which soon zigzags down to the boat cove and follow the sea wall to Dawlish Station.

From here it is possible at low tide to walk along the sea wall to Dawlish Warren, then at the start of the new promenade cross the railway by a footbridge to join the inland path and reach the main road. If the tide is high you must take the alternative route by turning left opposite the Railway Station and in 30 yards (27 m) turning right through an arch and ascending the steps. Continue forward, passing a new housing development on your left, and after passing through another two arches, you emerge onto the A379 road and continue forward. Shortly after passing the new Rockstone Flats turn right on the road signposted Dawlish Warren 0.75 mile (1 km) and immediately take the coastal footpath signed on your right to follow the Ladies Mile to Dawlish Warren. (You can in fact take a footpath immediately before the Rockstone Flats, although this is not signposted, then take the left fork to join the coast path.)

There is no official path along the Warren but if time and energy permit you can enjoy a circular walk round this sandy Nature Reserve.

You are now faced with crossing the River Exe and in the summer months there is a ferry from Starcross to Exmouth reached by walking along the road from Dawlish Warren. However this is a busy road and you can if you wish catch one of the frequent buses to Starcross.

Starcross/Exmouth (River Exe)   Mid April - end October.
Mr B Rackley,   Hourly, 7 days a week.
Starcross Pier & Pleasure Company   From Starcross Pier
26 Marine Parade,   on the hour from 1000 hrs.
Dawlish.   From Exmouth, Ferry Steps.
Tel: 01626 862452   on the half-hour from 1030 hrs.

Last Ferry	From Starcross	From Exmouth
April, May, Sept, Oct	1600	1630
June	1700	1730
July and August	1800	1815

We urge you to contact the ferry operator direct if you are relying on this service, particularly if you are anticipating a fairly late finish and need to confirm the time of its last run.

Alternative routes around the River Exe

1. Exe Water Taxis (1st April to 3rd September. Runs daily from 10 am to 5pm, weather permitting) will pick up passengers from the north-west end of Warren Point and take them to Exmouth. Please telephone 07970 918418 before relying on this service.

2. Turf/Topsham Ferry   Daily, 7 days a week Easter –
Dave McCabe   mid September. From Turf 1145 –1600
Tel: 077778 370582   From Topsham 11-30 1615.
      Evenings to be pre-booked.
(There is a train station at Topsham, with services running to Exmouth and Exeter.)

3. Topsham Ferry (River Exe)   Apr. - Sept. Daily except Tuesdays, from 1100 to
Exeter City Council Canals & Rivers Dept.   1700 hrs. Oct - Mar. Saturdays, Sundays and
Tel: 01392 274306 (Office)   Bank Holidays 1100 to 1700 hrs or sunset.
Tel: 0780 120 3338 (Ferryman)   Hail ferry to call service.

We urge you to contact the ferry operator direct if you are relying on this service, particularly if you are anticipating a fairly late finish and need to confirm the time of its last run.

(There is a train station at Topsham, with services running to Exmouth and Exeter.)

4. You can use the frequent bus services, changing routes at either Countess Wear or in Exeter.

5. You can catch a train at Dawlish Warren, changing at Exeter and going back down to Exmouth.

Once across the river you have to get to Exmouth and we are inclined to suggest the frequent bus service, but failing this the walk as far as Lympstone will be on the road except for a small footpath section between Clyst Bridge and Ebford. From Lympstone there is a riverside path to Exmouth, now part of the East Devon Way - look for the mauve markers featuring a foxglove.

67 | Exmouth to Budleigh Salterton (River Otter Car Park)   OS E115 (T) Exmouth (Trains)

| Grading: Moderate | Distance - | 9.9 | 838.1 | 6.2 | 520.8 |

Timing: 3 hours

See also our Shaldon to Sidmouth Path Description.

No real problems here for walkers but keep inland of the range at Straight Point. A necessary diversion around Sandy Bay caravans and another one going into Budleigh are currently in operation but are adequately waymarked.

68 | Budleigh Salterton to Sidmouth (River Sid)   OS E115 (T) Budleigh Salterton

| Grading: Moderate then strenuous | Distance - | 11.1 | 849.2 | 6.9 | 527.7 |

Timing: 3.5 hours

See also our Shaldon to Sidmouth Path Description.

The start is along a raised path inland to the River Otter Bridge at South Farm, then a riverside path back to the coast.

The path around High Peak is well marked but it does not unfortunately go over the top as you, and many others in the past, obviously expected. If you do battle your way to the top you will certainly not be disappointed with the views. The path on the top of Peak Hill immediately west of Sidmouth has been improved to give better seaward views.

The descent from Peak Hill towards Sidmouth takes you down through a wood and out on to the road. Turn right and keep to the right hand side of the road to pass through two kissing gates, then bear right through a gap in the hedge on to parkland for the descent into Sidmouth. At the bottom of the lawn, make your way onto the zigzag path which leads down between beach huts onto the small esplanade. Turn left and continue at sea level on the Clifton Walkway to the main esplanade.

69 | Sidmouth to Seaton (River Axe)   OS E115 & E116 (T) Sidmouth

| Grading: Severe then strenuous | Distance - | 16.7 | 865.9 | 10.4 | 538.1 |

Timing: 5.5 hours

See also our Sidmouth to Lyme Regis Path Description.

Please note that there are a number of quite considerable ascents and descents on this section, so do not judge the effort required purely on the distance. There are one or two places in this stretch where it is easy to come off the route but one is not likely to come to any severe harm. Landslips have caused diversions on this stretch, but the temporary route and the proposed alignments are well signed, and for the most part, enjoyable.

On leaving Sidmouth, dramatic cliff falls are the cause of a diversion, which is well marked.

After Branscombe Mouth there are alternative paths. The one over Hooken Cliffs gives superb views and is probably easier to walk. The undercliff path, apart from the beginning among the caravans is scenically better and we would recommend this if the weather is good. You have the interesting undercliff itself, the massive cliffs to the left, interesting rock formations ahead, and good views to seaward. At most states of the tide it is possible to walk along the beach from Seaton Hole to Seaton, avoiding some road work.

WATCH THE TIDE - YOU CAN GET CUT OFF

70 | Seaton to Lyme Regis (Town Car Park)

OS E116 (T) Seaton

Grading: Moderate

Distance -   **11.0**   **876.9**   **6.8**   **544.9**

Timing: 3.25 hours

See also our Sidmouth to Lyme Regis Path Description.

You leave Seaton across its bridge over the River Axe and have to turn inland. Go up the road to the golf course, then walk due east across the fairway into a lane, which you go along, turning to the coast in less than 0.25 mile (400 m).

The section through the Landslip is in a National Nature Reserve and can be very rewarding to some but extremely frustrating to others. Views are extremely limited and the path in places puts on a fair imitation of a corkscrew or helter-skelter; you are unlikely to get lost but most unlikely to know where you are. Small piles of brushwood have been placed on the former worn path to allow eroded areas to regenerate, but obvious alternative routes have been cleared. The time to walk the Landslip does vary depending on the walker. We have received reports from some who have taken about 4 hours whilst others report 2 hours. We thought you would like to be aware of this.

The path into Lyme Regis has now been improved and you can take a path directly down to The Cobb without having to come into the car park, and then down the road.

DORSET

From Lyme to Studland the geology is such that the cliffs are very vulnerable to slippage. During the very wet winter of 2000/01 a number of considerable cliff falls and landslips occurred on the Dorset section. These resulted in some major temporary diversions having to be put in place. We have no clear information on when solutions will be found and the various sections of the coast path reinstated. In this year's edition we have again included the details of both the coastal route and the temporary diversions which we hope may be removed by the time you walk the path. The diversions described start at the points in the text marked by a bold letter 'D' and a number e.g. **(D2)**. However at the time of writing we still do not know what further damage could occur during the winter of 2003/04 so you will need to be on the lookout for possible diversions not mentioned in the Guide. When walking the path the best advice we can give is to follow the signed route and any official notices or signs. For up to date details of temporary diversions you should visit the Association's website.

71 | Lyme Regis to Charmouth (River Char)

OS E116 (T) Lyme Regis

Grading: Moderate

Distance -   **4.4**   **881.3**   **2.7**   **547.6**

Timing: 1.25 hours

See also our Lyme Regis to Abbotsbury Path Description.

From Lyme Regis town centre take Church Street and Charmouth Road (A3052) until you reach Lyme Regis Football Club on the right, beyond which you will find a stile at the corner of a lane and take the footpath across fields to a lane where you turn left (yes west!) for 100 yards (90 m). At a finger post sign turn right up through the wood and near the top **[D1]** turn right onto the path that runs between the cliff edge and the golf course. Take the track downhill to Charmouth and at the first junction (with Old Lyme Hill) turn sharp right and follow the signposted route back to the cliff edge **[D2]**.

Alternatively at the end of the new promenade at Lyme Regis you may choose to walk along the firm sand on the beach to Charmouth, if the tide is well out. DO NOT attempt to walk upon the surface of the grey mud slide, and be aware of the state of the tide before starting out.

D1. Diversion 1 - Lyme Regis Golf Course. The diversion starts at the path junction in the wood at GR 3456 9330. Turn west on a path for 130 yards (120m) to a junction with a road named Timber Hill. Turn north on this road passing the golf course club house to join the A3052 road. Continue north on this road for about 110 yards (100m) and turn eastwards onto a public footpath (signposted to Fern Hill) across the golf course and bear north-east down through woods to rejoin the A3052 road. Turn south east down this road for some 550 yards (500m) to the roundabout with the main A35 road. Take the right hand fork, which is the local road into Charmouth, and follow it south-south-east into the village for about 760 yards (700m) to the second road junction. Here turn right into Higher Sea Lane (which later becomes a footpath) and proceed south-east for about 650 yards (600m) to rejoin the coast path at GR 3640 9305.

D2. Diversion 2 - Charmouth (Raffey's Ledge). If Diversion 1 has been lifted there is still the possibility of a further diversion on this section. From the end of the track (GR 3580 9345) at the west end of the road called Old Lyme Hill continue north-eastwards on the road to reach the main road through the village. Turn right down this road and in 110 yards (100m) turn right into Higher Sea Lane (which later becomes a footpath) and proceed south-east for about 650 yards (600m) to rejoin the coast path at GR 3640 9305.

72	Charmouth to West Bay (Bridport Arms)	OS E116 1 mile to (V) Charmouth

Grading: Strenuous	Distance -	11.2	892.5	7.0	554.6

Timing: 3.75 hours

See also our Lyme Regis to Abbotsbury Path Description.

This is a section of interesting walking with spectacular views from Golden Cap, the highest mainland point on the south coast of England, and later from Thorncombe Beacon. However, be warned, your good views are not obtained without effort! [D3]

When you get to what looks like the top of Golden Cap you have to turn left and go a little higher to the trig. point to find your way down, which starts at the north end before later bearing east again. [D4] There is a car park and a pub at Seatown.

D3. Diversion 3 - Charmouth (Stonebarrow). From Lower Sea Lane west of the footbridge over the River Char at GR 3652 9320 turn north east along a tarmac lane called River Way and at the end continue along a gravel footpath to reach Bridge Road. Carry on northwards up this road to the junction with the main village road, The Street. Turn eastwards along The Street to Newlands Bridge and fork right into Stonebarrow Lane. Continue up this narrow lane for nearly three quarters of a mile (1150 m) taking care of the traffic. At the top of this lane a car park is reached. Immediately turn sharp right to find a four directional signpost. Take the direction shown for the diverted coast path which is a grassy track south-eastwards towards Westhay Farm (the start of this path tends to get slightly obscured by bushes). After the track has started to descend in about 190 yards (170 m) turn south west through a barrier onto a footpath for another 190 yards (170 m) to rejoin the coast path at GR 3803 9301.

D4. Diversion 4 - Seatown. A minor diversion occurs on the western approach to Seatown. At the path junction at GR 4158 9197 following the signed diversion north-east and then easterly down to a road (Sea Hill Lane). Here turn southwards down the road to rejoin the coast path at GR 4199 9175.

73	West Bay to Abbotsbury (Swannery Car Park)	OS OL15 (V) West Bay; (V) Abbotsbury

Grading: Moderate	Distance -	15.2	907.7	9.4	564.0

Timing: 4.25 hours

See also our Lyme Regis to Abbotsbury Path Description.

SEE SECTION 80 FOR DETAILS OF THE ALTERNATIVE INLAND COAST PATH FROM WEST BEXINGTON TO OSMINGTON MILLS.

After you have walked round the back of West Bay harbour, pass to the right of St. John's Church and ahead to the West Bay Hotel, opposite which is the coast path sign pointing across to the foot of surprisingly steep cliffs.

Watch out for the inland loop at Burton Freshwater which is still shown on most OS maps. This has been changed and an improved route running between the caravan park and the beach has been installed and is well signed.

At Burton Beach, just east of the hotel, there is a café/toilet (open all year).

At Burton Mere, unless you are particularly interested in maritime flowers, the definitive route goes inland of the Mere, rather than going along the seaward side: you will get quite enough pebbles later.

There is a fair weather café and all year round toilets at West Bexington, and further on seasonal snack wagons in the car park where the road turns inland past Abbotsbury Gardens. Coast path walkers, however, should continue along the back of the beach for another 200 yards (185 m) before the route turns inland.

An alternative for the tough walker who wishes to stay on the coast all the way to Ferry Bridge avoiding all of section 74 is to use the Chesil Bank; you can do this by going onto the beach where the path turns inland at Abbotsbury but note you cannot 'get off' again until you reach the causeway from Wyke Regis to Portland. This is only a walk for the fit and not one to be attempted at times of severe gale! Please note that the Chesil Bank is closed to visitors from 1st May-31st August for the Schedule 1 bird nesting season. During the nesting season please keep to the seaward side of the beach so as not to interfere with nesting birds.

WARNING: If you intend to walk the whole length of Chesil Bank rather than going to Abbotsbury and along the edge of the Fleet (Section 74), you should telephone Major Hazard on 01305 783456 ext. 8132, to check whether the bank is safe to walk. There may be some firing at Chickerell Rifle Range and it is not unknown for the odd bullet to mis-target, and travel as far as the Bank. As a result, walkers will be sent back despite having walked half this gruelling hike.

The official route of the coast path runs to the south and east of Chapel Hill but avoiding Abbotsbury village. There is a short cut using a permissive path that leads to the Swannery car park.

There are refreshments, shops and B&Bs in Abbotsbury. If you have time, the climb up to St Catherine's Chapel is worth the effort.

74 | Abbotsbury to Ferry Bridge (Wyke Regis)   OS OL15 (T) Weymouth

| Grading: Easy. Chesil Beach: Strenuous | Distance - | 17.5 | 925.2 | 10.9 | 574.9 |

Timing: 4 hours (Official Route)

See also our Abbotsbury to Weymouth Path Description.

The coast path does not actually go into Abbotsbury. However if you visited the village the best route back to the coast is to leave by the path that you entered the village. That is the path going south from the B3157 (West Street) adjacent to Chapel Lane Stores. At a path junction in 220 yards (200 m) continue south to Nunnery Grove to rejoin the coast path.

The coast path now goes inland but is well marked and enjoyable to walk; part of it goes along a ridge and has some good views. You do not get back to the shores of the Fleet until Rodden Hive.

On the outskirts of Abbotsbury after Horsepool Farm keep going up the ridge; beguiling, much better tracks go round the hill to the right, but they will not bring you to the stile you need at the top. In about 1 mile (1500 m) turn south off to the ridge and after Hodder's Coppice turn sharp left. A track goes forward, but this is NOT the one you want. After you have crossed a minor road, the official path follows the field headland east and then south to the north east corner of Wyke Wood as signposted, and not in a direct line as shown on some older maps. Take particular care as you approach Rodden Hive - the path suddenly dives through a hedge on your left. There is an apparent track that might make you think that the path goes to the right of the stream, but it does not.

At Tidmoor Point, follow the red and white posts unless you have to divert as firing on the range is in progress across the coastal route. Near Wyke Regis the coast path deviates slightly inland around a MOD Bridging Hard.

Grading: Moderate

Distance - 21.3 946.5 13.2 588.1

Timing: 6 hours

See also our Isle of Portland Path Description.

The total distance includes walking Portland Beach Road (A354) twice (there and back).

In June 2003 the route in this section was officially designated as part of the SWCP National Trail. The circuit of the Isle of Portland is well worth the effort and should not be omitted although it is easy to do so. It is a fine walk, and while not beautiful it is rugged, spectacular, particularly in rough weather, and full of interest. The Island and Royal Manor of Portland still quarries its famous limestone, still 'hosts' H. M. Prison Services, but is replacing the Ministry of Defence with new port and tourism facilities. However there is still no immediate prospect of a reinstated and better route around the north-east section.

From Ferry Bridge you have a number of choices, none of them of much merit, for the first 2 miles (3 km). Using the shared footway/cycleway beside the busy A354 road; crossing over the car park beyond the Chesil Beach Centre to slog along the pebbles of Chesil Beach; or catching a bus to the roundabout at the south end of the causeway to alight at Victoria Square. Fourth, and probably best, is to cross the bridge to beyond the boatyard and on the eastern bank, walk along the raised bed of the old railway to near the end of the causeway at Mere Tank Farm, before returning to the footway/cycleway on the A354 to come to Victoria Square. Cross the road and follow signs for the Chesil Beach Gallery, turning left before the public toilets. Continue to the Cove House Inn and bear right up onto the promenade. About halfway along at the floodgates cut back sharp left and then right following Coast Path signs up a steep tarmac path past the school and up the steep path in the grass incline to the steps to the terraced path that was the old A354 road (that has been realigned).

Bear off right onto the coast path running between old quarry banks and the cliff face. Then should follow 3 miles (5 km) of spectacular and airy cliff top walking to Portland Bill. However at the time of writing a structural problem at the Blacknor Trailway has resulted in a temporary diversion **[D5]**.

On reaching Portland Bill with its lighthouse, obelisk, cafés, toilets and Pulpit Rock, continue around the end of the low headland. Then head northwards and pass to the seaward of wooden chalets to follow a winding path along the top of low cliffs to join a road above Freshwater Bay after about 1.5 miles (2.5 km).

Turn right up the road for 600 yards (550 m), past Cheyne Weares Car Park to a finger post on the right. Follow the zigzag path down into the rugged undercliff area, and follow the waymarks through the disused quarry workings down to Church Ope Cove.

From this point there is the choice of two routes. The newly designated route is signed and waymarked to run along the cliffs to the prison road, then through disused quarries before returning to the west side of the 'island' where the A354 road reaches the top of the hill. The route then retraces its outward route to Chiswell. However we think our preferred alternative route is better and is recommended. This route is described in the next three paragraphs. If following our route ignore other coast path signs and waymarks as the two routes do connect in two locations.

Before the 'West Cliff' and 'Coast Path' signs, turn right through a gap in the hedge with a 'Crown Estate' sign on to the undercliff path. Continue to seaward along the rugged path to Durdle Pier and bear up left to turn right onto a wide firm path (old track bed of the former Weymouth to Easton railway line). Continue along the track for 550 yards (500 m) to just before a 'rockfall' sign, where it is necessary to turn left over a bank to follow a rocky path that climbs up the cliffs to what appears to be an isolated chimney seen above on the skyline. A word of warning here - although the track continues northwards and appears to be well used, do not be tempted to continue as the way forward is eventually blocked by the perimeter security fence of the former MOD Establishments and there is no other route up the high cliffs.

Our preferred route is to turn sharp right at the chimney to go along a prison road, and follows a tarmac road northwards through a gap in a high wall. At the next road turn right and bear downhill toward the gates of the former MOD establishment, but shortly go left at a fork on an access road to compounds. Continue forward to a left hand bend, and carry on ahead on a grassy path towards a large pinnacle of rock (Nichodemus Knob) after which, at the 'rock falls' sign, bear left steeply up on to the higher escarpment heading for a large communications mast. At the high wire perimeter fence turn left and follow the fence along and then around to the north to the entrance of Verne Prison. Take a path through a little gap to the left of the entrance, passing beside railings and down steep steps. Bear right along a path that traverses under the grassy banks and by a waymark post, bear left down to a hairpin bend in the road (Verne Common Road).

Bear left down the road and after house number 90 turn left down a footpath. Emerging onto a road bear left, and take the path beside a 'No Entry' sign to Ventnor Road. Walk down to the main road (A354), and cross the road to a path through a park and turn right onto the road to the roundabout at Victoria Square, Chiswell. From here retrace your steps for 2 miles (3 km) to Ferry Bridge.

<u>D5. Diversion 5. Blacknor Tramway.</u> From the northern end of the closed section above Clay Ope turn south-east on a footpath and follow this to reach a main road (Wide Street). Turn right and follow the road southwards and shortly, at a junction, continue in the same direction down Weston Road. At the end of the cemetery on the right turn right onto a footpath that runs along the northern boundary of school playing fields. Continue on the path as it twice bears south and west to rejoin the coast path at Blacknor.

Please note that as yet there is no reference to the Isle of Portland Circuit in the National Trail Guide.

76 | Ferry Bridge to Lulworth Cove (Visitor Centre)   OS OL15 (T) Weymouth (Trains)

Grading: This section runs from easy to moderate to strenuous. Distance - 22.7   969.2   14.1   602.2

Timing: 6.25 hours

See also our Weymouth to Lulworth Cove Path Description.

SEE SECTION 80 FOR DETAILS OF THE ALTERNATIVE INLAND COAST PATH FROM WEST BEXINGTON TO OSMINGTON MILLS.

A footpath sign shows you where to continue on to Weymouth, using the track-bed of the old railway line from Portland (but take care as this is also a cycleway). After passing behind the sailing centre cut down to the right to continue into Old Castle Road. Opposite some new three-storey houses ignore a footpath sign pointing towards the coast. This now only leads to the beach and the continuing coastal footpath (known as Underbarn Walk) shown on most maps above Western Ledges has been permanently closed as a result of a landslip. The coast path is now unfortunately routed along residential roads. In 260 yards (240 m) from the footpath sign turn right into Belle Vue Road. Continue for about 600 yards (560 m) to a crossroads and turn right into Redcliff View. At the end of this road a path leads across a grassed area back onto the coast path at 6815 7814. **Westbound** walkers should turn sharp right after the Wyke Regis Coastguard lookout and turn westward on the northern leg of Redcliff View to then follow the eastbound route in reverse. Continue on the path close to the coast to Nothe Fort and bear sharp left down to the harbourside which is followed to the Town Bridge, which is crossed and the opposite side of the harbour is followed back to the Pavilion Complex. Here bear left to join The Esplanade. In summer a little ferry may run across the harbour to shorten the route.

Weymouth Harbour
Weymouth & Portland Borough Council,
Harbour Master's Office,
Municipal Offices, North Quay,
Weymouth, DT4 8TA
01305 838423

April to October daily - 1000 - sunset.
Weather permitting

Leave Weymouth along the new promenade and at Overcombe, go up the minor road to Bowleaze Cove. However, after passing the Spyglass Inn it is best to bear right to cross the grass public open space and follow the cliff edge to the Beachside Centre. From this point most maps show the coast path taking a route through the Beachside Centre and to the south of the Riviera Hotel (large white building).   However because of cliff falls the route of the coast path now continues along the road to the north of the hotel.   At the end of the road follow the signed coast path route back to the cliff edge near Redcliff Point.   Beyond a former holiday camp, now the 3D Education and Adventure Centre, follow the signed and waymarked route of a newly re-established section of coast path that avoids landslips.

On the downhill approach to Osmington Mills the route avoiding the landslide bears away from the cliff edge over a stile and down the right hand side of a field. At the bottom it joins the Inland Route just before it crosses two stiles to meet the narrow road that is followed down to the coast.

At Ringstead you are taken slightly inland, because the path shown on maps seaward of the houses does not exist. At the old coastguard cottages at White Nothe, be careful to take the left fork of the two yellow arrows, that being the correct route. From White Nothe onwards you will find that there are some quite severe gradients to be traversed before you reach Lulworth. West of Lulworth Cove the newly stone-pitched path will lead you down through the car park and past the Heritage Centre and onto a tarmac road to the cove.

Some maps show the coast path turning south from Hambury Tout. This is not correct and the route (that is not a right of way) is no longer able to be used. However lower down and before the main car park there is a signed route to the south that joins a minor road and is more convenient if you wish to take in the view into Stair Hole with its spectacular upturned rock formations.

However, some people turn even further inland than they need. Some signs indicate 'Youth Hostel – Coast Path' and contain the acorn logo. These signs are intended to indicate the route to the Youth Hostel at West Lulworth and are not the continuation of the coast path. Follow the signs for the Cove.

| 77 | Lulworth Cove to Kimmeridge, Gaulter Gap (Beach car park) OS OL15 (V) Lulworth

| Grading: Severe | Distance - | 11.8 | 981.0 | 7.3 | 609.5 |

Timing: 4 hours

See also our Lulworth to Kimmeridge Path Description.

The coastal path through the Army ranges is open at the times shown below, and is a very fine walk indeed, but a tough one. If closed, two alternative routes are shown on the next page.

The path behind the beach café is now open again. Higher up follow a short signed alternative to avoid an eroded area close to the cliff edge. Tide permitting, the beach route avoids a considerable ascent and descent. At most states of the tide, it is perfectly possible to walk along the pebble beach at Lulworth Cove, going up the path which rises diagonally on the far side of the beach. At the top of the steep ascent off the beach, the best route proceeds seawards and there the path turns south eastwards along the coast to the beginning of the Army Ranges, just by the Fossil Forest.

The village of Tyneham, church, school and historical information are worth going inland 0.5 mile (800 m) to see, between 1000 - 1600 hrs.

The route onwards is straight forward – just follow the yellow topped posts through the ranges to arrive at Kimmeridge Bay passing the 'nodding donkey' oil pump.

RAC Gunnery School Lulworth Ranges: No Firing and Firing Periods

1. *NON FIRING PERIOD.* The Range Walks will be open to the public during the following holiday periods, all dates are inclusive:

EASTER 2004	9 APR - 18 APR 2004
BANK HOLIDAY 2004	1 MAY - 3 MAY 2004
SPRING 2004	29 MAY - 6 JUN 2004
SUMMER 2004	24 JUL - 30 AUG 2004
CHRISTMAS/NEW YEAR 2004/2005	24 DEC 2004 - 3 JAN 2005

2. *FIRING PERIODS.* The Range Walks are normally open to the public every Saturday and Sunday except for some weekends in the year. For this year they have reserved the following six weekends for firing:

| FIRST WEEKEND | 31 JAN - 1 FEB 2004 |

SECOND	6 - 7 MAR 2004
THIRD	8 - 9 MAY 2004
FOURTH	12 - 13 JUN 2004
FIFTH	9 - 10 OCT 2004
SIXTH	20 - 21 NOV 2004

3. Experience has shown that it is sometimes possible to avoid firing on some of these reserved weekends and if this is the case, the Range Walks will be opened. Should this occur this year we will make every effort to publicise the fact.

4. Tyneham Church and the School are normally open for viewing 1000 hrs-1600 hrs when the walks are open.

5. Information is also available by ringing 01929 404819, which is a 24 hour answering service

Alternative Routes when Lulworth Range coast path is unavailable: Lulworth Cove to Kimmeridge, Gaulter Gap.

Option 1 - approx. 13.5 miles (22 km) on a safer, quieter but more strenuous route using mainly rights of way, and permissive paths through Lulworth Park (pre-plotting of given grid refs. onto a map will assist navigation).

Leave the Cove and take the 2nd road on the left (825 807).100 yards (90 m) on the right, a footpath leads north for 0.75 mile (1.2 km); turn right (east) and after 100 yards (90 m) turn left (north) to pass Belhuish Coppice and Belhuish Farm, and then across the B3071 at 835 832.

At 845 828 eastern boundary of Burngate Wood, use the permissive (blue) path north-east past Park Lodge, and go across the road (855 832) onto a bridleway.

Continue north-east along the bridleway to 865 839 where it veers north, and later north-east through the Highwood to meet the road at 872 862. On the road walk east, fork right (signposted Stoborough) at 882 855; over the crossroads with the B3070 at 886 855 east for further 1.5 miles (2.4 km) along Holme Lane to walk east 911 854.

(*) Turn right just before a railway bridge onto Dorey Farm bridleway at 911 854. After 1.25 miles (2 km) turn right onto Creech Road leading south-south-west towards the Purbeck Ridge. After another 1.5 miles (2.4 km) of road, walk up a steep gradient to a viewpoint car park. Beyond the car park 902 815 take the left road that turns back and down over the ridge to Corfe. (A short cut bridleway 905 817 zigzags down to meet the same road.) As the road levels out at a left hand bend 907 812, take the bridleway ahead that leads out south through Steeple Leaze Farm.

200 yards (185 m) south of the farm, a footpath leads south crossing another ridge bridleway, down a steep path, and across a field to Higher Stonehips, and on to Gaulter Gap, the easterly point of the range walks.

Option 2 - approx. 12 miles (19 km).

This route is mainly road walking, and care is needed on narrow bends. Leave the Cove to West Lulworth on the B3070, and then turn right to East Lulworth at 835 816 to continue on the B3070. After 3 miles (5 km), turn right (east) at grid reference 886 855 along Holme Lane, and then continue from * above, at 911 854.

78	**Kimmeridge, Gaulter Gap to Swanage (The Pier)**			**OS OL15**

| Grading: Severe and then moderate | Distance - | 21.4 | 1002.4 | 13.3 | 622.8 |

Timing: 7.25 hours

See also our Kimmeridge to South Haven Point Path Description.

From Gaulter Gap, Kimmeridge, the path is straightforward although care may be needed where small sections have slipped, cracked or may be close to the cliff top. After descending Hounstout the official route turns inland to avoid dangerous wet and unstable ground on what appears to be the direct route to St Aldhelm's Head. Take care to follow the signed and waymarked route even though it seems to be heading in the wrong direction to go inland to Hill Bottom cottages where the path turns south again, and beyond the gate climbs left up to a high level route which is well signposted. The climb up West Hill is away from the views, but as you gain height along Emmett's Hill, the views back along the Dorset coast are very good. The Royal Marines memorial is just to the left of the path.

From St Aldhelm's Head, there is fine high level walking all the way to Durlston Head, but not much accommodation along this stretch.

There is only minimal signing in the Durlston Country Park but improvements have been promised. However, you keep on the low level path all the way round Durlston Head but as you come up on the north side of it you take the second turning right, not the first which is a dead end into a quarry. [D6A]

After leaving Durlston Castle follow the broad stony coastal path north through the woods above Durlston Bay for some 760 yards (700 m) to reach a barrier and sign. From this point the coast path has been permanently diverted following a massive cliff fall. Turn left on a good path for some 125 yards (115 m) to reach Durlston Road at a kissing gate. Turn right and in about 185 yards (170 m) turn right again into Belle Vue Road. Just before a block of flats called Durlston Cliff the original coast path rejoined the road (the current path at this location now only leads to the foreshore), which is followed north-eastwards, to the grassed open space leading down to Peveril Point.

The section of the coast path through Swanage is not well signed. You are unlikely to go far wrong, and will soon be walking along the sea front promenade.

D6A. Diversion 6A. Durlston Castle. The section of coast path to the east and north of Durlston Castle is temporally closed because of a dangerous retaining wall. Work is due to start on this soon. Follow the signed short diversion that starts by The Globe.

79 | Swanage to Sandbanks (South Haven Point) OS OL15 (T) Swanage; (V) Studland

Grading: Moderate   Distance -   12.2   1014.6   7.6   630.4

Timing: 3.5 hours

See also our Kimmeridge to South Haven Point Path Description.

At the telephone box at the north end of Swanage Sea Front, sea state permitting, you may prefer to keep along the pedestrian promenade to the end and then walk 200 yards (185 m) along the stony beach turning up some steps to the official route. At high tide and in bad weather you have to leave the seafront on the main road (Ulwell Road) and where it bears left into a one-way system continue ahead into Redcliffe Road. At the sub post office turn right into Ballard Way and at the end do not be put off by the signs 'Ballard Private Estate'. Carry forward into the chalet estate and follow signs for the coast path to emerge on to a grassed area on the cliff edge.

From Ballard Down the path is obvious all the way to Handfast Point and the much photographed rocks of Old Harry.

When you reach a road by a public toilet, turn right up the road. Ignore the first footpath to the right, and shortly after passing the Bankes Arms, take a footpath on the right signposted as 'Middle Beach - Fort Henry'. On reaching the cliff edge turn left and follow the path to reach the beach access road at a barrier gate. Turn sharp right down to the beach and go left by the café. When the tide is out, this is firm, but when it is in more effort will be required.

Further up the beach, maybe we should mention there is a naturist beach, so you must not be put off if you find that on this last lap that you are the only one wearing clothes! The National Trust has also provided an alternative route, The Heather Walk, through the dunes, and this is marked by yellow-topped posts, however the naturist area is still partially in view and the soft sand underfoot is tiring at the end of a long walk.

Despite any notices you may see, dogs on leads may accompany coast path walkers along the shore line, but be sure to clean up after your dog if necessary.

Until the Autumn of 2002, the official finish of the path at the ferry road was undistinguished. Following years of pressure from this Association, there is now an impressive marker incorporating a steel mast and sail and a floor compass. Thanks are due to the efforts of the South West Coast Path Team and the generous donations made by our Association members and others.

At the South Haven Point Ferry you leave the South West Coast Path. You may meet someone about to start to walk the other way round. We know, from those who complete the coast path, their feelings of delight and disappointment, so how about planning your 'other way round' walk?

Shell Bay/Sandbanks (Mouth of Poole Harbour) Bournemouth-Swanage Motor Road & Ferry Company, Shell Bay, Studland. BH19 3BA.
Tel: 01929 450203.
www.sandbanksferry.co.uk

All year round. Daily every 20 mins.
Sandbanks 0700 - 2300 hrs
Shell Bay 0710 - 2310 hrs
Christmas Day every half hour.

Alfred Wainwright, at the end of his work on the Pennine Way said; 'You have completed a mission and achieved an ambition. You have walked the Pennine Way, as you dreamed of doing. This will be a very satisfying moment in your life. You will be tired and hungry and travel stained. But you will feel great, just great.' Dear reader, just substitute the South West Coast Path for the Pennine Way. We will add whether you have been lucky enough to walk the whole way from Minehead at one go, or simply, as most of us have, in bits and pieces over a period, nonetheless you will be glad you walked and have just finished Britain's longest and finest footpath. It's a longer step than most take in their lifetime!

If you are continuing to walk eastwards from Sandbanks see the notes following section 80 on page 92.

80 | Alternative Inland Coast Path: West Bexington to Osmington Mills OS OL15

Grading: Moderate   Distance - 27.0   16.8

See also our alternative Inland Route Path Description.

Although this is certainly not a coastal path it is an enjoyable walk along well-marked paths with good views seaward from the ridges. Because it is inland a more detailed route description is given. When walking this section bear in mind that we found no place on the route for obtaining refreshments between the start of the walk, where there is a cafe, and the village of Osmington.

At West Bexington car park turn inland up the road signposted 'Inland Route - Coast Path', and where the road turns left, continue forward up the stony track, signposted 'Hardy Monument $5^{1}/_{2}$ miles'. At top of the hill the footpath briefly joins the main road but you immediately leave it again over the stile on the right through a field, signposted `Hardy Monument 5 miles'. Take care, as the way across this field is not clear and you should, at first, keep parallel to the road and then bear right to a waymarked post. After you have crossed a wall, you can start to bear upwards to the left to the further signpost near the road, marked with the acorn symbol and the words 'Inland Route'. After about 300 yards (275 m) continuing through the field and by the corner of a wall there is a further signpost 'Hardy Monument $4^{1}/_{2}$, Osmington Mills 15'. Continue forward, very shortly emerging on to the B3157 road that you cross and leave through a gate, signposted `Hardy Monument $4^{1}/_{2}$'.

You now approach Abbotsbury Castle (hill fort). At a junction of paths take the upper slightly right-hand fork along the top of the southern earthwork of the fort past the trig point, from where you can get superb views in all directions. You should be able to see the Hardy Monument clearly in the distance. Proceed eastwards and cross a minor road and go forward, signposted `Hardy Monument 4'. Proceed in an approximate easterly direction along the ridge of Wears Hill and the crest of White Hill for about 2 miles (3.2 km) following the signposts and waymarks. However be careful not to follow signs (with the acorn symbol incorrectly shown) that indicate routes down to the village of Abbotsbury lying in the valley below, with the old chapel clearly visible. At the east end of White Hill bear north-east as signposted and leave in the inland corner through a gate on to a minor road. Turn left along this road for approximately 50 yards (46 m) and then turn right, signposted 'Inland Route - Hardy Monument 2'.

Follow the bridleway marked with blue arrows along the wire fence above the scrub to a path junction; where the bridleway carries on forward take the yellow waymarked footpath to the left and cross a stile. At the far side of the field the track then leads approximately 50 yards (46 m) to a further gate with a stile and waymark. Immediately adjacent to this gate is a stone circle which is an ancient monument and there is a sign to this effect. You now continue forward, leaving a small wood to the left, to reach the road from Portesham to Winterbourne Steepleton. Turn left along the road for approximately 60 yards (55 m) and then turn right into a field over a stile, signposted `Hardy Monument $1^{1}/_{2}$ - Osmington Mills 13'. On the far side of the field proceed forward, signpost `Hardy Monument 1'. At this point there is a signpost forking right to Hellstone only, with a return possible on a different path.

At Blackdown Barn turn left to climb up through the woods, signposted `Hardy Monument $1/_2$'. At the monument you will find a small signpost 'Inland Route-Osmington Mills 11 miles' with a blue arrow indicating the way forward. Cross the road to a further signpost with the acorn symbol and now descend through the bracken. You shortly reach the road again, turn left and in a few yards ignore the signpost on the right, cutting back indicating 'Bridleway to Coast Path' and continue forward, (signposted 'Coast Path East') and in another 100 yards (90 m) turn right, signposted `Inland Route to Corton Hill' on one side of the sign and `Osmington 12 - Corton Hill 2' on the other. Now there is a good ridgeway path without navigational problems for some 3 miles (4.8 km) and good views to seaward in the distance. After passing a radio mast you come to the B3159 road marked by the Borough of Weymouth boundary stone and continue across, signposted `Inland Route East'.

On approaching the main A354 road turn right immediately before it down the signposted track and after just over $1/_4$ mile (400 m) you will find a stile in the hedge on your left. The path leads across a narrow field to cross the busy A354. Before the farm with its adjacent radio mast take care to go through the gate on the right, marked with a blue arrow. After crossing the field, leaving two tumuli to your left, you reach a metalled road. Turn right and at the next junction there is a signpost surmounted by a symbol 'Dorset - Came Wood' which, unusually, carries the six-figure map reference of the locality (687 857). Here you turn right at the signpost `Bridleway to Bincombe'. At the end of the path join a metalled lane and at the road junction turn left, signposted 'Inland Route East'.

Drop down the road into the village of Bincombe and where the road turns right take the track forward leaving a small church on your right. Where the path splits take the left hand fork signposted again with a blue arrow and the acorn symbol. After the overhead high-voltage power lines pass through a small signposted wooden gate and then proceed forward through one field into the next to a footpath sign. Here turn left, following the line of the old indistinct curving grassy track until it meets the road at the bottom of Combe Valley. Turn left here and follow the road until you reach the Combe Valley road sign to `Sutton Poyntz' and take this turn to the right. After 70 yards (64 m) turn left through a gate, signposted `White Horse Hill - Osmington Mills'. The path now is easy to follow with extensive views to seaward over Weymouth and Portland. On passing a ruined building on your left you reach a broad track and turn right, signposted `Osmington $1^1/_2$' and after about 200 yards (185 m) go through a gate, signposted `Inland Route Osmington'. You will shortly pass a trig point on your right and at the next field gate bear left and follow the field boundary along White Horse Hill. Just beyond the next gate fork right, signposted 'Osmington 1, Lulworth 8'.

Descend to the village of Osmington and follow the signs through the village. When you reach the main Weymouth road near the Sun Ray Inn turn left and in about 250 yards (230 m) turn right at a signpost, over a stile and footbridge, and follow the field boundary on the left through two fields and at the top look back to see the Hardy Monument in the distance and also the white horse on the hillside. Go over the stile to the footpath sign, then turn half right to cross the field at an angle to a further stile. Cross it and turn left along the hedge side to the bottom. At the end of the field there is a very short length of enclosed footpath to the road; turn right along it, descending to Osmington Mills.

For those who wish to continue to walk eastwards

The South West Coast Path from Plymouth to South Haven Point (Poole Harbour entrance) is now also part of the British section of European Route E9. The British section continues to Dover and is predominantly a coastal walk as far as Portsmouth. The so-called Bournemouth Coast Path and then the Solent Way provide an onward coastal walk across the remainder of Dorset and all of Hampshire to the Sussex Border at Emsworth. The E9 route follows these two paths as far as Portsmouth where it turns inland.

The guidebook for the Bournemouth Coast Path is currently out of print but is being re-written with the view to publication in 2004. A new guide to the Solent Way has just been published and the linear route is included in Pub Walks Along the Solent Way by Anne-Marie Edwards and published by Countryside at £7.95. ISBN 1 85306 738 5.

Prior to the publication of the guidebook for Bournemouth (it also includes Christchurch to Milford-on-Sea) the Association's fact sheet on the route is still available, free to members for a stamped self-addressed envelope from the Administrator.

ACCOMMODATION

This list of accommodation has been prepared in path order.

The majority of our B & B addresses have been **reccommended by coast path walkers**. The fact that they are included in this book does not indicate a recommendation by The South West Coast Path Association. Their inclusion is merely for information purposes; they are there, if you want them. We cannot, for financial and practical reasons, introduce vetting, inspection or any form of `Star' rating. We do have a system whereby addresses can be removed from the list.

The following letter code is used.

Facilities

O	=	Open All Year	D	=	Drying facilities for wet clothes
EM	=	Evening Meal	PL	=	Packed Lunches
CP	=	Car Parking	LSP	=	Long Stay Parking
DW	=	Dogs Welcome	KT	=	Kit Transfer
PD	=	Pick Up/Drop Service	LT	=	Luxury Tent

Room Codes

D	=	Double	T	=	Twin
S	=	Single	F	=	Family
ES	=	En Suite			

Please note: The figure in brackets denotes the number of en-suite rooms e.g. 4d[2] = 4 double rooms, two of which are en-suite.

KT - Kit Transfer. A service being offered by some of our accommodation providers is to transfer your kit to your next accommodation. This could prove useful to you. Naturally a fee may be levied for this service.

PD - Pick Up/Drop. This code appears following the distance from the path and denotes a facility whereby your host is prepared to collect and return you to the coast path within reasonable distance. No fee should be charged for this service.

Distance from Path. Please remember these are only approximate and may not be accurate.

LT - Luxury Tent. Due to accommodation problems in the St Austell Bay area, some providers have installed superb tents in their gardens/paddocks. You will not need sleeping bags or any camping out gear.

The part of the address in CAPITALS is an aid to location; it does not signify the postal town. The extreme left-hand column refers to the appropriate section in the 'Trail Description'; we feel it may help you to find addresses quickly. The amount quoted gives an **indication of the starting rate** for bed and breakfast, and may well rise. If working on a tight budget, it is best to ask first.

Tourist Information Centres can be an additional source of accommodation addresses. We have provided a list of TICs along the coast path for your use on page 150.

Most of the B & B providers operate from their own private homes so do not expect plenty of staff as there are in hotels and large guesthouses. They work hard to make you comfortable, welcome, dry you out and make you feel like one of the family.

We wish to develop this list especially for many 'sparse' areas. Suggestions for inclusion in our next list will be welcome. Details of any new accommodation should be addressed to the Administrator. Our list is not comprehensive and walkers will find many B&B's in towns and villages along the coast path that are not recorded in this book.

It would not be out of place here to add a word of thanks from those who walk, to those who kindly board. How many times have we been thankful for a friendly welcome and good 'digs'? Maybe a note we had from one of our accommodation addresses puts it well. 'We have had quite a lot of walkers this year and we have usually managed to dry them out - and feed them up.'

Although there are a lot of addresses that state they are 'open all the year', some of these close for the Christmas period. Walkers should remember that during the holiday season many of our accommodation addresses could be fully booked up in advance by holidaymakers staying for a week or two. Conversely a walker could book for one night only in good time, thus preventing a guest house proprietor from taking a week or more booking later on. Accommodation problems can be frustrating to all parties concerned so bear these facts in mind when bed hunting **for one night only**.

Important If having booked ahead, and for any reason you are unable to get to your accommodation address, please telephone and explain your absence to your intended host. We have known instances where the host has become so worried about the non-appearance of walkers that they have informed the emergency services. The last thing we want is Police, Coastguards and Royal Navy helicopters out on a wild goose chase.

Sect.	Name and Address	Tel. No. Fax. No. Web / Email	Map Reference Opening Times	Distance from Path Starting Price Facilities Accommodation
1	Mr R Brooker 23 Chestnut Way Alcombe MINEHEAD TA24 6EB	01643 709913 sandraybrooker@tiscali.co.uk	972 452	1 km PD £17.00 O D EM PL CP KT PD 1T[1] 1S
1	Mrs D Morris Badgers 38 Summerland Road MINEHEAD TA24 5BS	01643 704583	969 461	400 mts £16.00 O D LSP 2D[2]2T[1] 1S 1F[1]
1	Mrs N Phillips The Old Ship Aground Quay Street MINEHEAD TA24 5UL	01643 702087 01643 709066 enquiries@oldshipaground.co.uk oldshipaground.co.uk	971 469	500 mts £25.00 O D EM PL CP LSP DW KT 2D 3T 2S 3F ALL ES
1	Mr & Mrs Smith 11 Glenmore Road MINEHEAD TA24 5BQ	01643 705253	973 462	1km O D CP KT 1D 3F
1	Mr & Mrs D Sanders Academy Guest House 1 Glenmore Road MINEHEAD TA24 5BQ	01643 706225 numberoneminehead@btopenworld.com	973 462	700 mts £20.00 O PL CP LSP DW KT 2D[1] 1T[1] 1S
1	Mr J Murray Marston Lodge Hotel St Michael's Road MINEHEAD TA24 5JP	01643 702510 As Phone	968 468 Mar-Oct	400 mts £25.00 D CP LSP 6D 2T 2S 1F ALL ES
1	Mr R Trott The Parks Guest House 26 The Parks MINEHEAD TA24 8BT	01643 703547 01643 709843 info@parksguesthouse.co.uk www.parksguesthouse.co.uk	965 467 Feb-mid Dec	800 mts £22.00 D PL CP DW KT PD 2D 2T 3F ALL ES LSP low season
1	Mrs A Green 24 Ponsford Road MINEHEAD TA24 5DY	01645 703945 Mar-Oct greenfinial@lineone.net	973 467	800 mts £17.00 D PL CP KT 1D 1T ALL ES
1	Mrs J Bakker Beverleigh Beacon Road MINEHEAD TA24 5SF	01643 708450 beverleigh@talk21.com	968 469	300 mts £22.00 O D PL CP LSP DW 2D 1T ALL ES EM on request
1	Mr & Mrs R Webber Hindon Organic Farm MINEHEAD TA24 8SH	01643 705244 info@hindonfarm.co.uk www.hindonfarm.co.uk	933 467	800 mts £25.00 D EM PL CP LSP DW 4D[3] 3T
1	Mr & Mrs G Lindley 20 Tregonwell Road MINEHEAD TA24 5DU	01643 702147 bactonleigh@aol.com	974 462	400 mts £20.00 O EM PL CP DW 5D 2T 1F ALL ES
1	Mrs H Harris Holnicote Cottage SELWORTHY TA24 8TJ	01643 863085 tbumble84@aol.com www.holnicote.com	909 463	800 mts £25.00 O D PL CP LSP KT PD 2D 1T
1	Exmoor Falconry & Animal Farm West Lynch Farm ALLERFORD Near Porlock TA24 8HJ	01643 862816 www.exmoorfalconry.co.uk	899 476 £25.00	500 mts O D PL CP LSP DW KT 2D 2T 1S

94

Sect.	Name and Address	Tel. No. Fax. No. Web / Email	Map Reference Opening Times	Distance from Path Starting Price Facilities Accommodation
1	Mr & Mrs J Winzer Cross Lane House ALLERFORD Minehead TA24 8HW	01643 862112 as phone crosslanehouse@aol.com www.restaurantguides.co.uk	905 469	800 mts PD £25.00 O D EM PL CP DW KT PD 1S 2F Single occupancy surcharge in season.
1	Mr & Mrs G Manning Lower House Farm BOSSINGTON TA24 8HF	01643 862693	896 479	on path £22.00 O PL D EM CP LSP KT 1D 1S 1F[1]
1	Mrs E Prescott Olands Bossington Lane BOSSINGTON TA24 8HQ	01643 862405	898 478 Easter-Oct	800 mts £20.00 D PL CP LSP 2D 1T
1	Mr & Mrs T V Stiles-Cox Leys The Ridge PORLOCK TA24 8HA	01643 862477 As Phone	892 469	2 km £22.00 O D PL CP LSP 3D 2S
1	Mr R G Steer Myrtle Cottage High Street PORLOCK TA24 8PU	01643 862978 As Phone bob.steer@talk21.com www.smoothhound@chelsoftdemon.com	885 467	100 mts PD £23.50 O D PL CP DW KT PD 5D 3T 5S 3F ALL ES Single £30.00
1	Mrs T Andrews Woodcocks Ley Farm PORLOCK TA24 8LX	01643 862502 as phone robandrews@c2812.fsnet.co.uk	881 450 Easter-Nov	3 km PD £20.00 D EM PL CP LSP KT PD 2D [1] 1T 1F £30 single occupancy
1	Mrs B Starr Sea View Cottage PORLOCK WEIR TA24 8PE	01643 862523	864 478	On path £19.00 O D PL CP DW KT 1D(1) 1T
2	Mrs E J Richards Silcombe Farm PORLOCK WEIR TA24 8JN	01643 862248	833 482	On path PD £20.00 O D EM PL CP LSP KT PD 1D[1] 2T[2] 1S
2	Mrs S Pile Coombe Farm COUNTISBURY Lynton EX36 6NF	01598 741236 as phone coombefarm@freeuk.com brendonvalley.co.uk/coombefarm	756 484 Mar-Nov	1.5 km £27.00 D PL CP LSP 13[1] 1T[1] 1S 2F[2]
2	The The Bath Hotel LYNMOUTH EX35 6EL	01598 752238 01598 752544 bathhotel@torslynmouth.co.uk www.torslynmouth.co.uk	722 495 Mar-Oct	20 mts £27.00 D EM PL CP DW 10D 7T 1S 4F ALL ES
2	Mr & Mrs A Francis Glenville House 2 Tors Road LYNMOUTH EX35 6ET	01598 752202 tricia@glenvillelynmouth.co.uk www.glenvillelynmouth.co.uk	727 494 March-Nov	300 mts £25.00 D PL 4D[3] 1T 1S
2	Miss D Smith Hillside House 22 Watersmeet Road LYNMOUTH EX35 6EP	01598 753836	725 493	400 mts £22.50 O D EM PL DW KT 3D[1] 1T 1S
2	Mr P Hood Woodlands Lynbridge Road LYNTON EX35 6AX	01598 752324 01598 753828 info@woodlandsguesthouse.co.uk www.woodlandsguesthouse.co.uk	720 487 Feb-Nov	£20.00 D EM PL CP 5D 1T 1S 5ES

Sect.	Name and Address	Tel. No. Fax. No. Web / Email	Map Reference Opening Times	Distance from Path Starting Price Facilities Accommodation
2	Mr & Mrs J McGowan The Denes Longmead LYNTON EX35 6DQ	01598 753573 As Phone j.e.mcgowan@btinternet.com www.thedenes.com	715 494	1km PD £18.00 O D EM PL CP KT PD 1D[1] 3T[2] 3F[2]
2	Mrs Mari Kirk 12 Crossmead LYNTON EX35 6DG	01598 753288	716 492	400 mts £20.00 O D PL DW 1D 1T 2S
2	Mrs P E Morgan Kingford House Longmead LYNTON EX35 6DQ	01598 752361 www.kingfordhouse.co.uk	715 493	200 mts £22.50 O D EM PL CP 4D 1T 2S ALL ES
2	Ms E Blake & E Rickey Lee House Lee Road LYNTON EX35 6BP	01598 752364 01598 752364 leehouse@freeuk.com www.smoothhound.co.uk/hotels/lee.html	717 495	400 mts £24.00 O D EM PL CP DW 7D 2T 1F ALL ES
2	Mr & Mrs C Wilkins Sinai House Lynway LYNTON EX35 6AY	01598 753227 01598 752633 enquires@sinaihouse.co.uk www.sinaihouse.co.uk	721 492 Feb - Dec	250 mts £23.00 D PL CP LSP 5D[5] 2T[1]1S
3	The Hunters Inn HEDDONS VALLEY Parracombe EX31 4PY	01598 763230 01598 763636 www.huntersinn.net	655 482	1 km PD £28.00 O D EM PL CP LSP DW KTPD 5D 1T 2F ALL ES
3	Mrs Dallyn Mannacott Farm Nr Hunters Inn MARTINHOE EX31 4QS	01598 763227	662 481 Apr-mid Oct	800 mts £17.00 D PL CP LSP 1D 1T
3	Mr & Mrs F J Barry Glendower King Street COMBE MARTIN EX34 0AL	01271 883449 01271 883449 francisb924@aol.com	578 471	100mts PD £17.00 O D PL CP DW KT PD 3D[2] 3T[2] 3S 1F[1]
3	Mrs J Bosley Hillview Guest House The Woodlands COMBE MARTIN EX34 0AT	01271 882331 hillviewgh@macunlimited.net	575 469 Easter-Oct	200 mts £18.00 D PL CP LSP KT 2D[2] 1T
3	Mr & Mrs Burbidge Mellstock House Woodlands COMBE MARTIN EX34 0AR	01271 882592 01271 882090 mary@mellstockhouse.co.uk www.mellstockhouse.co.uk	472 573	300 mts £20.00 O D EM PL CP KT PD 4D 1T 1S 1F ALL ES
3	Mrs A Waldon Idlehour Borough Road COMBE MARTIN EX34 0AN	01271 883217	577 472 March-Oct	80 mts £15.00 D CP DW 2D 1T 1F
3	Mrs M M Pawsey Blair Lodge Hotel Moory Meadow COMBE MARTIN EX34 0DG	01271 882294 info@blairlodge.co.uk www.blairlodge.co.uk	578 472 Feb-Nov	on path £23.00 D EM PL CP KT 6D[6] 2T[2]2S Open Xmas

Sect.	Name and Address	Tel. No. Fax. No. Web / Email	Map Reference Opening Times	Distance from Path Starting Price Facilities Accommodation
3	Mrs C Crawford Cobblestones Wood Lane COMBE MARTIN EX34 0NE	01271 882050 www.visitcombemartin.co.uk/cobblestones.htm	595 457	2 km PD £18.00 O D PL CP DW KT PD 1D 1S 1F
4	Mr & Mrs W J Millington Sherborne Lodge Hotel Torrs Park ILFRACOMBE EX34 8AY	01271 862297 01271 865520 113121-222@compuserve.com www.smoothhound.co.uk/hotels/sherborn.html	514 475	200 mts £20.00 O D EM PL CP LSP DW 5D[5] 3T[2]1S[1] 1F[1] LSP not August
4	Mr & Mrs C D Hewitt Norbury House Hotel Torrs Park ILFRACOMBE EX34 8AZ	01271 863888 info@norburyhousehotel.co.uk www.norburyhousehotel.co.uk	511 472 Mar-Nov	200mts £25.00 D EM PL CP LSP DW KT PD 3D[3] 1T[1]1S 3F[3]
4	Mrs R Franks The Cairn House Hotel ILFRACOMBE EX34 8EH	01271 863911 info@cairnhousehotel.co.uk www.cairnhousehotel.co.uk	517 464	1 km PD £18.00 O D EM PL CP LSP KT PD 5D 1T 1S 2F ALL ES
4	Mr & Mrs D Jenkins Avalon Hotel 6 Capstone Crescent ILFRACOMBE EX34 9BT	01271 863325 01271 866543 ann_dudley_avalon@yahoo.co.uk www.avalon.hotel.co.uk	523 479	200 mts £25.00 O D EM PL CP LSP DW 4D 2T 2F ALL ES £30 singles CP/LSP low season only,
4	Mrs W Grindlay Moles Farmhouse Old Berrynarbor Road Hele ILFRACOMBE EX34 9RB	01271 862099 info@molesfarmhouse.co.uk www.molesfarmhouse.co.uk	534 474	400 mts £20.00 O D PL CP 1D 1T 1F ALL ES
4	Mr & Mrs J Davies Seven Hills Hotel Torrs Park ILFRACOMBE EX34 8AY	01271 862207 01271 865976 holidays@sevenhillshotel.co.uk www.sevenhillshotel.co.uk	514 477	1 mts £25.00 O D EM PL CP LSP 8D 3T 2F ALL ES
5	Mr & Mrs T Jacobs Greyven House 4 St James Place ILFRACOMBE EX34 9BH	01271 862505 as phone sandratrevor@greyvenhouse.fsnet.co.uk www.ilfracombe.tourism.co.uk/greyvenhouse	571 429	50mts £19.50 O D PL CP KT 5D[4] 3T[2] 1S 1F[1]
5	Mrs M P Newcombe Sunnyside LEE Nr Ilfracombe EX34 8LW	01271 863189	487 463 Easter-	50 mts PD £18.00 D PL PD 2D[1] 1T 1S
5	Mrs G Potts The Orchard LEE Ilfracombe EX34 8LW	01271 867212 01271 865383 ginnypotts@hotmail.com www.theorchardlee.co.uk	487 463 Feb-Dec	on path £25.50 D EM PL CP LSP 2D[2] 1T 1S
5	Ms J Waghorn Grey Cottage LEE Ilfracombe EX34 8LN	01271 864360 info@greycottage.co.uk www.greycottage.co.uk	494 461	500 mts £26.00 O D EM PL CP DW KT PD 1D[1] 2T[1] 1F[1]

Sect.	Name and Address	Tel. No. Fax. No. Web / Email	Map Reference Opening Times	Distance from Path Starting Price Facilities Accommodation
5	Miss Georgina Manley Fuchsia Valley House LEE EX34 8LW	01271 866857 todS40@hotmail.com	487 463	200 mts £22.00 O D PL CP DW KT 2D[1]1T[1] 1F[1]
6	Mr T Cole Lundy House Hotel Chapel Hill MORTEHOE EX34 7DZ	01271 870372 01271 871001 info@lundyhousehotel.co.uk www.lundyhousehotel.co.uk	454 447 March-Oct	20 mts £24.00 D EM PL CP DW KT 5D 1T 4F ALL ES
6	Mr & Mrs S Lawn The Mortehoe Brasserie 2 The Crescent MORTEHOE EX34 7DX	01271 870610 01271 870610 stevedlawn@aol.com	456 451 14 Feb - 31 Dec	50 mts £27.50 D EM PL DW 3D[3]
6	Mr & Mrs S Oliver Gull Rock Hotel MORTEHOE Woolacombe EX34 7EA	01271 870534 simon.nicola@tiscali.co.uk www.thegullrockhotel.co.uk	457 446	200 mts £26.00 O D PL DW 2D 1T 2F ALL ES
6	Mrs A Braund Clyst House Rockfield Road WOOLACOMBE EX34 7DH	01271 870220	455 441 Mar-Oct	100 mts £24.00 D EM PL 1D 2T 1S
6	Mr & Mrs H J Riley Camberley Beach Road WOOLACOMBE EX34 7AA	01271 870231 info@camberleybandb.co.uk www.camberleybandb.co.uk	465 438	600 mts £24.00 O D PL CP KT 1D 1T 1F ALL ES
6	Mr & Mrs C Lewis Sandunes Guest House Beach Road WOOLACOMBE EX34 7BT	01271 870661 beaconbts@u.genie.co.uk	460 438	500 mts £24.00 O D PL CP 4D
6	Mr J Oakes Caertref Hotel Beach Road WOOLACOMBE EX34 7BT	01271 870361 info@caertref.co.uk www.caertref.co.uk	456 243	300 mts £23.00 O D PL CP 6D 3T 2F ALL ES EM, LSP, DW, KT, PD out of season
7	Mrs G Adams Combas Farm PUTSBOROUGH EX33 1PH	01271 890398 01271 890398	449 396	900 mts £20.00 O D EM PL CP LSP KT 2D[2] 1S 2F[2]
7	Mr & Mrs C Gedling West Winds Guest House Moor Lane CROYDE EX33 1PA	01271 890489 As Phone chris@croydewestwinds.freeserve.co.uk www.westwindguesthouse.co.uk	430 398 Mar-Nov	On path £29.00 D EM PL CP LSP KT 3D 1T 1S ALL ES
7	Mrs V Learmonth Chapel Farm Guest House Hobbs Hill CROYDE EX33 1NE	01271 890429 www.chapelfarmcroyde.co.uk	444 390	500 mts PD £20.00 O D PL CP PD 6 ROOMS ALL ES
7	Mr & Mrs G Casban Leadengate House CROYDE EX33 1PN	01271 890373	443 388	800 mts £26.00 O D PL CP DW KT 2D 1T 1S 1F ALL ES £30 high season

Sect.	Name and Address	Tel. No. Fax. No. Web / Email	Map Reference Opening Times	Distance from Path Starting Price Facilities Accommodation
7	Mr & Mrs A Baretta Shuna Down Road CROYDE EX33 1QE	01271 890537 as phone	436 386	100 mts £25.00 O D PL CP KT 4D 1T ALL ES
7	Mr & Mrs P Davis Moorsands Moor Lane CROYDE EX33 1NP	01271 890781 pladavis@onetel.net.uk www.croyde-bay.com/moorsands.htm	441 395	450 mts £23.00 O D PL CP KT 2D 1T 1F ALL ES
7	Mr R Tatman St Helens Priory Hobbs Hill CROYDE EX33 1NE	01271 890757 st_helens_priory@lineone.net www.sthelenspriory.co.uk	444 390 Mar-Dec	800 mts £27.50 D EM PL CP 3D 3T ALL ES
8	Mrs R C Saunders Stockwell Lodge 66 South Street BRAUNTON EX33 2AS	01271 814338	486 362	200 mts PD £20.00 O D PL CP LSP DW KT PD 3D[3] 4T[3] 1S 3F[3]
8	Mrs J Watkins North Cottage 14 North Street BRAUNTON EX33 1AJ	01271 812703 north_cottage@hotmail.com	485 367	200 mts £18.50 O D PL CP DW KT 2D[1] 1T[1] 1S
8	Mrs Smout Restormel Down Lane BRAUNTON EX33 2LE	01271 812124	492 366	500 mts £22.00 O D PL CP KT 1D 1T 1S 1F
8	Mr & Mrs J Harrison Cresta Guest House Sticklepath Hill BARNSTAPLE EX31 2BU	01271 374022 01271 374022 www.crestaguesthouse.com.uk	548 324	800 mts £19.00 O D CP DW KT 1D[1] 1T[1] 2S 2F[2]
8	Mr & Mrs C Allwood Mulberry House Barbican Terrace BARNSTAPLE EX32 9HH	01271 345387 mulberry@biscit.biz www.staynorthdevon.co.uk	559 335	500 mt £25.00 O D PL CP 2D 1S ALL ES
8	Mrs J Manning Herton Lake Hill BARNSTAPLE EX31 3HS	01271 323302	555 322	500 mts £20.00 O D CP LSP 3D[2] 1T[1] 1F[1]
8	Mr & Mrs P Thornton Ivy Lodge Goodleigh Road BARNSTAPLE EX32 7JS	01271 325000	582336	1800 mts PD £25.00 O D CP LSP DW KT PD 1D[1]
8	Mrs A Stoop Huish Moor Farmhouse Huish Lane INSTOW EX39 4LR	01271 860450 as phone huish.moor@btinternet.com www.silverstreamukfishing.com	500 292 Mar-Nov	4km PD £25.00 D EM CP LSP PD 1D 1T[1] 1S LSP low season only; PD from Instow
8	Mr & Mrs P Borg The Wayfarer Inn Lane End Road INSTOW Bideford EX39 4LB	01271 860342 01271 860066 wayfarerinn@tinyworld.co.uk www.instow.net	473 307	20 mts £25.00 O D EM PL CP 1D 2T
9	Mrs D E George Oakwood 34 Yelland Road FREMINGTON EX31 3DS	01271 373884	503 321	850 mts £12.50 O D EM PL CP LSP DW 4D

Sect.	Name and Address	Tel. No. Fax. No. Web / Email	Map Reference Opening Times	Distance from Path Starting Price Facilities Accommodation
9	Mrs P Bange Sunnymeade 26 Yelland Road FREMINGTON EX31 3BU	01271 346757 01271 346757 patbange@hotmail.com staynorthdevon.co.uk	507 324	500 mts £20.00 O D PL CP 2D 1T ALL ES
9	Mrs Saxby Greystones Church Hill FREMINGTON EX31 3BH	01271 326347	512 324	800 mts £18.50 O D PL CP LSP DW 2D[2] 1T
9	Mrs S Chapman Orchard Cottage Old Barnstaple Road BIDEFORD EX39 4ND	01237 422427	463 267	200 mts £26.00 O D CPKT 1F[1]
9	Mrs H Laugharne Mount Hotel Northdown Road BIDEFORD EX39 3LP	01237 473748 01237 373813 andrew@themountbideford.fsnet.co.uk www.themount1.cjb.net	449 269	500 mts O D PL CP LSP KT 3D 1T 2S 1F ALL ES
9	Mrs D Cope Conkers Durrant Lane NORTHAM EX39 2RL	01237 474794 dinny@homestaydevon.co.uk www.homestaydevon.co.uk	453 283	350 mts PD £28.00 O D EM PL CP LSP KT PD 1T[1] OR 1D[1] 10% discount for 2 or more nights
9	Mr G Bower Greysands Bed & Breakfast Long Lane WATERTOWN Appledore EX39 1NQ	01237 479310 glenncherie@greysands-bb.fsnet.co.uk www.greysands-bb.co.uk	454 303	on path £22.00 O D PL CP KT 1D[1] 1T 1F
9	Mrs S Clegg Mayfield Avon Lane WESTWARD HO! EX39 1LR	01237 477128 sallyclegg1@hotmail.com	435 291	400mts £16.00 O D PL CP LSP KT 3D 1T 1S
9	Mr & Mrs P Snowball Brockenhurst 11 Atlantic Way WESTWARD HO! EX39 1HX	01237 423346 As Phone snowball@brockenhurst1.freeser	432 290	200 mts PD £25.00 O D PL CP LSP DW KT PD 2D 1T ALL ES
9	Mrs C Pile Culloden House Hotel Fosketh Hill WESTWARD HO! EX39 1JA	01237 479421 01237 475628 enquiries@culloden-house.co.uk www.culloden-house.co.uk	432 290	200 mts £25.00 D PL CP LSP DW 2D[2] 6T[4] 2F[2]
9	Mr & Mrs G Panayiotou Broomhayes Manor 78 Atlantic Way WESTWARD HO! EX39 1JG	01237 477716 01273 477716 sue@broomhayes-manor.fsnet.co.uk www.stayanite.com	440 291	1 km £25.00 O D CP 2D 1T 1S 1F ALL ES
9	Mrs J K Wells Upper Lodge Stanwell Hill WESTWARD HO! EX39 1AE	01237 477527	432 288	180 mts £25.00 O D PL LSP 1D 1T[1]

Sect.	Name and Address	Tel. No. Fax. No. Web / Email	Map Reference Opening Times	Distance from Path Starting Price Facilities Accommodation
10	Mrs J Slee Sea Breeze West Goldsworthy Farm Horn's Cross NEAR BIDEFORD EX39 5DQ	01237 451650	553 822	300 mts £0.00 O D PL CP LSP PD 1D 1F ALL ES
10	Mrs D Staddon Coach & Horses Horns Cross BIDEFORD EX39 5DH	01237 451214 as phone	384 231	1 km £0.00 O EM PL CP KT 1D 1T 1F ALL ES
10	Mr & Mrs M Dunn 55 The Quay CLOVELLY Bideford EX39 5TF	01237 431436 01237 431919 mick@westcountry-walking-holidays.com www.westcountry-walking-holidays.com	318 248	500 mts £25.00 O D PL CP 1D[1] 1T
10	Mrs C Giddy Temple Bar High Street CLOVELLY EX39 5TE	01237 431438	318 248 Mar-Nov	500 mts £20.00 D CP LSP 1D 1T 1S
10	Mrs K Stuart The New Inn High Street CLOVELLY EX39 5TQ	01237 431303 01237 431636 newinn@clovelly.co.uk www.clovelly.co.uk	317 248	on path £17.50 O EM PL CP LSP 6D[6] 3T 1S[1] 1F[1] Hotel available £37 CP LSP 10 mins
10	Ms L J Simms Donkey Shoe Cottage 21 High Street CLOVELLY EX39 5TB	01237 431601	317 248	200 mts £20.00 O D PL CP LSP KT 2D 1T
10	Mr & Mrs T D Curtis Fuchsia Cottage Burscott Lane HIGHER CLOVELLY EX39 5RR	01237 431398 curtis@fuchsiacottage.fslife.co.uk www.clovelly-holidays.co.uk	313 242	1km PD £18.00 O D EM PL CP LSP KT PD 1D[1] 1T[1] 2S
10	Mrs B May Boat House Cottage 148 Slerra Hill HIGHER CLOVELLY EX39 5ST	01237 431209	310 243	600 mts £18.00 O D PL CP LSP DW KT 1D 1T 1S
10	Mrs P Vanstone High Banks Cottage Slerra Hill HIGHER CLOVELLY EX39 5ST	01237 431752	310 243	750 mts £17.00 O D PL CP KT PD 1D OR S
10	Mr & Mrs C West Pillowery Park Burscott HIGHER CLOVELLY EX39 5RR	01237 431668 as phone pc@pillowerypark.fsnet.co.uk Also phone 01237 431065 £28 singles;	315 241	2 kms PD £22.00 O D PL CP LSP KT PD 1D{1] 1T
11	Mr & Mrs J W George Gawlish Farm GAWLISH Hartland EX39 6AT	01237 441320 01237 441320	256 263	500 mts £20.00 O D EM PL CP 1D 2T ALL ES
11	Mrs Y Heard West Titchberry Farm WEST TITCHBERRY Hartland Point EX39 6AU	01237 441287 As Phone	242 271	250 mts PD £20.00 O D EM PL CP LSP KT PD 1D 1T 1F[1]

Sect.	Name and Address	Tel. No. / Fax. No. / Web / Email	Map Reference / Opening Times	Distance from Path / Starting Price / Facilities / Accommodation
11	Mrs W Currington Cheristow Cottages Cheristow HARTLAND EX39 6DA	01237 441522 01237 441522 wendy@cheristow-cottages.co.uk www.cheristow-cottages.co.uk	253 255	2.8 km PD £25.00 O D EM PL CP LSP DW KTPD 1D 4F ALL ES Cottage accommodation
11	Mr & Mrs C Johns Hartland Quay Hotel HARTLAND QUAY EX39 6DU	01237 441218 01237 441371 hartlandquayhotel@supanet.com www.hartlandquayhotel.com	235 246	On Path PD £30.00 O D EM PL CP LSP DW KTPD 5D[4] 3T[3] 2S[1] 6F[6]
11	Mrs B Slee Homeleigh STOKE EX39 6DU	01237 441465	235 247 Feb-Oct	500 mts £17.50 D PL CP LSP KT PD 1D 1T
11	Mrs R King Combe House STOKE Hartland EX39 6DU	01237 441427	235 246	250 mts £17.00 O D PL CP LSP KT 1D 1T
11	Mrs M Loveridge 2 Harton Manor The Square HARTLAND EX39 6BL	01237 441670 merlynl@email.com	258 245	4 km PD £22.00 O D PL CP LSP DW PD 1D[1] 1T 1S
11	Mrs T Goaman Elmscott Farm HARTLAND EX39 6ES	01237 441276 01237 441076	231 215	800mts PD £24.00 O D EM PL CP LSP KT PD 2D[2] 1T PTE BATH 1S
12	Mrs Heywood Cornakey Farm CORNAKEY Morwenstow EX23 9SS	01288 331260	208 160 Jan-Nov	500 mts £19.00 D EM PL CP LSP KT 1D 1T 1F[1]
12	Mrs J Hudson Little Bryaton MORWENSTOW Bude EX23 9SU	01288 331755 little.bryaton@dial.pipex.com www.little.bryaton.dial.pipex.com	221 156	1.2 km PD £25.00 O D EM PL CP DW KT PD 2D 1T ALL ES
12	Mrs E Tape Cory Farm MORWENSTOW EX23 9ST	01288 331151 01288 331758 tapeej@aol.com	557 820	1 km £25.00 O D CP LSP DW 1D 1F ALL ES
12	Mr & Mrs Cole Jays, WOOLLEY MORWENSTOW Bude EX23 9PP	01288 331540 cole.jays@talk21.com www.members.tripod.co.uk/jaysbarn/jaysbarn	254 168	4km PD £25.00 O D EM PL CP LSP DW KTPD 1D 1T 1S ALL ES
12	Mrs B Dunstan Strands STIBB Bude EX23 9HW	01288 353514	217 107	2.4 km PD £17.00 O D EM PL CP KT PD 1D[1] 1T 1F[1]
12	Mrs C White Trelawney Crosstown MORWENSTOW Bude EX23 9SR	01288 331453	208 150	800 mts £24.00 O D PL CP LSP KT 1D 1T

Sect.	Name and Address	Tel. No. / Fax. No. / Web / Email	Map Reference / Opening Times	Distance from Path / Starting Price / Facilities / Accommodation
12	Mr & Mrs Moore Crooklets Inn Crooklets BUDE EX23 8NF	01288 352335 01288 354779 gazcrooklets@aol.com	204 071	100 mts £17.50 O D EM PL CP LSP 3D 3T 2F ALL ES
12	Mr M E Payne Pencarrol Guest House 21 Downs View BUDE EX23 8RF	01288 352478	209 070 Jan-Nov	300 mts £22.00 D PL KT 3D[2] 1T[1] 2S 1F[1]
12	Mr D Robinson Stratton Gardens Hotel Cot Hill, Stratton BUDE EX23 9DN	01288 352500 strattongardes@aol.com www.cornwall-online.co.uk/stratton-gardens	231 065	1.5 km £25.00 O D EM PL CP LSP DW PD 5D[5] 2T[2] 1S
12	Mr & Mrs M Curtis Atlantic Calm 30 Downs View BUDE EX23 8RG	01288 359165 atlanticcalm@btinternet www.atlanticcalm.co.uk	206 071	200 mts PD £19.00 O D EM PL CP LSP KT PD 5D 2T 1S ALL ES
13	Mr & Mrs M Fly Fairway Guest House 8 Downs View BUDE EX23 8RF	01288 355059 fairwayhouse@kfly.freeserve.co.uk www.fairwayguesthouse.co.uk	209 070	200 mts £20.00 O D PL CP KT 4D[4] 2T[2] 2S
13	Mrs P Drew Surf Haven 31 Dows View BUDE EX23 8RG	01288 353923 As Phone info@surfhaven.co.uk www.surfhaven.co.uk	207 071	250 mts £22.00 D PL CP LSP DW 8D[6] 1T[1]
13	Mr & Mrs R Downes Tee-side Guest House 2 Burn View BUDE EX23 8BY	01288 352351 As phone info@tee-side.co.uk www.tee-side-co.uk	208 066	400 mts £24.00 O D EM PL CP LSP 2D[2] 4T[3] single in twin room £5 supplement
13	Mr & Mrs D Pooley Tresillian 10 Killerton road BUDE EX23 8EL	01288 356199	211 061	1 km £18.00 O D CP LSP KT 2D[2] 1T
13	Miss E Abbott St Merryn Coast View BUDE EX23 8AG	01288 352058 01288 359050 stmerryn@talk21.com www.stmerryn.org.uk	222 060	1.6 km PD £17.00 O D CP DW PD 1D 1T 1S 1F
13	Mr & Mrs P Collins Conna-mara Maer Down Road BUDE EX23 8NG	01288 356340 as phone conna-mara@btconnect.com www.visitwestcountry.com/connamara	206 071	200mts PD £19.00 O D EM PL CP LSP DW KTPD 1D 1T 1F ALL ES
13	Mr S Everett Northshore Bude 57 Killerton Road BUDE EX23 8EW	01288 354256 northshorebude@aol.com www.northshorebude.com	214 061	1 km PD £12.00 O D CP LSP PD 3D 1T 1F 8 DORMS Backpackers hostel
13	Mrs S Trewin Harefield Cottage UPTON Bude EX23 0LY	01288 352350 01288 352712 sally@coast-countryside.co.uk www.coast-countryside.co.uk	203 048	220 mts £22.00 O D EM PL CP LSP DW KTPD 2D 1T 1S ALL ES

Sect.	Name and Address	Tel. No. Fax. No. Web / Email	Map Reference Opening Times	Distance from Path Starting Price Facilities Accommodation
13	Bay View Inn Marine Drive WIDEMOUTH BAY EX23 0AW	01288 361273 enquiries@bayviewinn.co.uk www.bayviewinn.co.uk	201 022	100mts £18.00 O D EM PL CP LSP DW 3D[2] 2T[1] 3F[3] £10 extra for singles in season
13	Mr & Mrs J Cooper Coombe Barton Inn CRACKINGTON HAVEN EX23 0JG	01840 230345 01840 230788 info@coombebartoninn.com www.coombebartoninn.com	144 967 Mar-Nov	On Path £18.00 D EM PL CP LSP 4D[3] 1T 1S 1F{1]
13	Mr & Mrs R Anthony Shepherds Hallagather CRACKINGTON HAVEN EX23 0LA	01840 230276 as phone high season pre bookings difficult	150 954 Feb-Oct	1600 mts £26.50 D PL CP LSP KT PD 1F [1]
13	Mrs G Wilson Venn Park Farm CRACKINGTON HAVEN EX23 0LB	01840 230159 01840 230159	149 943	3 km PD £22.00 O D EM PL CP LSP KT PD 2D[2] 1F[1]
13	Mr & Mrs R Holmes Bears & Boxes Penrose DIZZARD, St Gennys EX23 0NX	01840 230318 rwfrh@btinternet.com www.bearsandboxes.com	171 985	500 mts £28.00 O D EM PL CP DW KTPD 2D 1T 1F ALL ES
14	Mrs J Horwell High Pennycrocker Farm ST JULIOT Boscastle PL35 0BY	01840 250488 As Phone Jackiefarm@aol.com www.higherpennycrockerfarmbandb.co.uk	127 927	1km £19.00 O D PL CP LSP 2D[1] 1T[1] 1F[1]
14	Mr & Mrs G Crown Tolcarne House Hotel Tintagel Road BOSCASTLE PL35 0AS	01840 250654 As Phone crowntolhouse@eclipse.co.uk www.milford.co.uk/go/tolcarne.html	097 905 Apr-Oct	800 mts £29.00 D EM PL CP LSP DW 5D 2T 1S ALL ES
14	Anne or Adrian Lower Meadows House Penally Hill BOSCASTLE PL35 0HF	01840 250570 stay@lowermeadows.co.uk www.lowermeadows.co.uk	101 913	200 mts £25.00 O D PL CP KT 4D 1T ALL ES
14	Mrs C Nicholls Treosewill Farm Paradise BOSCASTLE PL35 0BL	01840 250545 As Phone trerosewill@talk21.com trerosewill.co.uk	096 905 midFeb-mid Dec	500 mts PD £27.00 D PL CP LSP KT PD 3D 1T 2F ALL ES
14	Mrs D Johnson Tremorvah BOSCASTLE PL35 0AU	01840 250636 01840 250616 Jdrawingboard@aol.com www.cornwall-online.co.uk/tremorvah	096 915	200 mts PD £18.00 O D PL CP KT PD 1D 1T 1S
14	Mrs J Haddy Home Farm Minster BOSCASTLE PL35 0BN	01840 250195 jackie.haddy@btclick.com www.homefarm-boscastle.co.uk	105 906	2 km £19.00 D EM PL CP LSP KT PD 2D 1T ALL ES
14	Mr & Mrs P Templar The Riverside Hotel The Bridge BOSCASTLE PL35 0HE	01840 250216 01840 250860 reception@hotelriverside.co.uk www.hotelriverside.co.uk	099 912	250 mts £22.50 O D EM PL CP KT 4D 4T 2S 2F ALL ES

Sect.	Name and Address	Tel. No. Fax. No. Web / Email	Map Reference Opening Times	Distance from Path Starting Price Facilities Accommodation
15	Mrs A Jones Grange Cottage BOSSINEY Nr Tintagel PL34 0AX	01840 770487	065 888 Apr-Oct	200 mts £20.00 D PL CP KT 1D[1] 1T[1] 1S 1F
15	Mr L N Leeds Willapark Manor Hotel BOSSINEY Nr Tintagel PL34 0BA	01840 770782 nick@willapark.co.uk www.willapark.co.uk	069 891	150 mts £31.50 O D EM PLCP DW 6D 2T 2S 3F ALL ES
15	Mrs P Tinney Bossinney Cottage BOSSINEY Nr Tintagel PL34 0AY	01840 770327	066 888	200 mts £20.00 O D EM PL CP LSP KT 2D 1F
15	Mrs S Hawkins Bosayne Guest House Atlantic Road TINTAGEL PL34 0DE	01840 770514 clark@clarky100.freeserve.co.uk www.bosayne.co.uk	890 050	30 mts £23.00 O D PL CP 2D[2] 1T[1] 3S 2F[2]
15	Mr R D Howe Pendrin House Atlantic Road TINTAGEL PL34 0DE	01840 770560 As Phone pendrin@tesco.net www.penrinhouse.co.uk	056 888 Mar-Nov	400 mts £20.00 D EM PL CP 4D[3] 2T 1S 2F[1]
16	Mrs A May Challoch Guest House TREKNOW Tintagel PL34 0EN	01840 770273	057 867 Easter-Oct	400 mts £20.00 D PL CP 2D 1T 1F
16	Ms C Dollimore Mill House Inn TREBARWITH Tintagel PL34 0HD	01840 770932/770200 management@themillhouseinn.co.uk www.themillhouseinn.co.uk	058 864	800 mtrs £40.00 O D EM CP LSP DW 6D 1S 2F ALL ES
16	Port Gaverne Hotel PORT GAVERNE PL29 3SQ	01208 880244 01208 880151 pghotel@telinco.co.uk	003 807	200 mts £35.00 O D EM PL CP LSP DW 8D 6T 1S ALL ES
16	The Castle Rock Hotel 4 New Road PORT ISAAC PL29 3SB	01208 880300 01208 880219 info@castlerockhotel.co.uk www.castlerockhotel.co.uk	998 809	on path £31.00 O D EM PL CP LSP DW 8D[8] 5T[5] 2S[2] 5F[3]
16	Mrs L S Von Lintzgy Fairholme 30 Trewetha Lane PORT ISAAC PL29 3RW	01208 880397 01208 880189	001 805	200 mts £17.00 O D EM PL CP LSP DW 2D[1] 1T 2F[2]
16	Mrs M Andrews Hathaway Bed and Breakfast Roscarrock Hill PORT ISAAC PL29 3RG	01208 880416 marion.andrews1@btopenworld.com www.cornwall-online.co.uk/hathaway	995 807 Easter-Oct	30 mts £25.00 CP DW 1D 3T[2]
16	Mrs M Durston Anchorage 12 The Terrace PORT ISAAC PL29 3SG	01208 880629 As Phone	001 809 Feb - mid Dec	On path PD £23.00 O D EM PL LSP KT PD 3D[1] 1T[1] 2S 1F

Sect.	Name and Address	Tel. No. Fax. No. Web / Email	Map Reference Opening Times	Distance from Path Starting Price Facilities Accommodation
16	Mrs A Williams Kittiwake 7-9 Middle Street PORT ISAAC PL29 3RH	01208 880867 kittiwake@talk21.com	996 807	10 mts £25.00 O D EM PL KT 2D[1] 1T[1] 1S 1F[1] EM & KT winter months only
17	Mrs P White Seaways POLZEATH PL27 6SU	01208 862382 pauline@seaways99.freeserve.co www.seawaysguesthouse.co.uk	939 788	500 mts PD £25.00 O D CP LSP KT PD 2D[1] 2T[1] 1S 1F
18	Mr M Martin Silvermead ROCK Nr Wadebridge PL27 6LB	01208 862425 01208 862919	936 758	300 mts £30.00 O D CP LSP DW 2D[2] 2T[2] 2S 1F[1]
18	Roskarnon House Hotel ROCK Nr Wadebridge PL27 6LD	01208 862785	932 757 Mar-Oct	100 mts £30.00 D EM CP LSP 4D 2T 1S 1F ALL ES
18	Mr R Whittaker The Old Post Office Whitecross WADEBRIDGE PL27 7JD	01208 812620 as phone bywaysoldpostoffice@supanet.com www.bywaysactivityholidays.co.uk	966 722	8 km PD £15.00 O D PL CP LSP DW KTPD 1D 2T 1S 1F ALL ES
18	Mr E Champion Estuary Views 8 Treverbyn Road PADSTOW PL28 8DW	01841 532551 estuaryviews@hotmail.com www.smoothhouse.co.uk/hotels/estuaryviews	919 750	1km £27.50 O D PL CP LSP DW KT 2D 1T ALL ES
18	Mrs M R Romer 23 Barry's Lane PADSTOW PL28 8AU	01841 532178 maryrose@rhodesia.freeserve.co.uk	917 754 Apr-Oct	500 mts £25.00 D DW 1D 1T[1]
18	Mr P A Tamblin Hemingford House 21 Grenville Road PADSTOW PL28 8EX	01841 532806 peter@tamblin21.fsnet.co.uk www.padstow-bb.co.uk	913 751	1km £27.00 O D PL CP LSP KT 2D[1] 1T
18	Mrs A Humphrey 1 Caswarth Terrace PADSTOW PL28 8EE		917 750	£0.00
18	Mrs J Hull 24 Hawkins Road PADSTOW PL28 8EU	01841 533545 01841 532630 jim@jwhull.fsnet.co.uk	913 751	500 mts £27.50 O D CPLSP 1D 1F ALL ES
18	Mrs A Crowley Trealaw Guest House 22 Duke Street PADSTOW PL28 8AB	01841 533161 as phone	918 754	500 mts £25.00 O PL DW 1D 1T 1S ALL ES
18	Mrs A Reveley Kellacott 29 Church Street PADSTOW PL28 8BG	01841 532851 shaunreveley@compuserve.com www.padstow-paradise.co.uk	916 754	500 mts £22.00 O D LSP 2D[2]
19	Mr & Mrs J Stock Woodlands Close TREATOR Padstow PL28 8RU	01841 533109 john@stock65.freeserve.co.uk www.cornwall-online.co.uk/woodlands-close	904 751	1km £22.00 O D PL CP LSP KT 1D[1] 1T[1] 1S occasional PD

Sect.	Name and Address	Tel. No. / Fax. No. / Web / Email	Map Reference / Opening Times	Distance from Path / Starting Price / Facilities / Accommodation
19	Mrs J Ball Gwel-an-Nans Homer Park Road TREVONE PL28 8QU	01841 520769 As phone	894 757	400 mts £26.00 O D PL CP LSP 1D 1T PRIVATE BATHS
19	Mr & Mrs R Mills Well Parc Hotel TREVONE Nr Padstow PL28 8QN	01841 520318 sally@wellparc-demon.co.uk	893 755	400 mts PD £28.00 O D EM PL CP LSP KT PD 4D[2] 1T 1S 4F[4] £36.00 summer. PD only within 5 miles
19	Mrs J Loosemore Caradon Windmill TREVONE PL28 8QS	01841 520120	896 752	1.5 kms PD £16.00 O D CP LSP KT PD 1D 1T 1S 1F
20	Treyarnon Bay Hotel TREYARNON BAY PL28 8JN	01841 520235 01841 520239 www.treyarnon-bay-hotel.co.uk	859 740 Mar-Oct	100 mts £25.00 EM PL CP LSP DW KT 4D[3] 2T[2] 4F[4]
20	Mrs S Shadbolt Trelooan Treporth PORTHCOTHAN BAY PL28 8LS	01841 521158	858 716	300 mts £20.00 O D PL CPLSP KT 1D 1T 1S
20	Mrs J Cook Quoit Treburrick ST EVAL PORTHCOTHAN BAY PL27 7UR	01841 540935	862 707	1.5 km £18.00 O D CP LSP 2D
21	Mr M Ward Malmar Hotel TRENANCE Mawgan Porth TR8 4DA	01637 860324 as phone malmarhotel@supanet.com www.malmarhotel.com	851 679	400 mts £23.00 O D EM PL CP DW 4D[3] 3T[2] 2S[1] 1F[1]
21	Mrs L Bennett The Merrymoor Inn MAWGAN PORTH TR8 4BA	01637 860258 01637 860258 info@merrymoorinn.com www.merrymoorinn.com	849 671 Feb-Nov	45 mts £22.50 EM PL CP LSP DW 4D 1T 1S ALL ES
21	Mr & Mrs G Hope Seavista Hotel MAWGAN PORTH TR8 4AL	01637 860276 01637 860462 seavista@btopenworld.com www.seavista.co.uk	849 668 Mar-Oct	500 mts £21.00 D PL CP 4D[4] 1T[1] 4S[2]
21	Mr P Carthew Shore-Leas MAWGAN PORTH Nr Newquay TR8 4BA	01637 860851 pcarthew@ntlworld.com	851 670	100 mts £15.00 O D CP 1T[1]
21	Mr & Mrs Colwill Westwinds MAWGAN PORTH TR8 4DH	01637 860350	156 740 Mar-Oct	400 mts £17.00 D CP LSP KT PD 2D 1T 1F
21	Mr & Mrs R Brake Bre - Pen Farm BRE-PEN Mawgan Porth TR8 4AL	01637 860420 jill.brake@virgin.net www.bre-pen.co.uk	849 667	300 mts £20.00 O D CP LSP 3D[2] 1T

Sect.	Name and Address	Tel. No. / Fax. No. / Web / Email	Map Reference / Opening Times	Distance from Path / Starting Price / Facilities / Accommodation
21	Mr S Smith Tregurrian Hotel WATERGATE BAY TR8 4AB	01637 860280 01637 860540 tregurrian@holidaysincornwall.net www.holidaysincornwall.net	842 649 Mar-Nov	45 mts £22.00 EM PL CP 4D 4T 2S 7F ALL ES
21	Mr C Goss Porth Beach Hotel Beach Road PORTH Newquay TR7 3NE	01637 872447 01637 872469 enquire@porthbeach-hotel.co.uk www.porthbeach-hotel.co.uk	830 627 March-Nov	20 mts £20.00 D EM PL CP LSP DW KT 8D 6T 7F ALL ES Dogs by prior agreement
21	Mr A N Pedlar The Homestead Porthbean Road NEWQUAY TR7 3LU	01637 876918 neilpedlar@hotmail.com	830 627	20 mts £17.50 O D CP LSP KT 1D 1T 1S
21	Mr & Mrs D Youlden Bothwicks House 3 Bothwicks Road NEWQUAY TR7 1DY	01637 851580	812 619	On Path £25.00 O D PL CP LSP 1D 1T 1F[1]
21	Mrs J S Rowlands Crantock Plains Farmhouse Cubert NEWQUAY TR8 5PH	01637 830253	805 589	1.5km PD £20.00 O D PL CP LSP KT PD 1F[1]
21	Mrs S R Harper Chichester Interest Holidays & Accommodation 14 Bay View Terrace NEWQUAY TR7 2LR	01637 874216 As Phone sheila.harper@virgin.net http://freespace.virgin.net/sheila.harper	813 614 Mar-Nov	750 mts £18.00 D EM PL CP 3D[2] 2T[2] 1F[1]
21	Mrs P Williams Roma Guest House 1 Atlantic Road NEWQUAY TR7 1QJ	01637 875085 romaghnewquay@aol.com www.romaguesthouse.co.uk	803 616	500 mts £20.00 O D EM PL KT 2D[2] 1T[1] 1S 2F[2]
21	Mr D Grant The Corisande Manor Hotel Riverside Avenue Pentire NEWQUAY TR7 1PL	01637 872042 david@corisande.com www.corisande.com	794 613	On Path £77.00 O D EM PL CP DW 9D 1S ALL ES
21	Kev Stringer The Original Backpackers 16 Beachfield Avenue TOWAN BEACH Newquay TR7 1DR	01637 874668 www.originalbackpackers.com	809 616	100 mts £8.00 O D DW 6 DORMS[30BEDS]
21	Mr R Smith The Zone Backpackers Fistral Beach Headland Road NEWQUAY TR7 1HN	01637 872089 as phone thezone@backpackers.co.uk	804 622	500 mts £9.00 O D EM CP DW 11D 10T 7S 11 DORMS
22	Ms A Soltys & I Smithurst Sandbanks Beach Road CRANTOCK TR8 5RE	01637 830130	790 604 Easter-Sept	800 mts £18.00 D CP 2D[1] 1T
22	Mr & Mrs D Eyles Crantock Bay Hotel WEST PENTIRE Crantock TR8 5SE	01637 830229 01637 831111 stay@crantockbayhotel.co.uk crantockbayhotel.co.uk	777 607 Mar-Oct	50 mts £49.50 D EM PL CP LSP DW KT 8D 11T 10S 3F ALL ES Price includes dinner

Sect.	Name and Address	Tel. No. Fax. No. Web / Email	Map Reference Opening Times	Distance from Path Starting Price Facilities Accommodation
22	Mr & Mrs A Stevenson The Goose Rock Hotel WEST PENTIRE Crantock TR8 5SE	01637 830755 gooserock.hotel@virein.net	776 607 14 Mar-30 Sept	on path £21.50 EM CP LSP DW 4D 1S 4F ALL ES
22	Mrs J Robinson St Marys West Pentire Road CRANTOCK TR8 5RZ	01637 830257 As Phone joyrobinson@compuserve.com	788 602	400 mts PD £20.00 O D PL CP LSP KT PD 1D 1S ALL ES
22	Mr & Mrs R Boston Highfield Lodge Hotel Halwyn Road CRANTOCK Newquay TR8 5TR	01637 830744 01637 830568 info@highfieldlodge.co.uk www.highfieldlodge.co.uk	792 601	800 mts £20.00 O D EM CP LSP KT 6D[6] 1T 2S[1]
23	Mr & Mrs W Woodcock Chy An Kerensa Cliff Road PERRANPORTH TR6 0DR	01872 572470 As Phone	755 543	20 mts £18.00 O D PL CP DW KT 1D 1T 2S 1F ALL ES
23	Mrs M Crofts Tremore Liskey Hill Crescent PERRANPORTH TR6 0HP	0845 644 9487 As Phone tremore@totalise.co.uk www.tremore.co.uk	758 539 Easter-Oct	400 mts £23.00 D PL CP LSP KT 3D 1T ALL ES singles out of season only
23	Mr & Mrs R Honey Perranova Guest House Cliff Road PERRANPORTH TR6 0DR	01872 573440	754 544 Mar-Oct	100 mts £18.00 D PL CP KT DW 1D 1T 1S 1F
24	Mrs D Gill-Carey Penkerris Penwinnick Road info@penkerris.co.uk ST AGNES TR5 0PA	01872 552262 As Phone www.penkerris.co.uk	720 497	1 kmPD £20.00 O D EM PL CP LSP DW KTPD 3D[3] 1T 2S 2F
24	Mrs F Appleton Glen Cottage Quay Road ST AGNES TR5 0RP	01872 553546 glencott_2000@yahoo.co.uk	722 508	500 mts PD £17.00 O D PL CP LSP DW KT PD 2D 1T
24	Mr & Mrs G Treleaven Driftwood Spars Hotel Trevaunance Cove ST AGNES TR5 0RT	01872 552428 01872 553701 driftwoodspars@hotmail www.driftwoodspars.com	721 513	on path £38.00 O D EM PL CP LSP DW KT 8D 1T 1S 5F ALL ES
24	Mr & Mrs D Hart Groveview Cottage 9 Peterville ST AGNES TR5 0QU	01872 553199	723 506	800 mts £18.00 O D PL CP DW 2T 1S
25	Mrs V Parkinson Buzby View Forthvean Road PORTHTOWAN TR4 8AY	01209 891178 As Phone buzbyview@freenet.co.uk	691 473 Easter-Oct	500 mts £21.00 D PL 2D 1T 1S
25	Mrs S Hardwick The Beach Hotel O D EM PL CP KT PORTHTOWAN TR4 8AE	01209 890228 As Phone colin@hardwick63.freeserve.co.uk www.thebeachhotel.net	691 478	On Path £25.00 5D 2T 5F ALL ES

Sect.	Name and Address	Tel. No. Fax. No. Web / Email	Map Reference Opening Times	Distance from Path Starting Price Facilities Accommodation
26	Mr & Mrs A Keast Fountain Springs Glenfeadon House PORTREATH TR16 4JU	01209 842650 As Phone	658 451 Mar-Oct	100 mts £22.50 D CP LSP DW KT 2D[2] 1T 1S[1] 3F[3]
26	Mr & Mrs I B Austin Portreath Arms Hotel The Square PORTREATH TR16 4LA	01209 842259 portreatharms@aol	657 452	100 mts £25.00 O D EM PL CP LSP DW KT 2D[2] 5T[3]
26	Mr & Mrs P Smythe Benson's 1 The Hillside PORTREATH TR16 4LL	01209 842534 01209 843578 bensons@portreath.fsbusiness.co.uk www.shopincornwall.com	661 451	500 mts £22.50 O D PL CP LSP 2D 1T 1S ALL ES no LSP August
26	Mr C Symonds Suhaili 14 Forth-an-Nance PORTREATH TR16 4NQ	01209 842110	656 453	on path £18.00 O D CP LSP DW KT 2D(1) 1T(1) 1F
27	Mr T Greenaway Godrevy House GWITHIAN St Ives Bay TR27 5BW	01736 755493 as phone enquiries@gwithianholidays.com www.gwithianholidays.com	588 409	500 mts £25.00 O D CP LSP DW KT 5D 4T 2S 2F ALL ES
27	Mrs L Davies Nanterrow Farm GWITHIAN Hayle TR27 5BP	01209 712282 nanterrow@hotmail.com www.nanterrowfarm.co.uk	599 412	1.5km PD £22.00 O D PL CP LSP KT PD 1D 1F
27	Mr & Mrs A Hall Penpol Bed & Breakfast 34 Penpol Terrace HAYLE TR27 4BQ	01736 754484	558 373	15 mts £20.00 O D CP 1D[1] 1T
27	Mrs S Sowden-Semmens Beckside Cottage Treeve Lane Connor Downs HAYLE TR27 5BN	01736 756751 www.becksidecottage.demon.co.uk	582 396	1500 mts £27.50 O D CP KT 2D 1T ALL ES
27	Mrs A Cooper 54 Penpol Terrace HAYLE TR27 4BQ	01736 752855 annejohn@cooper827.fsnet.co.uk	558 378 Jan-Nov	500 mts £20.00 D PL CP LSP KT 1D 1T 1S
4	Mr & Mrs M Reffold Fernleigh 26 Commercial Road HAYLE TR27 4DG	01736 752166 mikelynreffold@fernleigh.fsbusiess.co.uk	562 377	400 mts £22.50 O D CP LSP KT PD 2D 1T ALL ES £30 single occupancy
27	Mrs McLeod Wheal Merth, Heather Lane CANONSTOWN Hayle TR27 6NQ	01736 740553	531 355	3 km PD £23.00 O D CP LSP DW KT PD 1D 1T
28	Mr & Mrs D O'Sullivan Hindon Hall LELANT St Ives TR26 3EN	01736 753046 As Phone hindonhall@talk21.com www.hindonhall.co.uk	543 369	on path £25.00 O D PL CP LSP 4D ALL ES

Sect.	Name and Address	Tel. No. Fax. No. Web / Email	Map Reference Opening Times	Distance from Path Starting Price Facilities Accommodation
28	Mr & Mrs D Heather Evergreen Lodge 12 Estuary View LELANT TR26 3ES	01736 755035 david.heather@tiscali.co.uk	545 369	3 mts £23.00 O D PL CP KT PD 1D[1] 1S 1F[1]
28	Thurlestone Hotel St Ives Road Carbis Bay ST IVES TR26 2RT	01736 796369 thurlestonehotel@aol.com www.thethurlestonehotel.co.uk	524 385	on path £21.00 O PL CP KT 5D 3T 3F ALL ES
28	Mrs A Timmins Bayside Parc Owles CARBIS BAY St Ives TR26 2RE	01736 795517 baysideparcowles@lycos.co.uk	525 388	200 mts £22.50 O D EM PL DW 1D[1] 1T 1S
28	Mr K R Weston The Grey Mullet 2 Bunkers Hill ST IVES TR26 1LJ	01736 796635 01793 834016 greymulletguesthouse@lineone.net www.touristnetuk.com/sw/greymullet	517 408	25 mts £22.00 O D PL 5D 1T 1S ALL ES
28	Mrs L Bowden Carlill 9 Porthminster Terrace ST IVES TR26 2DQ	01736 796738 lynne@lgpa.freeserve.co.uk www.travelcheck/hotel/1518.htm	517 402	250 mts £20.00 O PL CP LSP DW KT 4D[2] 1T 1S 2F[1]
28	Ms L Dean-Barrows Ten Steps 11 Fish Street ST IVES TR26 1LT	01736 798222 As Phone lydiadean-barrows@virgin.net	519 408	1.5km £27.50 O D PL LSP KT 2D 1T 2S 1F ALL ES Nov-Easter £25; KT when possible
28	Mr D S Tremelling Chy-An-Creet Hotel Higher Stennack ST IVES TR26 2HA	01736 796559 As Phone path@saint-ives.com www.saint-ives.com	507 399 Easter-Oct	1km PD £27.00 D EM PL CP LSP KT PD 4D 1T 1S 2F ALL ES
28	Mrs S Martin 6 Barnoon Terrace ST IVES TR26 1JE	01736 793172	517 407	100 mts £18.00 O D PL 1T 1S ALL ES
28	Mr R Smith St Ives Backpackers The Gallery Town Centre ST IVES TR26 1SG	01736 799444 As Phone st.ives@backpackers.co.uk www.backpackers.co.uk	516 404	100 mts £10.00 O D 2D 4T 1S 9 DORMS
28	Ms K Daines Chy Lelan Bunkers Hill ST IVES TR26 1LJ	01736 797560 As Phone chylelan@dainesk.fsnet.co.uk	518 407	800 mts £18.00 O 4D 1T 2S 1F
28	Mrs Clifford Seagulls Guest House Godrevy Terrace ST IVES TR26 1JA	01736 797273 seagullsstives@aol.com www.seagullsstives.com	516 407	20 mts £25.00 O D PL CPLSP 6D[4] 1T[1] 2S 1F[1]
28	Mr A Biss Primrose Valley Hotel Primrose Valley Porthminster Beach ST IVES TR26 2ED	01736 794939 info@primroseonline.co.uk www.primroseonline.co.uk	519 399 Feb-Nov	50 mts £27.50 D EM PL CP LSP KT PD 5D 4F Also open Xmas & New Year EM high

Sect.	Name and Address	Tel. No. Fax. No. Web / Email	Map Reference Opening Times	Distance from Path Starting Price Facilities Accommodation
28	Mr & Mrs A Popplestone The Toby Jug 1 Park Avenue ST IVES TR26 2DN	01736 794250 enquiries@tobyjogstives.co.uk www.tobyjog@stives.co.uk	516 402	500 mts £25.00 PL CP LSP KT 3D 2T 1S 1F
29	Mrs O Parish Tamarisk Burthallan Lane ST IVES TR26 3AA	01736 797201 enquiries@tamarisk-bb.co.uk www.tamarisk-bb.co.uk	508 406	500 mts £22.00 O D PL CP LSP 2D
29	Mrs N Mann Trewey Farm TREWEY Zennor TR26 3DA	01736 796936	454 384	1.5kms £21.00 O D PL CP 2D 1T 1S 2F
29	Mr P Whitelock The Old Chapel Backpackers Hostel ZENNOR TR26 3BY	01736 798307 As Phone zennorbackpackers@btinternet.com www.backpackers.co.uk	455 385	500 mts £10.00 O D EM PL CP LSP 1F 5 DORMS Dorms 6 beds
29	Mrs S Wilson Tregeraint House ZENNOR TR26 3DB	01736 797061 as phone sueewilson@yahoo.co.uk	451 378	1500 mts £25.00 O D CP 2D 1T 1F
29	Dr Gynn Boswednack Manor BOSWEDNACK Zennor TR26 3DD	01736 794183	443 378 Easter-Sept	1 km £19.00 D PL CP LSP KT 2D[2] 1T 1S1F
29	Mr & Mrs I Hamlett Rosmorva BOSWEDNACK Zennor St Ives TR26 3DD	01736 796722 www.rosmorva.freeuk.com	443 378	900 mts £20.00 O D PL CP 1T 1F[1]
29	Mrs Berryman Treen Farm GURNARDS HEAD Zennor TR26 3DE	01736 796932	436 377 Mar-Oct	400 mts £18.00 D PL CP LSP DW KT 1D 1T
29	Mrs J Kell The Gurnards Head Hotel TREEN Zennor TR26 3DE	01736 796928 01736 795313 enquiries@gurnardshead.free-on www.gurnardshead.fsnet.co.uk	436 377	800 mts £27.50 O D EM PL CP LSP DW KT 4D 1T 1F ALL ES
29	Mrs J Davey Pendeen Manor PENDEEN TR19 7ED	01736 788753 As Phone	384 355	250 mts PD £19.00 O D PL CP LSP KT PD 3D[2] 1T[1] 1S 1F[1]
29	Mrs P W Cass The Radjel Inn PENDEEN TR19 7DS	01736 788446 theradjelinn@aol.com	385 344	850 mts PD £20.00 O D EM PL CP LSP KT PD 1D 1T 1S 1F Also camping
29	Mr E J Coak The North Inn PENDEEN TR19 7DN	01736 788417 ernestjohncoak@aol.com	383 344	2 km £22.00 O D EM PL CP DW KT 3D 3T ALL ES Also camping

Sect.	Name and Address	Tel. No. Fax. No. Web / Email	Map Reference Opening Times	Distance from Path Starting Price Facilities Accommodation
29	Mr & Mrs T Dymond The Old Count House BOSCASWELL DOWNS Pendeen TR19 YED	01736 788058	383 344 Easter-Oct	1.2kms £20.00 D PL CP LSP 2D
30	Mrs V A Westfoot Field House TREWELLARD Pendeen TR19 7ST	01736 788097 As Phone fieldhousetrewellard@talk21.com www.cornwall-online.co.uk	338 377	1.5kms £25.00 O D EM PL 2D[2] 1T EM April-Sept not Tues,Sat or Sun
30	Mrs H Kirkman Scilly View 9 Trewellard Road TREWELLARD Penzance TR19 7ST	01736 786367 hilary.kirkman@tesco.net cornwallfarwest.co.uk	338 377	1km PD £25.00 O D CP LSP DW KT PD 1D 1T
30	Mr & Mrs N Griffiths Boswedden House Hotel CAPE CORNWALL St Just TR19 7NJ	01736 788733 As Phone relax@boswedden.org.uk www.boswedden.org.uk	359 318	200 mts £28.00 O D PL CP LSPKT PD 2D 4T 2S 1F ALL ES
31	Mrs J Cargeeg Botallack Manor BOTALLACK St Just TR19 7QG	01736 788525	368 328	300 mts £25.00 O CP LSP 2D 1T ALL ES
31	Mrs E Lawry Llawnroc 1 Truthwall Villa BOTALLACK TR19 7QL	01736 788814	368 325	400 mts £16.00 O D PL CP KT 3D 2T 1F
31	Mr & Mrs P Michelmore 2 Fore Street St JUST TR19 7LL	01736 787784 As Phone	372 313	1.5 km PD £22.50 O PL PD 1D 1T Dogs by Arrang.
31	Mrs C Collinson Bosavern House BOSAVERN St Just TR19 7RD	01736 788301 info@bosavern.com www.bosavern.com	371 305	1 km PD £24.00 O D PL CP KT PD 3D[3] 2T[1] 1S[1] 2F[2]
31	Mr M Evans Myrtle Cottage Old Coastguard Row SENNEN COVE TR19 7BZ	01736 871698	350 262	£18.00 O PL 2D[1] 1S
31	Mr & Mrs M Adams Homefields MAYON Sennen TR19 7AD	01736 871418 01736 871666 homefield1BandB@AOL.com www.homefieldsguesthouse.co.uk	356 255 Mar-Oct	500 mts £20.00 CP DW 4D[4] 1T
31	Mr & Mrs R Hack The Mayon Farmhouse SENNEN Penzance TR19 7AD	01736 360605 01736 330922	356 255	800 mts PD £25.00 O D EMPL CP LSP KT PD 2D[2] 1T single occupancy £30; beauty & holistic
32	Mr T Ellison Whitesands Lodge SENNEN TR19 7AR	01736 871776 As Phone info@whitesandslodge.co.uk www.whitesandslodge.co.uk	366 264	400 mts £11.00 O D EM PL CP LSP DW KT 2D[1] 1T 1S 2F[1] 25 Dorm Beds

113

Sect.	Name and Address	Tel. No. Fax. No. Web / Email	Map Reference Opening Times	Distance from Path Starting Price Facilities Accommodation
32	Mrs P Jones Sunnycroft SENNEN TR19 7AP	01736 871744 as phone	365 260	1000 mts £18.00 O D EM PL CP LSP DW KT 1D 1T 1S ALL ES
32	Ms L Trenary Treeve Moor House Sennen LAND'S END TR19 7AE	01736 871284 info@firstandlastcottages.co.uk www.firstandlastcottages.co.uk	353 251	400 mts £20.00 O D KT PD 1D[1] 1T
32	Mr & Mrs R Davis Sea View House The Valley PORTHCURNO TR19 6JX	01736 810638 seaview.porthcurno@tinyworld.co.uk www.seaviewhouseporthcurno.com	383 227 Mar-Oct	350 mts PD £26.00 D EM PL CP LSP KT PD 3D 2T 1S ALL ES
32	Mr & Mrs T Goss The Porthcurno Hotel The Valley PORTHCURNO TR19 6JX	01736 810119 01736 810711 mail@porthcurnohotel.co.uk www.porthcurnohotel.co.uk	383 226	250 mts £27.50 O D EM PL CP LSP DW KT 6D[4] 5T[3] 1F[1]
32	Mrs R Thomas Grey Gables PORTHCURNO TR19 6JT	01736 810421 As Phone	380 221 Easter-Sept	100 mts £24.00 D EM PL CP LSP 3D[3] 1T
32	Mr T Goss & Mr G Dowe Mariners Lodge Hotel PORTHCURNO TR19 6JU	01736 810236 01736 810840 themarinerslodge@aol.com www.marinerslodgehotel.co.uk	384 222	50 mts £22.00 O D EM PL CP LSP DW KT 3D[2] 1T[1] 2S 1F[1]
33	Mrs E Jilbert Penver Houses Farm TREEN Nr Porthcurno TR19 6LG	01736 810778 As Phone	394 231 April to Oct	750 mts £18.50 O D PL CP LSP KT PD 1D[1] 1T
33	Mrs P Hall Treen Farmhouse TREEN Nr Porthcurno TR19 6LF	01736 810253 paulachrishall@treenfarm.fsnet.co.uk	394 231	750 mts £15.00 O D PL CP LSP DW 2D[2] 1T
33	Mr K Fraser Annand Burnewhall House NEAR ST BURYAN Penzance	01736 810650 as phone burnewhall@btconnect.com TR19 6DN	406 236	800 mts £35.00 O D PL CP 1D[1] 1T £15 single supplement
33	Mrs S White Cove Cottage ST LOY St Buryan Penzance TR19 6DH	01736 810010	424 232	on path £30.00 O D EM CP 1D[1]
33	Mrs D Hardy Pridden ST BURYAN Penzance TR19 6EA	01736 810801 01736 810054 doana.hardy@priddenfarm.co.uk www.priddenfarm.co.uk	415 265	8 km PD £17.00 O D EM PL CP LSP DW KTPD 1D[1] 1T 1F
33	Mrs B Trembath Lamorna Lodge LAMORNA Nr Penzance TR19 6XL	01736 732517 As Phone	446 244	500 mts £24.00 O D PL CP KT 2D[2] 1S 1F[1]
34	Mr M Male Lowenna Raginnis Hill MOUSEHOLE TR19 6SL	01736 731077 mm4lowenna@aol.com	468 262	On path £22.50 O D PL 1F[1]

Sect.	Name and Address	Tel. No. Fax. No. Web / Email	Map Reference Opening Times	Distance from Path Starting Price Facilities Accommodation
34	Mr M Maiden 1 Paul Lane MOUSEHOLE TR19 6TR	01736 731406 As Phone	468 266 Jan-mid Dec	250 mts £20.00 D PL CP 1D 2T
34	Mrs E Reynolds Renovelle 6 The Parade MOUSEHOLE TR19 6PN	01736 731258	469 264 Easter - Oct	on path £17.00 D PL CP 2D 1S
34	Mrs A J Waters Sunrise Commercial Road MOUSEHOLE TR19 6QG	01736 731457	469 264	100 mts £17.50 O D PL DW 2D 1S
34	Mrs T M Harvey Thatched Cottage Ragrunts Farm MOUSEHOLE Penzance TR19 6NJ	01736 731333 thatched.cottage@task21.com	465 258	250 mts £25.00 O D EM PL CP LSP KT 2D[1]
34	Mr & Mrs P Schofield 17 Mennaye Road PENZANCE TR18 4NG	01736 361395 pbschofield@btinternet.com	469 297	200 mts £22.00 O D PL 1T[1]
34	Mr & Mrs P George The Yacht Inn Green Street PENZANCE TR18 4AU	01736 362787 anita@loganrockinn.com	475 299	10 mts £30.00 O EM PL CP LSP DW KT 5D 2T ALL ES
34	Mrs L G G Ash Torre Vene Lescudjack Terrace PENZANCE TR18 3AE	01736 364103	475 308	1 km £18.00 O D PL CP 2D 2T 2S 2F
34	Mrs Buswell Penalva Alexandra Road PENZANCE TR18 4LZ	01736 369060 As Phone	298 468	500 mts £16.00 O D CP LSP 2D[2] 1T[1] 1S 1F[1]
34	Mr & Mrs J Leggatt Cornerways 5 Leskinnick Street PENZANCE TR18 2HA	01736 364645 As Phone enquires@cornerways-penzance.co.uk www.penzance.co.uk/cornerways	475 308 Mar-Jan	800 mts £23.00 1D 1T 2S ALL ES
34	Mr & Mrs D & Peach Woodstock House 29 Morab Road PENZANCE TR18 4EZ	01736 369049 01736 369049 info@woodstockguesthouse.co.uk www.woodstockhouseguesthouse.co.uk	471 299	200 mts £18.00 D PL DW KT PD 3D[2] 1T 3S[2] 1F[1]
34	Mr & Mrs R Stacey Lynwood Guest House 41 Morrab Road PENZANCE TR18 4EX	01736 365871 As Phone lynwoodpz@aol.com www.lynwood-guesthouse.co.uk	471 299	200 mtrs £14.00 O D PL DW 2D[1] 2T[1] 2S[1] 2F[2]
34	Mr R Halling Penzance Backpackers Blue Dolphin PENZANCE TR18 4LZ	01736 363836 01736 363844 pzbackpack@ndirect.co.uk www.penzancebackpackers.ndirect.co.uk	467 299	400 mts £10.00 O D 2D 5 DORMS
34	Mr & Mrs D Smith Chy-an-Mor 15 Regent Terrace PENZANCE TR18	01736 363441 As Phone reception@chyanmor.co.uk www.chyanmor.co.uk	475 298 Feb-Nov	100 mts £28.00 CP LSP 4D 5T 1SALL ES

Sect.	Name and Address	Tel. No. Fax. No. Web / Email	Map Reference Opening Times	Distance from Path Starting Price Facilities Accommodation
34	Ms J Cavangh Warwick House Hotel 17 Regent Terrace jules@warwickhouse.fsworld.co.uk PENZANCE TR18 4DW	01736 363881 as phone www.warwickhouse.co.uk	475 298 £23.00	30 mts O D EM PL CP LSP KT PD 4D[3] 2T[2] 2S[1] 1F[1] £30 single occupancy
34	Mr & Mrs R Peterson Kimberley House 10 Morrab Road PENZANCE TR18 4EZ	01736 362727 As Phone enquiries@kimberleyhouse.fsnet.co.uk www.smoothhound.co.uk	471 299	250 mts £20.00 O D CP DW 2D[2] 2T[1]1S 1F
34	Mr & Mrs I Webb Richmond Lodge 61 Morrab Road PENZANCE TR18 4EP	01736 365560 ivor@richmondlodge.fsnet.co.uk www.geocities.com/richmondlodge_uk	470 300	£19.00 O PL CP KT 2D[1] 2T[1] 1S 2F[1]
34	Mr & Mrs C Hatton Relubbas House Relubbas PENZANCE TR20 9EP	01736 762796 as phone info@relubbushouse.co.uk www.Trelubbushouse.co.uk	566 319 Mar-Dec	3 km PD £20.00 D EM PL CP LSP KT PD 2D[2] 2
34	Ms H Cahalane Glencree House Mennay Road PENZANCE TR18 4NG	01736 362026 as phone stay@glencreehouse.co.uk www.glencreehouse.co.uk	469 297	50 mts £18.00 O D PL CP LSP DW KT 4D[3] 1T[1] 2S[1] 1F[1]
34	Mrs C Ahearne-Bates Heartlodge 4 Leskinnick Street PENZANCE TR18 2HA	01736 351872 kennis@batestennis.fsnet.co.uk	475 306	300mts £25.00 O 1D 1T
34	Mr R Halling Penzance Backpackers Blue Dolphin PENZANCE TR18 4LZ	01736 363836 01736 363844 pzbackpack@ndirect.co.uk www.penzancebackpackers.ndirect.co.uk	467 299 Mar-Jun	400 mts £10.00 D 2D 4DORMS[3]
34	Mr J Smalley Chy Bowjy CHY SAUSTER Penzance TR20 8XA	01736 368815 01736 363440 jj@jj-associates.co.uk www.chy-bowjy.co.uk	350 470	4.5 km PD £22.00 O D EM PL CP LSP KT PD 1D
35	Mr & Mrs R Tucker The Corner House Fore Street MARAZION TR17 0AD	01736 711348	520 306	£20.00 O EM PL CP 3D 1T 1F ALL ES £30 single occupancy
35	Mr & Mrs P Vincent Blue Horizon Fore Street MARAZION TR17 0AW	01736 711199 holidaybreaksmarazion@freeola.com www.holidaybreaksmarazion.co.uk	521 306 Jan-Oct	500 mts £25.00 D PL CP LSP PD KT 3D[3] 2T[2] 1S 1F[1] £27 single room all year round
35	Mr & Mrs M Trevillion Mount Haven Hotel Turnpike Road MARAZION Near Penzance TR17 0DQ	01736 710249 01736 711658 reception@mounthaven.co.uk www.mounthaven.co.uk	526 306 Feb-Xmas	100 mts £40.00 D EM PL CP LSP 8D 7T 3F ALL ES
36	Mrs S Brazier Victoria Inn Churchtown PERRANUTHNOE Penzance TR20 9NP	01736 710309 01736 719284 www.victoriainn-penzance.co.uk	538 295	250 mts £27.50 O EM PL CP 2D[2] 2S[1] single £35

Sect.	Name and Address	Tel. No. Fax. No. Web / Email	Map Reference Opening Times	Distance from Path Starting Price Facilities Accommodation
36	Mrs M Foy Mzima Penlee Close PRAA SANDS TR20 9SR	01736 763856 marionfoy@prussia-cove-holiday.com	588 281	800mtrs PD £17.00 O D PL CP KT PD 1T 1F
36	Mr & Mrs K Allen Gwynoon Guest House Chy-An-Dour Road enquiries@gwynoon.co.uk PRAA SANDS TR20 9SY	01736 763508 www.gwynoon.co.uk	581 280	50 mts £26.00 O D PL CP KT 2D 2T 2S 2F ALL ES
36	Mrs B Harris Grove Cottage Trescowe GERMOE TR20 9RW	01736 763623/4 harris@westcornwallhampers.co.uk	577 308 Easter-Sept	1.5 kms PD £20.00 D PL CP LSP KT PD 2D single occupancy supplement high seas
37	Mr F P Hallam Seefar Peverell Terrace PORTHLEVEN TR13 9DZ	01326 573778 eefar@talk21.com www.seefar.co.uk	630 255 Feb-Nov	200 mts £20.00 D PL CP LSP DW KT 2D[1] 1T[1] 1S
37	Miss S Kelynack & Mr R Perkins An Mordros Hotel Peverell Terrace PORTHLEVEN TR13 9DZ	01326 562236 info@anmordroshotel.com www.anmordroshotel.com	630 255	On Path £27.50 O D EM PL KT 3D 1T 2F ALL ES
37	Mr & Mrs P Ingham Anchor Cottage Cliff Road PORTHLEVEN TR13 9EZ	01326 574391	629 254	On Path £20.00 O D PL KT 1D[1] 1T
37	Ms S Flanagan The Copper Kettle Tea Rooms 33 Fore Street PORTHLEVEN TR13 9HQ	01326 565660 01326 564772 tsue@davisck.fsnet.co.uk www.cornish-holiday.com	629 259	100 mts £19.00 O D PL CP 2D[1] 1T 1S 2F[1]
37	Mrs C Budd Sandpipers Loe Bar Road PORTHLEVEN TR13 9EL	01326 564542	630 253 April to Sept	On path £21.00 D PL KT 1D 1T 1S
37	Mr & Mrs R Williams Rosemorran B&B 14 The Crescent PORTHLEVEN TR13 9LU	01326 574855	630 262	1 km £23.00 O D 2D £21 more than 1 night; £30 single
38	Mr & Mrs T Tucker Lyndale Guest House 4 Greenbank Meneage Road HELSTON TR13 8JA	01326 561082 01326 565813 enquiries@lyndale1.freeserve.co.uk www.lyndale1.freeserve.co.uk	662 269	4.5 km PD £17.00 O D EM PL CP LSP DW KTPD 3D[2] 1T[1] 1S 1F
38	Mrs J Tyler-Street Trenance Farmhouse MULLION TR12 7HB	01326 240639 As Phone info@trenancefarmholidays.co.uk www.trenancefarmholidays.co.uk	673 185 Apr-Sept	500 mts £22.50 PL CP LSP 4D 1T ALL ES
38	Mrs J Valender The Old Vicarage Nansmellyon Road MULLION TR12 7DQ	01326 240898 jacqui@mullionoldvicarage.freeserve.co.uk	677190	750 mts £27.00 O CP KT 2D[1] 2F[2] single £29 low season

Sect.	Name and Address	Tel. No. Fax. No. Web / Email	Map Reference Opening Times	Distance from Path Starting Price Facilities Accommodation
38	Mr & Mrs P Dann Ridgeback Lodge Hotel & Restaurant Nansmellion Road MULLION TR12 7DH	01326 241300 As Phone Ridgebacklodge@compuserve.com www.business.thisiscornwall.co.uk/ridgeback	677 185	100 mts £19.50 O D EM LSP DW KT 3D[1] 1T[1] 1S 2F[2]
38	Mr M Bolton Criggan Mill MULLION COVE TR12 7EU	01326 240496 0870 1640549 info@crigganmill.co.uk www.crigganmill.co.uk	667 180	200 mts £18.00 O DEM PL CP LSP DW KTPD 6D 6T 6S 6F ALL ES
39	Mrs I Sowden The Most Southerly House LIZARD POINT TR12 7NU	01326 290300 As Phone	702 115 Mar-Sept	25 mts £20.00 D PL CP LSP KTPD 1D[1] 1T
39	Mrs P Hocking Bayview Cross Common THE LIZARD TR12 7PD	01326 290369	707 126 May-Sept	600 mts £18.00 D CP LSP DW 2D
39	Mr & Mrs B Charity Parc Brawse House Penmenner Road. THE LIZARD TR12 7NR	01326 290466 benjocharity@aol.com www.cornwall-online.co.uk/parcbrawsehouse	701 121	300 mts £18.00 O PL CP LSP DW KT 4D[3] 2T[2] 2S[2] 1F[1]
39	Mr D Macbride Kynance Bay House Penmenner Road THE LIZARD TR12 7NR	01326 290498 as phone david.macbride@btinternet.com kynancebayhouse@btopenworld.com	700 120	400 mts £30.00 O D EM PL CP LSP KT 2D 1T ALL ES
39	Mrs J Grierson Carmelin Pentreath Lane THE LIZARD TR12 7NY	01326 290677 pjcarmelin@aol.com www.carmelin.ukf.net	699 126	500 mts £25.00 O D PL CP DW KT 1D[1]
39	Mrs K Thirlaway Green Cottage THE LIZARD TR12 7NZ	01326 290099	703 126	1 km £18.00 O D PL CP LSP DW 1D 1T
39	Mrs G Rowe Trethvas Farmhouse THE LIZARD Helston TR12 7AR	01326 290720 As phone	709 136 Mar-Oct	300 mts £21.00 D PL CP LSP 1D 1T 1F ALL ES
39	Mrs H Peake The Caerthillian THE LIZARD TR12 7NQ	01326 290019 as phone hpeake@caerthillian.fsnet.co.uk www.thecaerthillian.co.uk	703 125	500 mts £18.00 O D CP 3D[3] 1T[1] 1S 1F[1]
40	Mrs I Hickey Poltesco Way RUAN MINOR TR12 7JW	01326 290735	721 153	 £20.00 O D EM CP LSP KT PD 1D 1T 1S
40	Mrs J Baird Porthbeer Chynhalls Point COVERACK TR12 6SB	01326 280680 jane@porthbeer.fsnet.co.uk porthbeer.fsnet.co.uk	782 176	100 mts £20.00 O D PL CP LSP KT PD 2D 1F ALL ES
40	Mrs T Carey Tamarisk Cottage COVERACK TR12 6TG	01326 280638	783 188 Easter-Oct	On path £19.00 D CP LSP DW 1D 1T 1S

Sect.	Name and Address	Tel. No. Fax. No. Web / Email	Map Reference Opening Times	Distance from Path Starting Price Facilities Accommodation
40	Mrs M E Daw Bakery Cottage Polcoverack Lane COVERACK TR12 6TD	01326 280474	780 184	On path £18.50 O D EM PL CP LSP DW 1D 1F
40	Mrs W Watters Boak House COVERACK TR12 6SA	01326 280608	782 180 Mar-Nov	50mts £19.00 D EM CP DW KT 2D 1T 2F
40	Mrs A Rogers Fernleigh Chymbioth Way COVERACK TR12 6TB	01326 280626	781 183	50 mts £20.00 O D EM PL CP DW KT 2D[1] 1T[1]
40	Ms T Hone Trevenwith Farm Near Gwenter COVERACK TR12 6SL	01326 290873 tracyhone@onetel.net.uk	740 171 Apr-Oct	400 mts £18.50 EM CP LSP DW 1F[1]
41	The White Hart Inn The Square whitehart@easynet.co.uk ST KEVERNE TR12 6ND	01326 280325 www.white-hart-hotel.co.uk	791 212	1 km £25.00 O EM PL CP LSP DW 1D 1T 2S ALL ES
41	Mrs R Kelly Trevinock PORTHOUSTOCK St Keverne TR12 6QP	01326 280498 www.trevinock_guesthouse_thelizard.co.uk	802 216 Easter-Oct	1.5 km £21.00 D EM PL LSP KT 2D[1] 2S
41	Ms A Strickland Gallen-Treath Guest House PORTHALLOW TR12 6PL TR12 6PL	01326 280400 01326 280400 gallentreath@btclick.com www.gallen-treath.com	797 232	150 mts PD £22.00 O D EM PL CPDW KT PD 2D 1T 1S 1F ALL ES evening meal by arrangement
41	Mrs J A Penman Little Pengarrock PORTHALLOW TR12 6PL	01326 280872 littlepengarrock@tesco.net	799 225 Mar-Nov	200 mts £23.00 D EM PL CP LSP KT PD 1D[1] 1T[1] 1S 1F[1]
41	Mr N Dobson Parc-an-Tidno PORTHALLOW TR12 6QH	01326 281080 Mad-house@parc-an-tidno.freeserve.co.uk	798 226	on path £18.00 O D EM PL CP 2D[1]
41	Mrs P Peters Rose Cottage PORTHALLOW St Keverne TR12 6PP	01326 280360	796 230 Feb-Dec	on path £0.00 CP 1D 1T
41	Mrs P Hawthorne Valley View House PORTHALLOW COVE St Keverne TR12 6PN	01326 280370 As Phone hawthorne@valleyviewhouse.freeserve.co.uk www.smoothhound.co.uk/hotels/valleyvi.html	796 232	20 mts PD £19.00 O D EM PL CP LSP KT PD 2D[1] 1T
41	Mrs E Whale Porthvean GILLAN TR12 6HL	01326 231204	792 252	£0.00 O D CP LSP DW 1T[1]
41	Mrs L Jenkin Landrivick Farm MANACCAN Helston TR12 6HX	01326 231686	750 245	2 km PD £25.00 O D EM PL CP LSP PD 1D[1] 1T

Sect.	Name and Address	Tel. No. Fax. No. Web / Email	Map Reference Opening Times	Distance from Path Starting Price Facilities Accommodation
41	Mrs P Julian Landrivick Farm LANDRIVICK Manaccan TR12 6HX	01326 231249	750 245	1.6 km PD £25.00 O D PL CP LSP PD 1D 1T 1S1F
41	Mrs J Davies Pengwedhen HELFORD TR12 6JZ	01326 231481 nandjdavies@hotmail.com	755 265	500 mts £25.00 O D PL CP LSP DW KT 1D 1T 2S
41	Mrs P Royall POINT Helford Nr Helston TR12 6JY	01326 231666 info@helfordcottages.co.uk www.helfordcottages.co.uk	758 262	on path £27.50 O D CP 1T[1]
42	Mr & Mrs T Cooke Hideaway Rosevear MAWGAN TR12 6AZ	01326 221392 jean.cooke@amserve.net	697 245 Feb-Oct	2 km £22.50 D CP 2D 1T ALL ES
42	Mrs C Spike Carwinion Vean Grove Hill MAWNAN SMITH TR11 5ER	01326 250513 www.carwinionveanbb.uklinux.net	777 283	1.6 km £22.00 O D PL CP LSP DW 3D[1] 2T[1] 1F DW if own pet bed provided
42	Mrs S P Annan Chynoweth Carwinion Lane MAWNAN SMITH TR11 5JB	01326 250534 01326 251010 sannan@lineone.net	781 283	800 mts PD £27.50 O D CP PD 2T
42	Mrs C Lake Gold Martin Carlidnack Road MAWNAN SMITH Falmouth TR11 5HA	01326 250666 gold_martin@hotmail.com	778 291	1.6 km PD £26.00 O D PL CP KT PD 2D[1] 1S
42	Mr & Mrs G Cumins Grove Hotel Grove Place FALMOUTH TR11 4AU	01326 319577 As Phone guests@grovehotel.freeserve.co.uk grovehotel.freeserve.co.uk	811 325	On path £25.00 O D EM PL CP 6D 5T 2S 2F ALL ES
42	Mr & Mrs I Carruthers The Clearwater 59 Melvill Road FALMOUTH TR11 4DF	01326 311344 clearwater@lineone.net www.theclearwater.co.uk	809 319 Feb-Nov	500 mts £23.00 D PL CP 5D[5] 2T 2S 2F[1]
42	Mr & Mrs G Warring Rosemary Hotel 22 Gyllyngvase Terrace FALMOUTH TR11 4DL	01326 314669 As Phone rosemaryhotel@lineone.net www.rosemaryhotel.co.uk	810 318 Feb-Oct	50 mts £29.00 D PL DW 6D 1T 1S 2F ALL ES high season bookings difficult
42	Ms C Mitchell Falmouth Lodge Backpackers 9 Gyllyngvase Terrace FALMOUTH TR11 4DL	01326 319996 charlotte@mitchell999.fsworld.co.uk falmouthbackpackers.co.uk	811 319	100 mts £13.00 O D CP 1T 1S 3 DORMS
42	Mr & Mrs R Picken The Lerryn Hotel De Pass Road FALMOUTH TR11 4BJ	01326 312489 thelerrynhotel@btconnect.com www.thelerrynhotel.co.uk	813 319	20 mts £35.00 O EM PL CP LSP DW KT 6D 8T 4S 2F ALL ES

Sect.	Name and Address	Tel. No. Fax. No. Web / Email	Map Reference Opening Times	Distance from Path Starting Price Facilities Accommodation
42	Mr & Mrs D Burd Esmond House Emslie Road FALMOUTH TR11 4BG	01326 313214	812 318	100mts £23.50 O D PL KT 4D 1T 1S ALL ES
42	Mr & Mrs P Crocker The Dolvean Hotel 50 Melvill Road FALMOUTH TR11 4DQ	01326 313658 01326 313995 reservations@dolvean.co.uk www.dolvean.co.uk	809 319	300 mts £30.00 O D CP LSP 7D 1T 3SALL ES
42	Mr & Mrs D Bowerman Arwenack Hotel 27 Arwenack Street FALMOUTH TR11 3JE	01326 311185 arwenack@hotmail.com www.falmouth-hotels.co.uk	810 325	 £25.00 O D CP LSP DW 2D 2T 5S 3F[1]
42	Mrs J Barclay Chelsea House Hotel 2 Emslie Road FALMOUTH TR11 4BG	01326 212230 info@chelseahousehotel.com www.chelseahousehotel.com	813 319	100 mts £23.00 O D CP LSP 5D 2T 1S 2F ALL ES
43	Mrs K Moseley Braganza Grove Hill ST MAWES TR2 5BJ	01326 270281 as phone braganzakf@aolcom Open Jan-Oct and Dec but not	846 331	300 mts £32.50 D CP KT 2T[2] 2S
44	Mrs C Sewell 2 Springfield PORTSCATHO TR2 5HS	01872 580024	875 354	100 mts £25.00 O D PL CP DW KT PD 2D
44	Mrs W A Penhaligon Trewithian Farm PORTSCATHO Truro TR2 5EJ	01872 580293 penhaligon@trewithian.freeserve.co.uk www.trewithianfarm.co.uk	878 372	800mts £25.00 O D PL CP LSP DW KT 2D 2T 1S 2F ALL ES
44	Mrs D Weale Glenlorcan 9 Tregassick Road Gerrans PORTSCATHO TR2 5ED	01872 580343 weale@glenlorcan.fsnet.co.uk www.visitus.co.uk	873 351 Mar-Oct	400 mts £22.00 D PL CP 1D 1T 1F ALL ES
44	Mrs A Palmer Trenestrall RUAN HIGH LANES Portscatho TR2 5LX	01872 501259	886 399 Mar-Oct	2.5km PD £25.00 DCP DW PD 2D 1T 1F ALL ES
45	Mr & Mrs M Rawling Treverbyn House Pendower Road VERYAN TR2 5QL	01872 501201 holiday@treverbyn.fsbusiness.co.uk www.cornwall-online.co.uk/treverbyn	914 393	2 km PD £25.00 O D PL CP PD 1D 1T 1S ALL ES
45	Mr & Mrs K Righton Broom Parc Camels PORTLOE TR2 5PJ	01872 501803 01872 501109 www.broomparc.freeserve.co.uk	930 390	On Path £25.00 O D EM PL CPLSP DW KT PD 1D 2T ALL ES
45	Mrs P Ollerearnshaw Fuglers The Gow PORTLOE TR2 5RE	01872 501482	940 395 March-Dec	On Path £25.00 D PL KT PD 2T 1F ALL ES £30 single occupancy

Sect.	Name and Address	Tel. No. Fax. No. Web / Email	Map Reference Opening Times	Distance from Path Starting Price Facilities Accommodation
45	Mrs B Leach Carradale PORTLOE TR2 5RB	01872 501508 www.cornwalltouristboard.co.uk	935 394	250 mts £25.00 O D PL CP LSP 1D[1] 1T 1F[1]
47	Mr & Mrs A Freeman Llawnroc Inn GORRAN HAVEN PL26 6NU	01726 843461 01726 844056 llawnroc@mevagissey.com www.llawnroc.mevagissey.com	010 416	200 mts £20.00 O D EM PL CP LSP DW 3D 3T 2F ALL ES
47	Ms G Mott Piggy Pantry The Willows GORRAN HAVEN PL26 6JG	01726 843545 piggyspantry@hotmail.com www.piggyspantry.co.uk	011 415	200 mts £20.00 1D 1T O D PL CP DW
47	Mr & Mrs R J Smith Homestead 34 Chute Lane GORRAN HAVEN PL26 6NU	01726 842567	010 416	On Path £27.50 O D CP 1D 1T ALL ES
47	Mr & Mrs P Calcraft Grenville 1 Quilver Close GORRAN HAVEN PL26 6JT	01726 843243 www.cornish-riviera.co.uk/grenville	011 414	300 mts £20.00 O D PL CP LSP KT PD 1D 1T1F
47	Mrs P Bamford Bumblebees Foxhole Lane GORRAN HAVEN PL26 6JP	01726 842219 bumblebees@foxhole.vispa.com www.bumblebees.biz	013 414	200 mts £21.00 O D PL CP KT 2D 1T 1F
47	Miss S Chubb The Granary BOSWINGER Gorran Haven PL26 6LL	01726 844381 holidays@thegranaryboswinger.freeserve.co.uk www.cornwallbandb.co.uk	991 410	500 mts £22.50 O D PL CP 3D[1] 1T Single rate £28
47	Mrs J O Lucas Mount Pleasant Farm GORRAN HIGH LANES Gorran Haven	01726 843918 jill@mpfarm.vispa.com www.vegetarian-cornwall.co.uk	987 432 April-Oct	2 km PD £23.00 D EM CP LSP KT PD 2D[2] 1T 1S
48	Ms J Connolly Mandalay Hotel School Hill MEVAGISSEY PL26 6TQ	01726 842435 as phone joe@mandalayhotel.freeserve.co.uk	014 452 Jan-Nov	300 mts £23.00 D PL CP LSP DW KT 5D[5] 3T[3] 1S 2F[2]
48	Mr & Mrs A Parsloe Tregorran Guest House Cliff Street MEVAGISSEY PL26 6QW	01726 842319 patricia@parsloep.freeserve.co.uk www.tregorran.homestead.com/home.html	015 451 Jan-Nov	100 mts PD £20.00 D PL KT PD 4D 1T 1F ALL ES KT by arrangement
48	Mrs C J Avent Wild Air Polkirt Hill MEVAGISSEY PL26 6UX	01726 843302	016 444	On path £25.00 O D PL CP KT 3D[2]
48	Mrs W Bennett Mount Pleasant House Cross Park Terrace MEVAGISSEY PL26 6TA	01726 843777 wenbennett2@classicfm.net	013 453	500 mts £19.00 O D PL CP LSP KT PD 1D[1] 1T 1S

Sect.	Name and Address	Tel. No. Fax. No. Web / Email	Map Reference Opening Times	Distance from Path Starting Price Facilities Accommodation
48	Mrs J Rudge 51 Church Street MEVAGISSEY PL26 6SP	01726 843751	014 450	100 mts £20.00 O D PL CP LSP DW 2D 1S 1F
48	Woodleys Bed & Breakfast 5 Prospect Terrace MEVAGISSEY PL26 6SU	01726 844133 info@woodleysbb.co.uk www.woodleysbb.co.uk	013 451	500 mts £0.00 O D PL KT 3D[1]
48	Mrs F Thomas Kervernel 35 Cliff Street MEVAGISSEY PL26 6QJ	01726 844656 www.lightsoft.co.uk/cornwall	015 448	100 mts £20.00 O D PL KT PD 2T[1]
48	Mrs A Thomlinson Haven Cottage HE WAS WATER PL26 7JF	01726 882169 havencott@aol.com www.havencottage.co.uk	965 498	5 km £25.00 O D EM PL CP KT PD
48	Mr & Mrs P Jenkin Treburthick HIGHER PORTHPEAN St Austell PL26 6AY	01726 73689 pamattreburthick@hotmail.com	029 505 Mar-Oct	300 mts PD £20.00 D EM CP LSP KT PD 2D[2] 1T 1S Non smoking
49	Mr M I Christie T'Gallants Guest House 6 Charlestown Road CHARLESTOWN PL25 3NJ	01726 70203	252 536	200mtrs £22.50 O CP LSP 6D[6] 2T
49	Mr & Mrs R Callis Ardenconnel 179 Charlestown Road CHARLESTOWN PL25 3NN	01726 75469 ardenconnel@tiscali.co.uk	036 520	400 mts £23.00 O D PL CP LSP KT 1D[1] 2T[1] 1S 2F[1]
49	Mrs D A Best Broad Meadow House Quay Road CHARLESTOWN PL25 3NX	01726 76636 As Phone best.tribe@btopenworld.com	039 517	100 mts £25.00 O D PL CP LSP KT PD 1D[1] Also luxury tents available £15 "tent &
50	The Cliff Head Hotel Sea Road CARLYON BAY PL25 3RB	01726 812345 01726 815511 cliffheadhotel@btconnect.com www.cornishriviera.uk/cliffhead	053 520	on path £45.00 O EM PL CP LSP 17D 17T 16S 8F ALL ES
50	Mr & Mrs N Sedgley Copper Beeches Lodge 52 Truro Road ST AUSTELL PL25 5JJ	01726 74024 as phone enquiries@copperbeecheslodge.co.uk www.copperbeecheslodge.co.uk	007 523 Feb-Nov	4 kms £30.00 D CP 4D 3T ALL ES
50	Mrs S Clyne Boslowen 96 Par Greet PAR PL24 2AG	01726 813720 enquiries@boslowen.co.uk www.boslowen.co.uk	079 536	10 mts £25.00 O D CP LSP KT PD 3D[1]
50	Mrs B D Burgess 55 Polmear Road PAR PL24 2AW	01726 812967	086 535	500 mts £20.00 O D CP LSP 1T 2S

Sect.	Name and Address	Tel. No. Fax. No. Web / Email	Map Reference Opening Times	Distance from Path Starting Price Facilities Accommodation
50	Mrs M.H Ball Polbrean House Woodland Avenue TYWARDREATH PL24 2PL	01726 812530 polbrean@lineone.net www.smoothhound.co.uk	082 543	2 km £22.50 O D PL CP 2D 1S
51	Mr S Hardinge & Mrs Davis Trevanion Guest House 70 Lostwithiel Street FOWEY PL23 1BQ	01726 832602 As Phone stephen.hardinge@btopenworld.com www.users.globalnet.co.uk/~trefoy/fowey.htm	124 518	800 mt2 £25.00 O D EM PL CP DW KT PD 1D[1] 1S 2F[2]
51	The Ship Inn Trafalgar Square FOWEY PL23 1AZ	01726 832230 As Phone	125 515	On path £20.00 O EM 2D 2T 2F[1]
51	Mr & Mrs D Turner Topsides Esplanade FOWEY PL23 1HZ	01726 833715 gemmaturner@fowey66.freeserve.co.uk	123 515	50 mts £20.00 O D PL DW 2D 1S
52	Mrs T Paull Coombe Farm FOWEY PL23 1HW	01726 833123 As phone tessapaull@hotmail.com	110 511	on path £25.00 O D CP LSP 2D[2]
52	Mrs B Blamey Holly House 18 Fore Street POLRUAN PL23 1PQ	01726 870478	123 508 Feb-Oct	1 km £15.00 DW 3T
52	Mrs P Moore Chyavallon Landaviddy Lane POLPERRO PL13 2RT	01503 272788 as phone www.polperro.org	205 510	350 mts £23.00 O D PL CP 2D 1T ALL ES price based on two sharing
52	Mrs P Wilcox The Watchers The Warren POLPERRO PL13 2RD	01503 272296 as phone www.polperro.org	210 509	On Path £23.00 O D PL DW KT 2D 1T ALL ES DW by Arrang.
52	Mr S Shephard The House on Props Talland Street POLPERRO PL13 2RE	01503 272310	208 509	on path £35.00 O EM PL LSP DW KT 2D 1T ALL ES
52	Mr & Mrs D Foster The Cottage Restaurant The Coombes POLPERRO PL13 2RQ	01503 272217	205 511	400 mts £26.00 D EM CP 5D[5]
52	Mr A Taylor Crumplehorn Inn POLPERRO PL13 2RJ	01503 272348 host@crumplehorn-inn.co.uk www.crumplehorn-inn.co.uk	201 205	800 mts £25.00 O D EM PL CP LSP DW 9D 3T 8F ALL ES

Sect.	Name and Address	Tel. No. Fax. No. Web / Email	Map Reference Opening Times	Distance from Path Starting Price Facilities Accommodation
53	Mr & Mrs P Barlow Schooner Point 1 Trelawney Terrace WEST LOOE PL13 2AG	01503 262670 enquiries@schoonerpoint.co.uk www.schoonerpoint.co.uk	252 536	150mtrs £15.00 O D PL CP DW 3D[2] 1T 2S
53	Mr & Mrs C Eveleigh Grasmere St Martins Road EAST LOOE PL13 1LP	01503 262556 grasmerelooe@btopenworld.com	254 544	400 mts £18.00 O D EM PL CP 3D[1] 1T[1] 1S 2F[1]
53	Mr E Mawby Marwinthy Guest House East Cliff EAST LOOE PL13 1DE	01503 264382 eddiemawby@lineone.net www.marwinthy.co.uk	256 533 Mar-Nov	On Path £18.00 D DW 2D[2] 1T 1F
53	Mr & Mrs J Jenkin Sea Breeze Lower Chapel Street EAST LOOE PL13 1AT	01503 263131 johnjenkin@sbgh.freeserve.co.uk www.cornwallexplore.co.uk/seabreeze	256 531	100 mts £18.00 O D PL DW 4D[3] 1T
53	Mr & Mrs Andrews St Johns Court East Cliff EAST LOOE PL13 1DE	01503 262301 stjohnscourtlooecornwall.freeserve.co.uk stjohnscourt.com	256 532	10 mts £25.00 O D 3D 2T 3F ALL ES
53	Mr & Mrs D Bulley Deganwy Hotel Station Road EAST LOOE PL13 1HL	01503 262984 01503 262461 enquiries@deganwyhotel.co.uk www.deganwyhotel.co.uk	254 536 Jan-Nov	50 mts £20.00 D PL CP LSP KT 3D[1] 1T[1] 1S[1] 3F[3]
54	Mrs P Rowlandson Blue Haven Looe Hill SEATON PL11 3JQ	01503 250310 bluehaven@btinternet.com www.smoothhound.co.uk/hotels/bluehave.html	262 551	300 mts £22.00 O D EM PL CP DW 3D[3] 1T[1] 1S 1F[1] EM PL DW by arrange.
54	Mrs M A Chamberlain Bay Cottage DOWNDERRY PL11 3JZ	01503 250617 lesaloneman@aol.com	315 540	on path £17.00 CP 1D 1T
54	Mr D Maynard The Inn On The Shore Seafront DOWNDERRY PL11 3JY	01503 250210 01503 250660	314 539	800 mts O EM PL CP LSP 2D 2T 1S ALL ES
54	Mrs A J Harvey The Bungalow Cliff Road PORTWRINKLE PL11 3BY	01503 230334	355 541 Mar-Oct	220 mts £17.50 D PL CP LSP 1D 1T
54	Mrs D Hughes B & B by the C 39 Whitsand Bay View PORTWRINKLE PL11 3DB	01503 230947 01503 230946 darrylhughes@hotmail.com www.bandbbythec.com	356 529	90 mts £20.00 O D CP LSP 2D[2] 1T 1S
54	Mrs K Ridpath Fir Cottage LOWER TREGANTLE PL11 3AL	01752 822626 As Phone	392 536	200 mts £20.00 O D EM PL CP LSP KT PD 1D 1T 2F

Sect.	Name and Address	Tel. No. Fax. No. Web / Email	Map Reference Opening Times	Distance from Path Starting Price Facilities Accommodation
55	Mr Collins Sea Edge The Bound CAWSAND PL10 1PB	01752 822229 collins@cawsand.f9.co.uk	435 502	25 mts £48.00 O D PL DW 1D 1T 1F ALL ES
55	Mrs D Goodwright Clarendon Garrett Street CAWSAND PL10 1PD	01752 823460 www.crabpot.co.uk	435 502	On Path £18.00 O 1D 1T 1S
55	Mr & Mrs H Honig The Halfway House Inn Fore Street KINGSAND PL10 1NA	01752 822279 01752 823146 www.connexions.co.uk/halfway	434 505	500 mts £30.00 O D EM PL DW 3D 1S 1T 1F ALL ES/
55	Ms T Williams Westcroft Market Street KINGSAND PL10 1NE	01752 823216	434 505	200 mts £12.50 O D PL CP DW 1D 1T 1F
55	Ms A Heasman Cliff House KINGSAND PL10 1NJ	01752 823110 01752 822595 chkingsand@aol.com www.cliffhse.abel.co.uk	434 506	20 mts £27.50 O D EM PL CP 3D 3T ALL ES
55	Mrs B Graham Weir Cottage Lower Anderton Road MILLBROOK PL10 1HP	01752 822050 joeandbinna.graham@virgin.net	438 523	1.5 km PD £25.00 O D EM PL CP LSP PD 1D/T[1]
56	Mrs J Moulds Berkeley's of St James 4 St James Place East PLYMOUTH PL1 3AS	01752 221654 As Phone www.smoothhound.co.uk/hotels/berkely2.html	474 541	on path £22.50 O D CP 3D[2] 1T[1] 1S[1] £30 single occupancy
56	Mr J Lovell Plymouth Backpackers Hotel 172 Citadel Road PLYMOUTH PL1 3BD	01752 225158 01752 207847 plymouthback@hotmail.com www.plymouthbackpackers.co.uk	473 540	On Path £10.00 O D 3D 8 DORMS(SLEEP 2-8) Also 1 Female En Suite Dorm sleeps 6
56	Mrs M Emery Acorns & Lawns Guest House 171 Citadel Road PLYMOUTH PL1 2HY	01752 229474 As Phone	478 541	100 mts £18.00 O D PL 5D[5] 3T[2] 1S 1F[1]
56	Mr & Mrs B Penn Sunray Hotel 3-5 Alfred Street The Hoe PLYMOUTH PL1 2RP	01752 669113 01752 268969 info@sunrayhotel.freeserve.co.uk www.devon-hotel.co.uk	475 541	750 mts £25.00 O D EM PL CP 5D[5] 1T[1] 5S[3] 8F[8]
56	Mrs C M Hawton Edgcumbe Guest House 50 Pier Street West Hoe PLYMOUTH PL1 3BT	01752 660675 01752 666510 hawton@clara.co.uk www.hawton.clara.net	473 537	20 mts £25.00 O CP DW 5D 3T 1S 1F ALL ES
56	Mr S Jones The Old Pier Guest House 20 Radford Road WEST HOE Plymouth PL1 3BY	01752 268468 enquire@oldpier.co.uk www.oldpier.co.uk	472 537	100 mts £18.00 O D PL 2D[1] 2T[1] 1S 1F

Sect.	Name and Address	Tel. No. Fax. No. Web / Email	Map Reference Opening Times	Distance from Path Starting Price Facilities Accommodation
57	Nr Wembury Beach Road Heybrook Bay Private HEYBROOK BAY PL9 0BS	01752 862345	496 488 Mar-Nov	On path £18.00 CP LSP 4D 2T
57	Mr & Mrs A J Farrington Bay Cottage 150 Church Road WEMBURY PL9 0HR	01752 862559 As Phone thefairies@aol.com www.bay-cottage.com	520 485	200 mts £29.00 O D PL CP DW 2D(2) 2T(1) 1S Closed Xmas & New Yr
57	Mrs M R Denby Knoll Cottage 104 Church Road WEMBURY PL9 0LA	01752 862036	523 489	500 mts £18.00 O D EM PL CP LSP 2D[2] 1S
58	Mrs J Cross Wood Cottage Brigend NEWTON FERRERS PL8 1AW	01752 872372 jillx@wdcott.freeserve.co.uk	555 482	on path PD £20.00 O D EM PL CP DW KT PD 2D 1F[1]
58	Mr & Mrs J Urry Barnicott Bridgend Hill NEWTON FERRERS Plymouth PL8 1BA	01752 872843	551 482	2 km PD £18.00 O D PL CP LSP KT PD 2D 1T
58	Mrs J Williams 32 The Coombe NOSS MAYO PL8 1EN	01752 872261 mikelw@freedelta.net	548 478 Apr-Nov	1 km £22.50 D PL CP LSP KT 1D[1]
58	Mrs J Rogers Higher Shippen WORSWELL BARTON Noss Mayo PL8 1HB	07152 872977 as phone Bedbreakworswell@aol.com	550 464	800 mts £20.00 O D CP LSP 2D 1F
58	Mrs J Stockman Bugle Rocks, The Old School BATTISBOROUGH Holbeton PL8 1JX	01752 830422 01752 830558	601 473 Mar-Dec	500 mtrs £28.00 D PL CP LSP 3D[2] 1T[1] 2S 1F[1] price based on 2 sharing
58	Miss F Kempt West Hanover Lodge HOLBETON PL8 1JN	01752 830582	617 502 Easter-Oct	4.5kms £18.00 D CP 1D(1)
58	Miss L Price Mildmay Colours Inn HOLBETON Plymouth PL8 1NA	01752 830248 01752 830432 www.mildmay-colours.co.uk	613 501	2 km £27.50 O D EM PL CP DW 3D 3T 2F ALL ES Single £35 best Devon Village award 20
58	Mrs L Wallis Windlestraw Penquit ERMINGTON PL21 0LU	01752 698384 As Phone wallispenquit@beeb.net	646 544	2 km PD £22.00 O D PL CP LSP KT 1T 1S Will PD Yealm Erme Avon
58	Mrs E Dodds Ayrmer House RINGMORE Nr Kingsbridge TQ7 4HL	01548 810391	651 459	1.2 km £25.00 O D CP LSP 1D[1] 1T

Sect.	Name and Address	Tel. No. Fax. No. Web / Email	Map Reference Opening Times	Distance from Path Starting Price Facilities Accommodation
58	Mr M Walker Blackadon Barns NEAR IVYBRIDGE PL22 0HB	01752 897034 mwalkone@aol.com www.blackadonbarns.co.uk	665 577	12 km PD £25.00 O D CP LSP DW KT PD 4D[3] 9T[5] Will Pick Up/Drop
58	Mrs C Walsh Folly Foot CHALLABOROUGH Bigbury-On-Sea TQ7 4JB	01548 810036 carolwalsh@freenet.co.uk www.freenetpages.co.uk/hp/follyfoot	652 447	50 mts PD £25.00 O D PL CP LSP KT PD 2D[1] 1S 1F[1]
58	Mr & Mrs M A Farrell Warren Cottage Marine Drive BIGBURY-ON-SEA TQ7 4AS	01548 810210 As Phone	650 444	On path £18.00 O D EM PL CP LSP DW KT 1T 1S
58	Mrs R van der Heiden Avonlea 6 Folly Hill BIGBURY ON SEA TQ7 4AR	01548 810926 01548 810153 hansvheiden@eurobell.co.uk	656 443	20 mts PD £25.00 O D PL CP LSP KT PD 2D[1] 1T 1S
58	Mrs V Walker The Milking Parlour 9 Combe Farm Barn ASHFORD TQ7 4NH	01548 830958	487676	6 km PD £23.00 O EM PL CP KT PD 2D[1] 1T
59	Mr J Asden Beacon Point Hotel THURLESTONE SANDS TQ7 3JY	01548 561207	676 411	on path £23.00 O D PL CP LSP DW KT PD 2D[2] 4F[2]
59	Mr & Mrs G Clack Ley House SOUTH MILTON TQ7 3JR	01548 560050 grahamandliz@tiscali.co.uk www.leyhouse.co.uk	676420	100 mts £20.00 O D CP KT 2D[1] 1F[1]
59	Mrs T Wilson 2 Horswell Cottages SOUTH MILTON TQ7 3JU	01548 561328	691423	1.5 kms PD £23.00 O D EM PL CP KT PD 1D 1T
59	Mr & Mrs C Barclay The Sand Pebbles Hotel Grand View Road HOPE COVE Kingsbridge TQ7 3HF	01548 561673	677 402 Apr-Oct	250 mts £30.00 D EM PL CP DW 8D 3T 1F ALL ES
59	Mrs L Dixon Smiley Lodge 9 Weymouth Park HOPE COVE TQ7 3HD	01548 561946 as phone enquiries@smileylodge.co.uk www.smileylodge.co.uk	680 399	350 mts £25.00 O D PL CP DW 2D[1] DW depending on other bookings
59	Miss S Ireland The Cottage Hotel HOPE COVE info@hopecove.com Kingsbridge TQ7 3HJ	01548 561555 01548 561455 www.hopecove.com	675 400 Feb-Dec	25 mts £26.00 D EM PL CP LSP DW 2D[2] 22T[18] 5S 6F[5]
60	Mr & Mrs R Petty-Brown Rocarno Grenville Road SALCOMBE TQ8 8BJ	01548 842732 rocarno@aol.com	736 389	500 mts £22.50 O D PL 2D 2T ALL ES

Sect.	Name and Address	Tel. No. Fax. No. Web / Email	Map Reference Opening Times	Distance from Path Starting Price Facilities Accommodation
60	Mrs P Snelson Lyndhurst Hotel Bonaventure Road SALCOMBE TQ8 8BG	01548 842481 as phone lyndhursthotel@salcombe_online.co.uk www.salcombeinformatione.co.uk/lyndhurst.html	737 389 Mar-Oct	400 mts £25.00 D PL CP 3D 3T 1S 1F ALL ES
60	Mr & Mrs R Vaughan Trennels Hotel Herbert Road SALCOMBE TQ8 8HR	01548 842500 trennels_hotel@btinternet.com www.btinternet.com/~r.vaughan/trennels-hotel	737 388 Mar-Oct	400 mts £26.00 CP 5D ALL ES
60	Mrs E M Weymouth Motherhill Farm Main Road SALCOMBE TQ8 8NB	01548 842552 As Phone djw@dweymouth.fsnet.co.uk	730 393 Easter-Oct	1.5 km £19.00 D CP LSP 1D 1T 1S
60	Ms A Woodhatch Rainbow's End 11 Platt Close SALCOMBE TQ8 8NZ	01548 843654 thewoodhatches@hotmail.com	730 393	800 mts PD £19.50 O D PL CP LSP DW KT PD 1T 1F ALL ES
60	Mrs S Davies Castle Combe Sandhills Road SALCOMBE TQ8 8JP	01548 843361 01548 843361 sueandjohn.davies@virgin.net	731 382	25 mts £25.00 O D PL CP LSP 1D 1T[1]
61	Mr & Mrs N Alen Ashleigh House Ashleigh Road KINGSBRIDGE TQ7 1HB	01548 852893 as phone reception@ashleigh-house.co.uk www.ashleigh-house.co.uk	731 439	6 km £24.00 O D EM CP LSP DW 5D 1T 2F ALL ES
61	Mr C Richards The Gara Rock Hotel GARA ROCK East PortlemoutH TQ8 8PH	01548 842342	752 371	D EM PL CP LSP DW 10D 20F ALL ES
61	Mr & Mrs P Barber Maelcombe House§ MAELCOMBE East Prawle TQ7 2DE	01548 511521	790 363	100 mts £40.00 O D CP LSP DW KT PD 2D[1] 1T 1S KT by arrangement
61	Mrs J Foss Down Farm START POINT Kingsbridge TQ7 2NQ	01548 511234 As Phone downfarm@btinternet.com	806 377	600 mts £20.00 O D PL CP LSP 1D[1] 1T
61	Mrs P Wolstenholme Widget NORTH HALLSANDS Kingsbridge TQ7 2EX	01548 511110	819388	50 mts £20.00 O D CP 2D[1] 1T
61	The Cricket Inn Mrs R Simon BEESANDS TQ7 2EN	01548 580215 www.thecricketinn.co.uk	819 402	on path £60.00 per room O EM PL CP LSP 3D[3] 1F[1]
61	Mrs B Honeywill Marybank House BEESON Kingsbridge TQ7 2HW	01548 580531 marybankhouse@hotmail.com www.marybankhouse.com	811 408 Mar-Nov	500 mts £25.00 D PL CP DW 2D[2] 1T 1S 1F[1]
61	Mr & Mrs R Rose-Price Startlea House TORCROSS Kingsbridge TQ7 2TQ	01548 580724 Rose-Price@startlea.co.uk www.startlea.co.uk	823 422	5 mts £25.00 O D CPPD 1D 1T ALL ES

Sect.	Name and Address	Tel. No. Fax. No. Web / Email	Map Reference Opening Times	Distance from Path Starting Price Facilities Accommodation
61	Ms C Ley Linger Lodge TORCROSS TQ7 2TJ	01548 580599 www.lingerlodge.co.uk	822 421	300mts PD £27.00 O D CP LSP PD 3D [3]
61	Mr & Mrs P Wagstaff Sea Breeze Cottage TORCROSS TQ7 2TQ	01548 580697 peter@seabreeze-cottage.co.uk	823 421	on path £19.50 O D CP PD 3D[2] 1T[1]
61	Mrs A Lansdale Bay House TORCROSS TQ7 2TQ	01548 580771 as phone	821 421 May-Oct	on path £25.00 D CP 1D[1] 1T
61	Mrs L Raeburn Malston Barton Sherford NEAR TORCROSS TQ7 2BB	01548 531794 01548 531694 david.raeburn@farmersweekly.net	774 452	6 km PD £20.00 O D EM PL CP LSP KT PD 2D[1] 1T[1] 2F[1] Camping also available
62	Mrs V A L Mercer Old Walls SLAPTON Nr Kingsbridge TQ7 2QN	01548 580516	822 449	1 km PD £20.00 O D PL DW KT PD 1T 1S 1F[1]
62	Mrs J Makepeace Skerries STRETE Nr Dartmouth TQ6 0RH	01803 770775 01803 770950 jamskerries@rya-online.net www.skerriesbandb.co.uk	842 470	500 mts £29.00 O D PL CP KT 2D 1T ALL ES
62	Mr & Mrs C Tonkin Fairholme Bay View Estate STOKE FLEMING Dartmouth TQ6 0QX	01803 770356 As Phone	861 481	500 mts £20.00 O D CP DW 3D[3] £30 single occupancy
62	Mr & Mrs K Scott Little Weeke House Weeke Hill DARTMOUTH TQ6 0JT	01803 835922 kayceek@aol.com	875 499	1200 mts £30.00 O PL CP KT 2D[2]
62	Miss S Leach Sunny Banks Guest House 1 Vicarage Hill DARTMOUTH TQ6 9EW	01803 832766 As Phone sue@sunnybanks.com www.sunnybanks.com	874 513 Feb-Dec	1 km £22.50 PL CP DW 5D[4] 2T[2] 1S 2F[2]
62	Mr & Mrs P Walton Westbourne House 4 Vicarage Hill DARTMOUTH TQ6 9EW	01803 832213 01803 839209 peterwalton@westbourne-house.co.uk www.westbourne-house.co.uk	874 513	1.5 kms £34.00 O D CP LSP 4D[4]
62	Mrs A Cardwell The Maitland 28 Victoria Road DARTMOUTH TQ6 9SA	01803 835854	875 513	500 mts £20.00 O D CP 3D[2]
62	Mr & Mrs P Croad Agincourt House 27 Lower Street DARTMOUTH TQ6 9AN	01803 839278	878 511	10 mts £30.00 O D PL DW 1D 1T 1S ALL ES
63	Mr & Mrs L Congdon Carlton House Higher Street KINGSWEAR TQ6 0AG	01803 752244	882 510	100 mts £16.50 O D PL CP LSP DW 2D 2T 1S 1F

Sect.	Name and Address	Tel. No. Fax. No. Web / Email	Map Reference Opening Times	Distance from Path Starting Price Facilities Accommodation
63	Mrs C Haddock Coleton Barton Farm Brownstone Road KINGSWEAR TQ6 0EQ	01803 752795 01803 752241 caroline.haddock@btopenworld.com	915 512	500 mts £18.50 O D EM PL CP LSP DW 2D[1] 1T
63	Mr & Mrs P Hancock Melville Hotel 45 New Road BRIXHAM TQ5 8NL	01803 852033 melvillehotel@brixham45.fsnet.co.uk	920 559 March-Nov	500 mts £17.50 D EM PL CP 3D[3] 1T 3S 2F[2]
63	Mr&Mrs T Watson Sampford House 57/59 King Street BRIXHAM TQ5 9TH	01803 857761 01803 858697 sampfordhouse@supaworld.com	927 562	50 mts £20.00 O D PL CP DW 5D[4] 1T[1] 1F[1] limited CP
64	Mr & Mrs P Gibbs Benbows Hotel 1 Alta Vista Road ROUNDHAM Paignton TQ4 6DB	01803 558128 benbowshotel@aol.com www.benbowshotel.co.uk	894 599	200mts £16.00 O EM CP DW 6D[2] 1T[1] 1S 2F[1]
64	Mrs P Kingdon Bruce Lodge Guest House 2 Elmsleigh Road PAIGNTON TQ4 5AU	01803 550972 As Phone roger_kingdon@lineone.net www.paigntondevon.co.uk/brucelodge	888 603 Easter-Sept	500 mts £16.00 D CP 2D 3T 1SF
64	Mr & Mrs M Gosling Cayton House 53 Upper Morin Road Preston PAIGNTON TQ3 2HX	01803 520663 lyn@caytonhouse.fsnet.com www.visitsouthwest.com/cayton	892 614	100 mts £20.00 O D CP LSP 1D 1T ALL ES
64	Mrs D Powell Sunnybank Hotel 2 Cleveland Road PAIGNTON TQ4 6EN	01803 525540 sunnybankpowvtb@supanet.com	893 601	500 mts £18.00 O D EM PL CP 3D[1] 2T[1] 2F[2]
64	Mrs F Dwane The No Smoking Clifton Hotel 9 Kernou Road PAIGNTON TQ4 6BA	01803 556545 as phone freda@cliftonhotelpaignton.co.uk www.cliftonhotelpaignton.co.uk	891 607 Easter-Oct	100 mts £24.00 D EM PL CP 5D 4T 4S 2F ALL ES no single nights in August
64	Mrs R Leysinger Cedar Court 3 St Matthews Road CHELSTON Torquay TQ2 6JA	01803 607851 01803 607851 enquiries@cedarcourt-hotel.co.uk www.cedarcourt-hotel.co.uk	903 634	700 mts £22.00 O D EM PL 5D 1T 3S 1F ALL ES
64	Mr & Mrs M French Fairmount House Hotel Herbert Road CHELSTON Torquay TQ2 6RW	01803 605446 as phone enquiries@fairmounthousehotel.co.uk www.fairmounthousehotel.co.uk	898 638	1 km £24.00 O D EM PL CP DW 4D 1T 1S 2F ALL ES
64	Miss L Cooper Mulberry House 1 Scarborough Road TORQUAY TQ2 5UJ	01803 213639	910 642	1 km £30.00 O D EM PL CP LSP 2D 1T ALL ES
64	Mrs J Hodgson Torquay Backpackers 119 Abbey Road TORQUAY TQ2 5NP	01803 299924 jane@torquaybackpackers.co.uk www.torquaybackpackers.co.uk	912 642	1km £9.00 O D CP DW 1D 9 DORMS

Sect.	Name and Address	Tel. No. Fax. No. Web / Email	Map Reference Opening Times	Distance from Path Starting Price Facilities Accommodation
64	Ansteys Cove Hotel 327 Babbacombe Road TORQUAY TQ1 3TB	01803 200900 01803 211150 info@torquaydevon.com www.torquaydevon.com	931 647	On Path £32.00 O EM CP LSP 6D 1T 2S ALL ES
65	Ms J Hobday Beech Close Guest House 53 Babbacombe Road BABBACOMBE TQ1 3SN	01803 328071	925 654	100 mts £19.00 O D PL CP LSP KT PD 4D[1] 1S
65	Mr T P Pinder Birch Tor 315 Babbacombe Road TORQUAY TQ1 3TB	01803 292707 As Phone terry@birchtor.co.uk www.birchtor.co.uk	932 648	50 mts £18.00 O PL CP 3D[1] 1T[1] 1S[1] 1F
65	Mr & Mrs D Blenkinsopp Aveland Hotel Aveland Road BABBACOMBE TQ1 3PT	01803 326622 01803 328940 avelandhotel@aol.com www.avelandhotel.co.uk	921 652	800 mts £20.00 O D EM PL CP 4D 2T 1S 3F ALL ES
65	Mr & Mrs K A James Suite Dreams Hotel Steep Hill MAIDENCOMBE TQ1 4TS	01803 313900 01803 313841 suitedreams@suitedreams.co.uk www.suitedreams.co.uk	926 685	200 mts £23.00 O D CP DW 9D 3T ALL ES £38 upper price limit
65	English House Hotel English House Hotel Teignmouth Road MAIDENCOMBE TQ1 4SY	01803 328760	919 682	1 km £30.00 O D EM PL CP 3D 1T 1F ALL ES
65	Mrs B Cook Green Willow Stoke Road MAIDENCOMBE Torquay TQ1 4TN	01803 329764 cook@greenwillow.freeserve.co.uk	922 690	1km PD £17.00 O PL CP PD 1T
65	Ms J Beckett West Wing Ringmore Lodge Salty Lane SHALDON TQ14 0AP	01626 872754	927 722 Mar-Nov	1.1 km PD £24.00 D PL CP KT PD 1D 1F ALL ES
65	Mr P Hockings Brunswick House 5 Brunswick Street TEIGNMOUTH TQ14 8AE	01626 774102 margrethehockings@hotmail.com	941 727	100 mts £20.00 O D PL DW 4D 3T 1S 1F ALL ES Dogs by arrangement
65	Mr & Mrs B Mesley Leicester House 2 Winterbourne Road TEIGNMOUTH TQ14 8JT	01626 773043 01626 879055 info@leicesterhouse.com www.leicesterhouse.com	940 732	500 mts £26.00 O D CP 2D 1T ALL ES
66	Mr I Dunnington & Mrs A Wright West Hatch Hotel 34 West Cliff DAWLISH EX7 9DN	01626 864211 /862948 westhatchhotel@aol.com www.smoothhound.co.uk/hotels/westhatc.html	962 763	100 mts £26.00 O CP 7D 2T ALL ES
66	Mrs A Ferris The Blenheim 1 Marine Parade DAWLISH EX7 9DJ	01626 862372 theblenheim@btinternet.com	962 765	10mts £23.00 O D PL CP DW 1D 2T ALL ES

Sect.	Name and Address	Tel. No. Fax. No. Web / Email	Map Reference Opening Times	Distance from Path Starting Price Facilities Accommodation
66	Mrs H M Hobson Two Farthings Long Lane ASHCOMBE Near Dawlish EX7 0QR	01626 864847 as phone hobsonhm@yahoo.co.uk www.twofarthings.co.uk	944 789	3 km PD £25.00 O D PL EM CP LSP PD 1T 1F[1] Also self contained chalet (single occ.
66	Mr & Mrs M Hayes The Old Vicarage STARCROSS EX6 8PX	01626 890206 As Phone maggie@theoldvicarage.clara.co.uk www.theoldvicarage.clara.net	976 813 March-Oct	On path £21.00 D CP LSP 2D 1T ALL ES
66	Mr I Stewart The Croft Guest House Cockwood Harbour STARCROSS EX6 8QY	01626 890282 01626 891768	975 808	On Path £22.00 O D CP DW 1D 4T 1S ALL ES single from £30
66	Mrs M Lambert Wixels Ferry Road TOPSHAM EX3 0JH	01392 876785	964 880	On path £16.00 O D DW 1D
66	Mr & Mrs G & Dawe 24 Highfield Clyst Road TOPSHAM Exeter EX3 0DA	01392 874563 geoffdawe50@hotmail.com	965 892	1km PD £18.00 O D PL CP LSP PD 1D 1S
66	Mr J Dobinson The Barn Hotel EXMOUTH EX8 2DF	01395 224411 01395 225445 info@barnhotel.co.uk	014 801	100 mts £30.00 O EM PL CP KT 3D 4T 2S 2F ALL ES
66	Mrs P M Garwood St Aubyns 11 Hartley Road EXMOUTH EX8 2SG	01395 264069	004 806	1km £21.00 O D PL CP LSP 2D 1T 1S
66	Ms A Jones Sholton Guest House 29 Morton Road EXMOUTH EX8 1BA	01395 277318	999 807	100 mts £19.50 O D CP 3D[2] 2T 1S 1F[1]
67	Mrs S Freeman 10 Knowle Village BUDLEIGH SALTERTON EX9 6AL	01395 445807	050 825	1.5 km PD £20.00 O D PL CP LSP DW PD 1D 1T[1] 1S
67	Mrs H J Simmons Chapter House 6 Westbourne Terrace BUDLEIGH SALTERTON EX9 6BR	01395 444100	059 818	10 mts £20.00 O D PL CP LSP DW 1D 1T 1S 1F ALL ES
67	Mrs S Taylor Rosehill 30 West Hill BUDLEIGH SALTERTON EX9 6BU	01395 444031 rosehill@bnbrelaxed.demon.co.uk www.devon-health-spa.co.uk	057 819	400 mts £25.00 O D PL CP DW KT 3D[3] 1T
67	Mr & Mrs K Coles Lilac Cottage 1 Knowle Hill BUDLEIGH SALTERTON EX9 7AL	01395 442417 kenlin@eclipse.co.uk	048 822	750 mts £20.00 O D EM PL CP 2D 1T

Sect.	Name and Address	Tel. No. Fax. No. Web / Email	Map Reference Opening Times	Distance from Path Starting Price Facilities Accommodation
68	Mrs F Cameron-Jones Anchoring Farm Ottery Street OTTERTON Budleigh Salterton EX9 7HW	01395 567198 mark@cameronjones.fsnet.co.uk www.anchoringfarm.co.uk	085 855	1 km PD £22.50 O D EM PL CP KT PD 1D 1F ALL ES
68	Mr & Mrs Griffiths Rock Cottage Peak Hill SIDMOUTH EX10 8RZ	01395 514253 tomgriffiths@rockcottage.co.uk www.rockcottage.co.uk	121 870	on path £30.00 O D 3D[1]
68	Mr & Mrs M C Penaluna Canterbury Guest House Salcombe Road SIDMOUTH EX10 8PR	01395 513373 cgh@eclipse.co.uk	127 878	600 mts £20.00 O D EM CP DW 2D 2T1S 3F ALL ES
68	Mrs L Lever Larkstone House 22 Connaught Road SIDMOUTH EX10 8TT	01395 514345	125 878	500 mts £19.00 O D CP DW 1D 1T[1] 1S
68	Mrs J Young Avalon Guest House Vicarage Road SIDMOUTH EX10 8UQ	01395 513443 owneravalon@aol.com www.avalonsidmouth.co.uk	127 880	500 mts £23.00 O D CP 3D 1T ALL ES
68	Mr & Mrs D Haslam Bramley Lodge Guest House Vicarage Road SIDMOUTH EX10 8UQ	01395 515710 haslam@bramleylodge.fsnet.co.uk	127 880	700 mts PD £23.00 O D EM PL CP DW KT PD 2D[2] 1T[1] 2S[1] 1F[1]
68	Mr D Leach Newland Guest House Temple Street SIDMOUTH EX10 9BA	01395 514155 mobile: 07855 953739	126 881	2 km PD £20.00 O E PL CP LSP KT PD 2D[2] 2T[1] 1S 2F[1]
69	Mrs K Smith The Masons Arms BRANSCOMBE EX12 3DJ	01297 680300 01297 680500 reception@masonsarms.co.uk www.masonsarms.co.uk	203 888	2 km £25.00 O EM PL CP DW 19D[18] 1T 2F[2] Room rate £50 pppn
69	Mr & Mrs P R Manning Pendennis South Down Road BEER EX12 3AE	01297 23395	228 889 Easter-Sept	30mts £21.00 D EM PL CP LSP 3D[2] 2T[1] 1S
68	Mr & Mrs B Rosewarne Sea Glimpses Burrow Road SEATON EX12 2NF	01297 22664 01297 22664 liz@glimpses.fsnet.co.uk	250 899	30 mts £20.00 O D PL CP LSP 1T 1F
69	Mr M Christopher Mariners Hotel The Esplanade SEATON EX12 2NP	01297 20560	247 898	on path £28.00 O D EM CP DW 7D 2T 1S ALL ES
69	Mr T Willis and Andy Wise Beach End Trevelyan Road SEATON EX12 2NL	01297 23388 01297 625604	251 899	on path £25.00 O D 2D 1T ALL ES

Sect.	Name and Address	Tel. No. Fax. No. Web / Email	Map Reference Opening Times	Distance from Path Starting Price Facilities Accommodation
69	Mrs E D Jordan Lyndhurst Manor Road SEATON EX12 2AQ	01297 23490	244 902	800 mts £17.00 O CP LSP DW 1D 1T 1S
69	Mr & Mrs A Pearson Millhaven House 52 Fore Street SEATON EX12 2AD	01297 22456 01297 22616 andrewevents@aol.com	245 901	300 mts £17.50 O D PL CP DW 1D 2T[2] 1S 1F Tropical tea garden
69	Mr & Mrs R Webber Axe Farm AXMOUTH Seaton EX12 4BG	01297 24707 axe.farm@ic24.net www.axefarm.co.uk	256 911	1km £18.00 O D PL CP LSP DW 1D 1F ALL ES
69	Mrs J Calvert 13 Southcombe Terrace AXMOUTH Seaton EX12 4AT	01297 22749 Jkmacalvert@yahoo.co.uk	260 910	500mts £15.00 O D CP 1D 1T
69	Mr & Mrs P Tansley Dairy Cottage Stedcombe Vale AXMOUTH EX12 4BJ	01297 20366 as phone	263 919	2 kms PD £25.00 O D PL CP KT PD 1D 1T ALL ES
70	Ms M Bolton Cliff Cottage Tea Garden Cobb Road LYME REGIS DT7 3JP	01297 443334 merry.bolton@btinternet.com	336 918 Easter-Oct	25 mts £20.00 D EM PL LSP DW 2D 1F ALL ES
70	Mr & Mrs W Bradbury Charnwood Guest House 21 Woodmead Road LYME REGIS DT7 3AD	01297 445281 enqswcp@lymeregisaccommodation.com www.lymeregisaccommodation.com	339 924	500 mts £25.00 O D PL CP 3D 2T 1S 1F ALL ES
71	Mrs A Thomas Swansmead River Way CHARMOUTH DT6 6LS	01297 560465 anthea@swansmead.co.uk www.swansmead.co.uk	366 932	100 mts £21.00 O D CP 1D(1) 1F £30.00 single occupancy
71	Mr & Mrs M J Bomford Stonebarrow Manor Stonebarrow Lane CHARMOUTH DT6 6RA	01297 560212 01297 560234 stonebarrowmanor@hotmail.com	371 936	on path £25.00 O D PL CP DW 6D 5T 2S 1F ALL ES
72	Mrs Backhouse Chimneys Guest House Main Street CHIDEOCK DT6 6JH	01297 489368	424 928	200 mts £25.00 O PL CP DW 3D[2] 1T[1] 1F[1]
72	Mrs C Jones Heatherbell Cottage Hill Close West Cliff WEST BAY DT6 4HW	01308 422998 heatherbell4bnb@onetel.net.uk infoonwww.westcountrynow.com	459 906 Jan-Nov	300 mts £28.00 3D[3] no pre-booking for July & August
72	Mr A Hardy Britmead House West Bay Road BRIDPORT DT6 4EG	01308 422941 01308 422516 britmead@talk21.com www.britmeadhouse.co.uk	465 913	800 mts £25.00 O D CP DW KT PD 4D 2T 2F ALL ES

Sect.	Name and Address	Tel. No. / Fax. No. / Web / Email	Map Reference / Opening Times	Distance from Path / Starting Price / Facilities / Accommodation
72	Mr D Walker Eypeleaze 117 West Bay Road BRIDPORT DT6 4EQ	01308 420228 enquiries@eypeleaze.co.uk www.eypeleaze.co.uk	466 911	1.2 km PD £17.00 O D PL CP LSP KT PD 1T[1]
72	Mrs G R Bramah 143 Victoria Grove BRIDPORT DT6 3AG	01308 456617 ramblingrose@bramah3.freeserve.co.uk	467 934	3km PD £18.00 O D CP KT PD 1T
72	Mrs V A Moore Eggardon View 261 St Andrews Road BRIDPORT DT6 3DU	01308 459001 valamoore@hotmail.com	477 942	4.5 kms PD £19.00 O D CP LSP PD 1T[1]
72	Mrs P Bales Highway Farm West Road BRIDPORT DT6 6AE	01308 424321 as phone bale@highwayfarm.co.uk www.highwayfarm.co.uk	443 928	1.5 km £0.00 O D EM CP LSP 3F[3] on bus route
73	Mr M B Hoare Burton Cliff Hotel BURTON BRADSTOCK DT6 4RB	01308 897205 01308 898111 burtoncliffhotel@btopenworld.com www.burtoncliffhotel.co.uk	487 891	on path PD £21.00 O D EM PL CP LSP DW KTPD 7D(5) 8T(6) 3S(1)
73	Mrs N Millard Blegberry Swyre Road WEST BEXINGTON DT2 9DD	01308 897774 01308 898300 normamillard@aol.com Single bookings difficult July & Aug.	532 872	500 mts £20.00 O D PL CP LSP 1D 1F
73	Mrs M Harman Linton Cottage ABBOTSBURY DT3 4JL	01305 871339 queenbee@abbotsbury.co.uk www.lintoncottage.co.uk	578 852	1km £26.00 O D PL CP 3D(3)
73	Mrs W Wood East Farm ABBOTSBURY DT3 4JN	01305 871363 as phone wendy@eastfarmhouse.co.uk www.eastfarmhouse.co.uk	578 853	£15.00 O EM PL CP DW 2D 1T ALL ES
73	Mr & Mrs G Roper The Swan Lodge ABBOTSBURY DT3 4JL	01305 871249 as phone	579 853	1km £24.00 O D EM PL CP LSP DW 3D[2] 2T[1] single from £33
73	Mr & Mrs F Harber The Keep Back Street ABBOTSBURY DT3 4JP	01305 871294 mayling.thirlaway@which.net	578 854	50 mts £20.00 O D CP LSP KT 1D(1) 1S
73	Mrs P Crockett 21 Rodden Row ABBOTSBURY DT3 4JL	01305 871465	579 855	750mtrs £19.00 O D 1D 1T
73	Mr & Mrs J Cooke Abbey House Church Street ABBOTSBURY DT4JJ	01305 871330 01305 871088 www.theabbeyhouse.co.uk	577 852	50 mts £30.00 O D CP 1D 3T 1F ALL ES

Sect.	Name and Address	Tel. No. Fax. No. Web / Email	Map Reference Opening Times	Distance from Path Starting Price Facilities Accommodation
74	Mrs A Martin The Old Fountain 36 Front Street PORTESHAM DT3 4ET	01305 871278 as phone martann981@aol.com	603 860	2 km PD £22.00 O D PL CP LSP KT PD 1D 1T
74	Mr & Mrs G Tatlow The Old Ship Inn 7 The Redgeway UPWEY DT3 5QQ	01305 812522 01305 816533	669 850	2.25 km PD £25.00 O D EM PL CP KT PD 2D 2T
75	Mr D Fox The Pulpit Inn PORTLAND DT5 2JT	01305 821237	678 687	on path £25.00 O D EM CP LSP 2D 1S 1F
75	Mr G Bisogno Alessandria Hotel & Restauraunt 71 Wakeham Road PORTLAND DT5 1HW	01305 822270/820108 01305 820561 alessandriahotel@hotmail.com	694 716	300 mts £25.00 O D PL CP LSP KT 6D[4] 3T[3] 3S 2F[2]
76	Mr & Mrs S Green Florian 59 Abbotsbury Road WEYMOUTH DT4 0AQ	01305 773836 clare@florian-guesthouse.co.uk www.florian-guesthouse.co.uk	671 791	500 mts £19.00 O D CP 3D 3T 1S 1F ALL ES
76	Miss V Clark Oaklands Edwardian Guesthouse 1 Glendinning Avenue WEYMOUTH DT4 7QF	01305 767081 01305 767379 andrew@oaklands-guesthouse.co.uk www.oaklands-guesthouse.co.uk	678 801	500 mts £20.00 O D CP 5D[4] 2T[2] 1F[1] LSP at quiet times
76	Mrs K Jones Kimberly Guest House 16 Kirtleton Avenue WEYMOUTH DT4 7PT	01305 783333	679 802	£15.00 O D EM PL CP LSP PD 4D[1] 1T 1S 1F
76	Mr & Mrs Penman Horizon Guest House 16 Brunswick Terrace WEYMOUTH DT4 7RW	01305 784916 info@horizonguesthouse.co.uk www.horizonguesthouse.co.uk	682 799	on path £19.00 O D EM PL 3D[2] 2T 1S 1F[1]
76	Miss K Amos Double Three Guest House 33 Rodwell Road WEYMOUTH DT4 8QP	01305 786259 doublethree16762@aol.com www.doublethree.co.uk	675 785 Feb-Nov	100 mts £18.00 D PL CP LSP DW 1D 1T 3S 2F[1]
76	Mrs K Legg Rosedale Church Lane OSMINGTON DT3 6EW	01305 832056	723 832 Mar-Oct	on path £18.00 D PL LSP 2D[1] 1T
76	Miss B Leigh Rosthwaite Church Lane OSMINGTON DT3 6EW	01305 833621	723 832 £17.00	on path O D PL CP KT PD 1D 1T
76	Smugglers Inn Smugglers Inn OSMINGTON MILLS DT3 6HF	01305 833125	735 817	£32.50 O D EM PL CP LSP 2D 3T 1S 1F 7ES

Sect.	Name and Address	Tel. No. Fax. No. Web / Email	Map Reference Opening Times	Distance from Path Starting Price Facilities Accommodation
76	Osmington Mills Holidays Osmington Mills Holidays The Ranch House OSMINGTON MILLS DT3 6HF	01305 832311 01305 835251 holidays@osmingtonmills.fsnet.co.uk osmington-mills-holidays.co.uk	738 817 Easter-Oct	300 mts £20.00 EM CP DW 2D 2F ALL ES
76	Mrs J Ravensdale Elads-Nevar West Road WEST LULWORTH BH20 5RZ	01929 400467	824 806	800 mts £17.00 O D PL CP DW 2D 1T
76	Ms J Emery Lulworth Cove Hotel WEST LULWORTH BH20 5RQ	01929 400333 01929 400534 hotel@lulworth-cove.com www.lulworth-cove.com	382 080	on path £27.50 O D EM PL CP LSP DW 12D[10]1T[1]1S[1]1F[1]
76	The Hambury WEST LULWORTH Nr Wareham BH20 5RL	01929 400358 01929 400167 durdle@aol.com www.thehambury.co.uk	824 806	400 mts £39.00 O D EM PL CP 11D 3T 1S ALL ES
76	Mr & Mrs B Burrill Graybank Main Road WEST LULWORTH BH20 5RL		822 802 Feb-Nov	250 mts £18.00 D PL CP KT 3D 2T 1S 1F
76	Mrs C Miller Cromwell House Hotel WEST LULWORTH BH20 5RJ	01929 400253 01929 400566 catriona@lulworthcove.co.uk www.lulworthcove.co.uk	821 801	on path £35.00 OD EM PL CP LSP DW 8D 5T 1S 3F ALL ES
76	Mr & Mrs J Bickerton Breach House LULWORTH COVE BH20 5RJ	01929 400777 info@lulworthcovebandb.co.uk www.lulworthcovebandb.co.uk	821 801	on path £35.00 O CP DW 3D[2]
76	Mrs H Cooper April Thatch COOMBE KEYNES Lulworth Cove BH20 5PP	01929 463412 admin@aprilthatch.co.uk www.aprilthatch.co.uk	842 843	4.8 km PD £25.00 O D PL CP PD 1D[1]1T[1]1S
77	Mr M Francis East Burton House WOOL Wareham BH20 6HE	01929 463857 01929 463026	870 834	3 km £25.00 O D PL DW 2D 1T
77	Mrs E Braisby Blackmanston Farm STEEPLE Kimmeridge BH20 5NZ	01929 480743 01929 480743 mail@swanage.gov.uk memberslyco5.co.ukblackmanstonfarm	916 808	1.5km PD £24.00 O D EM PL CP LSP DW KTPD 1T 1F
78	Mrs G Hole Bradle Farm CHURCH KNOWLE Kimmeridge BH20 5NU	01929 480712 01929 481144 bradlefarmhouse@farmersweekly.net www.bradlefarmhouse.co.uk	930 805	3.5 km PD £25.00 O D PL CP LSP KT PD 2D 1T ALL ES
78	Mrs A Fry Kingston Country Courtyard Greystone Court KINGSTON Wareham BH20 5LR	01929 481066 annfry@kingstoncountrycourtyard.co.uk www.kingstoncountrycourtyard.co.uk	962 793 Feb-Nov	500 mts £26.00 D PL CP DW 5D 1T 2S 1F ALL ES

Sect.	Name and Address	Tel. No. / Fax. No. / Web / Email	Map Reference / Opening Times	Distance from Path / Starting Price / Facilities / Accommodation
78	Mr & Mrs A Clevett 13 Colletts Close CORFE CASTLE Wareham BH20 5HG	01929 480124 01929 480457 amclevett@supanet.com	965 813	7 km PD £30.00 O D CP DW PD 1D 1T[1]
78	Mr D Joseph Kamloops Haycrafts Lane Near Swanage LANGTON MATRAVERS BH19 3EE	01929 439193	983 791	2 km PD £25.00 O D PL CP KT PD 3D[3] Rooms dbl or twin
78	Mrs A Stiles Langton Manor Farmhouse LANGTON MATRAVERS BH19 3EU	01929 421247 alexstyles999@aol.com	003 789	2 km PD £30.00 O D CP LSP KT PD 1F[1]
78	Mr & Mrs A Preston Sunny Bay House 17 Cluny Crescent SWANAGE BH19 2BP	01929 422650 gillgc@aol.com.	031 784 Jan-Oct	200 mts £18.00 O D PL 1D 1T[1] 1F[1]
78	Mrs E Hine Perfick Piece Springfield Road SWANAGE BH19 1HD	O1929 423178 perfick-piece@supanet.com www.perfick-piece.co.uk	028 788	400 mts £16.00 O D EM PL CP 1D 1T 1S 1F[1] EM winter only
78	Mr & Mrs M D Buckley Amberlea 36 Victoria Avenue SWANAGE BH19 1AP	01929 426213 swanage@yahoo.co.uk	026 792	500 mts £19.00 O D EM PL CP 4D 1T 1S 1F ALL ES
78	Mr & Mrs M S Cooper Sunny South 118 Kings Road West SWANAGE BH19 1HS	01929 422665 SunnySouth@btinternet.com www.sunnysouth.btinternet.co.uk	023 790	812 mts £16.00 O D PL KT PD 1D1] 1S/T/D
79	Mrs J Small 11 Durlston Point 78 Park Road SWANAGE BH19 2AE	01929 421717 je.small@virgin.net 1D[1] 1T	033 782	100 mts £20.00 O D EM PL CP LSP KT
79	Ms L Fegan The Limes Hotel SWANAGE BH19 2AE	01929 422664 0870 054 8794 info@limeshotel.demon.co.uk www.limeshotel.demon.co.uk	033783	200 mts £28.00 O D PL CP DW 2D[2] 4T[4] 3S 3F[3]
79	Mrs North The Laurels 60 Britannia Road POOLE BH14 8BB	01202 265861 laurels@fsmail.net thelaurelsbandb.freeservers.com	033 913	1km £23.00 O D CP 1D[1] 1T[1] 1S 1F[1] £25 single occupancy

CAMPSITES

A list of campsites has been prepared in path order.

The following letter code is used;

T	=	Toilets	S	=	Showers
G	=	Grocery Shop	CP	=	Car Parking
LSP	=	Long Stay Parking	LY	=	Laundry
O	=	Open All Year	DW	=	Dogs Welcome
KT	=	Kit Transfer	PD	=	Pick Up/Drop

KT - Kit Transfer. A service being offered by some of our accommodation providers is to transfer your kit to your next accommodation. This could prove useful to you. Naturally a fee may be levied for this service.

PD - Pick Up/Drop. This code appears following the distance from the path and denotes a facility whereby your host is prepared to collect and return you to the coast path within reasonable distance. No fee should be charged for this service.

Distance from Path. Please remember these are only approximate and may not be accurate.

The part of the address in CAPITALS is an aid to location; it does not signify the postal town. The extreme left-hand column refers to the appropriate section in the 'Trail Description'; we feel it may help you to find addresses quickly. The amount quoted gives an **indication of the starting rate** per night, and may well rise. If working on a tight budget, it is best to ask first.

Individuals - but we stress **not parties** - usually find no problem in obtaining leave to camp away from official camp sites if they request permission to do so. In fact, our correspondence has many examples of extra kindnesses extended by farmers and others to campers. We would, however, very much emphasize the requesting of permission first. It would be so easy for the thoughtlessness of a few to undo the good relationships of many others built up over some years.

This list is thin in many areas. Suggestions for inclusions in future lists will always be welcome. Information of any new sites should be addressed to the Administrator.

Sect.	Name and Address	Tel. No. Fax. No. Web / Email	Map Ref. Distance from Path	Facilities Starting Price Opening Times
1	Mr P R Weaver Sparkhayes Farm Camp Site Sparkhayes Lane PORLOCK TA24 8NE	01643 862470 01643 862470	446 469 on path	T S LY G CP LSP DW KT £4.50 Apr to Oct
3	Mr & Mrs T Greenaway Newberry Farm Touring Caravans & Camping Woodlands COMBE MARTIN EX34 OAT	01271 882334 01271 882880 enq@newberrycampsite.co.uk www.newberrycampsite.co.uk	574 470 200 mts	T S LY £7.00 Easter - End Oct
3	Mr M Richards Napps Campsite Old Coast Road BERRYNARBOR EX34 9SW	01271 882557 as phone bookings@napps.fsnet.co.uk www.napps.co.uk	565 475 on path	T S LY G CP LSP DW KT PD £6.00 No PD high season, pool & café
3	Mrs M Malin Mill Park Campsite Mill Lane BERRYNARBOR EX34 9SH	01271 882647 01271 882667 millpark@globalnet.co.uk www.millpark.co.uk	558 470 500 mts	T S LY G CP LSP DW £6.00
4	Mr & Mrs D S Dovey Hele Valley Holiday Park HELE BAY Ilfracombe EX34 9RD	01271 862460 01271 867926 holidays@helevalley.co.uk www.helevalley.co.uk	533 472 600 mts	T S LY DW £8.00 Apr-Oct S/C Cottage and Static Caravans also avail.
4	Mr D L Wassell Big Meadow Camp Site WATERMOUTH Ilfracombe EX34 9SJ	01271 862282 www.big-meadow.co.uk	558 483 On path	T S LY G CP LSP DW £3.00 Easter-Oct
4	Mr N Barten Little Meadow Campsite Lydford Farm WATERMOUTH Near Ilfracombe EX34 9SJ	01271 866862 info@littlemeadow.co.uk www.littlemeadow.co.uk	554 479 250 mts	T S G CP LSP DW £4.50
4	Mr & Mrs M Fletcher Hidden Valley Park WEST DOWN Nr Ilfracombe EX34 8NU	01271 813837 01271 814041 relax@hiddenvalleypark.com www.hiddenvalleypark.com	180 133 6 km	OT S LY G CP LSP DW £6.00
6	Mr P Richards Easewell Holiday Parc Mortehoe Road MORTEHOE EX34 7EH	01271 870343 01271 870089 goodtimes@woolacombe.com www.woolacombe.com	465 454 1 km	T S LY G DW £4.00
6	Mr & Mrs B Gilbert North Morte Farm Campsite MORTEHOE EX34 7EG	01271 870381 01271 870115 holidays@northmortefarm.co.uk www.northmortefarm.co.uk	459 455 500 mts	T S LY G CP DW £4.50
7	Mr S Malin Little Roadway Farm Camping Park WOOLACOMBE EX34 7HL	472 425 01271 870313	T S CP LSP DW 500 mts	 £7.00
7	Mr P Richards Golden Coast Holiday Village Station Road WOOLACOMBE EX34 7HW	01271 870343 01271 870089 goodtimes@woolacombe.com www.woolacombe.com	480 435 800 mts	OT S LY G £4.00

Sect.	Name and Address	Tel. No. Fax. No. Web / Email	Map Ref. Distance from Path	Facilities Starting Price Opening Times
7	Mr P Richards Twitchen Holiday Parc Mortehoe Road WOOLACOMBE EX34 7AS	01271 870343 01271 870089 goodtimes@woolacombe.com www.woolacombe.com	470 437 500 mts	T S LY G DW £4.00
7	Mr P Richards Woolacombe Bay Holiday Village Sandy Lane WOOLACOMBE EX34 7AH	01271 870343 01271 870089 goodtimes@woolacombe.com www.woolacombe.com	467 441 1 km	T S LY G DW £4.00
7	Lobb Field Caravan & Camping Park Saunton Road BRAUNTON EX33 1EB	01271 812090 as phone info@lobbfields.com www.lobbfields.com	475 378 1600 mts	T S LY DW CP £5.00
7	Mr G Ingleby Myrtle Moor Lane CROYDE EX33 1NN	01271 890233 guy@croydebay.co.uk www.croydebay.co.uk	442 394 500 mts	T S CP LSP £7.90 28-31 May; 18-20 June; July weekends
8	Mrs S Massey Chivenor Cross Caravan Park BARNSTAPLE EX31 4BN	01271 812217 01271 812644 chivenorcp@lineone.net chivenorcaravanpark.com	505 350 100 mts 15 Mar-15 Nov	T S LY G DW £6.50
8	Mr D Fry Midland Holiday Park Braunton Road Ashford BARNSTAPLE EX31 4AU	01271 343691 01271 326355 enquiries@midlandpark.co.uk www.midlandpark.co.uk	533 346 1.6 kms Mar-Nov	O T S LY G CP DW £5.50
8	Mr G Ingleby Mitchums Meadow Campsite Heanton Farm Heanton Punchardon BARNSTAPLE EX31 4DQ	01271 890233 guy@croydebay.co.uk www.croydebay.co.uk	501356 on path	T S CP LSP £7.90
10	Mr & Mrs R Croslegh Steart Farm Touring Park HORNS CROSS Bideford EX39 5DW	01237 431836 as phone steart@tiscali.co.uk	356 229 1 km Easter-30 Sept	T S LY CP LSP DW £3.00
11	Mrs H Davey Stoke Barton Farm STOKE Hartland EX39 6DU	01237 441238	234 246 700 mts	T S CP LSP DW KT £3.50 Easter - End Sept Tearoom on site
11	Mrs L Allin Hartland Caravan & Camping Park South Lane HARTLAND Bideford EX39 6DG	01237 441242 01237 441034	263 243 2.5 km	O T S G CP LSP DW KT PD £4.00
12	Mr & Mrs J M Cloke Upper Lynstone Camping & Caravan Park BUDE EX23 0LP	01288 352017 01288 359034 reception@upperlynstone.co.uk www.upperlynstone.co.uk	205 053 100 mts	T S LY G CP DW £7.50 Easter - Oct Shop end May - mid Sept

Sect.	Name and Address	Tel. No. Fax. No. Web / Email	Map Ref. Distance from Path	Facilities Starting Price Opening Times
12	Mr S Everett Northshore Bude 57 Killerton Road BUDE EX23 8EW	01288 354256 northshorebude@aol.com www.northshorebude.com	214 061 1km PD	O D CP LSP PD £12.00 Also B&B
13	Mrs J Onions Coxford Meadow St Gennys CRACKINGTON HAVEN EX23 0NS	01840 230707 01840 230451	161 967 1 km	T S CP LSP DW £3.50 Easter - Oct
13	Mrs S Weller Hentervene Camping & Caravan Park CRACKINGTON HAVEN EX23 0LF	01840 230365 contact@hentervene.co.uk www.hentervene.co.uk	155 944 3.2 km PD	T S LY CP LSP DW PD £4.30 Open All Year
17	Mrs R Harris South Winds Camping & Caravan Park POLZEATH PL27 6QU	01208 863267 01208 862080 www.rockinfo.co.uk	948 790 on path	T S LY CP LSP DW £12.00 Mar to Sept
17	Mr R Harris Tristram Caravan & Camping Park POLZEATH PL27 6UG	01208 862215 01208 862080 www.rockinfo.co.uk	948 790 On path	T S LY CP LSP DW £15.00 Mar to Nov
18	Mr D Zeal Dennis Cove Camping Dennis Cove PADSTOW PL28 8DR	01841 532349 denniscove@freeuk.com www.denniscove.co.uk	920 745 500 mts	T S LY CP DW £6.50 Apr - Sept
20	Carnevas Farm Holiday Park PORTHCOTHAN BAY PL28 8PN	01841 520230 as phone	862 728 800 mts	T S LY G CP DW £6.50 1 Apr to 31 Oct Price based on 2 people
21	Mr K Stringer Original Backpackers 16 Beachfield Avenue TOWAN BEACH Newquay TR7 1DR	01637 874668 www.originalbackpackers.com	809 616 100 mts	O D DW £8.00
24	Ms J. Sawle Beacon Cottage Farm Touring Park Beacon Drive ST AGNES TR5 ONU	01872 552347/553381 beaconcottagefarm@lineone.net www.beaconcottagefarmholiday.co.uk	705 505 400 mts	T S G CP DW £6.00 Apr to oct Mobile 07879 413862
25	Mr J Barrow Rosehill Touring Park PORTHTOWAN Truro TR4 8AR	01209 890802 reception@rosehillcamping.co.uk www.rosehillcamping.co.uk	693 473 800 mts	T S LY G CP £7.50 Apr-End Oct
26	Mr H Williams & Son Magor Farm Caravan Site TEHIDY Camborne TR14 0JF	01209 713367 www.magorfarm.co.uk	632 427 1200 mts	T S LY CP LSP DW £6.00 Apr - Oct
27	Mr B Frost Gwithian Farm Camping & Caravan Park GWITHIAN Hayle TR27 5BX	01736 753127 as phone	586 412 500 mts	T S LY G CP LSP DW KT £6.00 Also open Easter

Sect.	Name and Address	Tel. No. Fax. No. Web / Email	Map Ref. Distance from Path	Facilities Starting Price Opening Times
28	Mr R Smith St Ives Backpackers The Gallery ST IVES TR26 1SG	01736 799444 stives@backpackers.co.uk www.backpackers.co.uk	516 404 100 mts	O D £10.00
29	Mr R Osborne Trevalgan Holiday Farm ST IVES TR26 3BJ	01736 796433 01736 799798 trevalgan@aol.com www.trevalganholidayfarm.co.uk	490 402 400 mts	T S LY G CP LSP DW £7.00 1 May to 30 Sept
28	Miss K Sharps Ayr Holiday Park ST IVES TR26 1EJ	01736 795855 01736b 798797 kerry@ayrholidaypark.co.uk	511 405 350 mts	O T S LY DW £8.50
30	Mr J Boyns Levant House Camp Site TREWELLARD Pendeen TR19 7SX	01736 788795	375 337 500 mts	T S CP DW £2.50 1 Apr to 31 Oct
30	Mr E J Coak The North Inn PENDEEN TR19 7DN	01736 788417 ernestjohncoak@aol.com	383 344 2 km PD	O T S G CP LSP DW KT PD £3.50 Also B&B
30	Mr & Mrs P Whitelock The Old Chapel Backpackers Hostel ZENNOR TR26 3BY	01736 798307 As Phone zennorbackpackers@btinternet.com www.backpackers.co.uk	455 385 500mtrs	O T S LY CP LSP £10.00 Open All Year. Winter by
30	Mrs W Nicholas Trevedra Farm Caravan & Campsite SENNEN TR19 7BE	01736 871835	368 279 1 km	T S LY G CP LSP DW KT PD £3.50 KT & PD low season only. Path to campsite from Gwenver Beach
31	Mr S Edwards Kelynack Caravan & Camping Park KELYNACK Penzance TR19 7RE	01736 787633 As Phone steve@kelynackholidays.co.uk www.ukparks.co.uk/kelynack	372 301 1.5 km PD	T S LY G CP LSP DW PD £3.50 Bunk Barn also avail from £7 pppn DW camping only
30	Mr P Eachus Trevaylor Camp Site BOTALLACK Penzance TR19 7PU	01736 787016 bookings@trevaylor.com www.trevaylor.com	370 328 500 mts	T S LY G DW £8.00 Apr to Oct
31	Mr T Ellison Whitesands Lodge Lands End Backpackers SENNEN TR19 7AR	01736 871776 As Phone info@whitesandslodge.co.uk www.whitesandlodge.co.uk	366 264 400 mts	O T S LY CP LSP DW KTPD £6.50 Open All Year
33	Mr J Hall Treen Campsite TREEN Nr Penzance TR19 6LF	01736 810526	392 228 100 mts	O T S G CP LSP DW £5.00 end Mar - end Oct
33	Mrs H Gwennap Treverven Camp Site Treverven Farm ST LOYE St Buryan TR19 6DG	01736 810200 as phone www,drycor.co.uk/camping/treverven	419 245 800 mts	T S LY G CP LSP DW £6.50

Sect.	Name and Address	Tel. No. Fax. No. Web / Email	Map Ref. Distance from Path	Facilities Starting Price Opening Times
35	Mr R Halling Penzance Backpackers Blue Dolphin PENZANCE TR18 4LZ	01736 363836 01736 363844 pzbackpack@ndirect.co.uk www.penzancebackpackers.ndirect.co.uk	467 299 400 mts	D £10.00
38	Mr A B Thomas Tenerife Farm Caravan & Camping Park Predannack MULLION TR12 7EZ	01326 240293 as phone	672 166 800 mts	T S LY LSP DW £6.50 Easter to Oct
39	Mr & Mrs R H Lyne Henry's Campsite Caerthillian Farm THE LIZARD TR12 7NX	01326 290596	125 701 500 mts PD	O T S CP LSP DW KT PD £4.00 Open all year
40	Mr & Mrs B Fagan Chycarne Holiday Park KUGGAR Ruan Minor Helston TR12 7LX	01326 290200 01326 290854 kennacksands@ukonline.co.uk	725 163 200 mts	T S LY G CP LSP DW £3.50
40	Mr & Mrs C W Pullinger Silver Sands Holiday Park Gwendreath KENNACK SANDS Ruan Minor, Helston TR12 7LZ	01326 290631 As Phone enquiries@silversandsholidaypark.co.uk www.silversandsholidaypark.co.uk	729 169 1km	T S LY CP DW £8.00 May to Sept
40	Mr T Gibson Gwendreath Farm Caravan Park KENNACK SANDS Helston TR12 7LZ	01326 290666 tom.gibson@virgin.net www.tomandlinda.co.uk	729 168 1km	T S LY G CP DW £4.50 Easter to Oct
41	Mr B Roskilly Penmarth Farm Caravan Site COVERACK TR12 6SB	01326 280389	782 176 30 mts	T S LY G CP LSP DW £0.00
40	Mrs M Mita Little Trevothan Caravan & Camping Park COVERACK TR12 6SD	01326 280260 As Phone mmita@btopenworld.com www.littletrevothan.com	770 180	T S LY G CP DW 1000 mts £6.50 Apr-Oct
42	Mr & Mrs A J Jewell Pennance Mill Farm Chalet & Camping MAENPORTH Falmouth TR11 5HJ	01326 312616 www.pennancemill.co.uk	791 307 800 mts	T S LY G CP LSP DW £5.00 Easter to Oct
42	Mrs F Harris Tregedna Farm MAEN PORTH Falmouth TR11 5HL	01326 250529	784 304 700 mts	T S LY CP LSP DW £4.00
43	Ms C Mitchell Falmouth Lodge Backpackers 9 Gyllyngvase Terrace FALMOUTH TR11 4DL	01326 319996 charlotte@mitchell999fsworld.com falmouthbackpackers.co.uk	811 319 100 mts	O D CP £12.00
45	Mr & Mrs V Barry Treloan Coastal Farm PORTSCATHO Truro TR2 5EF	01872 580989/99 01872 580989 holidays@treloan.freeserve.co.uk www.coastalfarmholidays.co.uk	874 348 300 mts PD	O T S LY CP LSP DW KT PD £6.00 Camping Barn available

Sect.	Name and Address	Tel. No. Fax. No. Web / Email	Map Ref. Distance from Path	Facilities Starting Price Opening Times
47	Dr J Whetter Trelispen Camping Park GORRAN HAVEN PL26 6NR	01726 843501 As Phone trelispen@care4free.net	005 421 750 mts Apr to Oct	T S LY CP DW £7.00 £20 high season
47	Mrs J McIntosh Journeys End Cottage EAST PORTHOLLAND Gorran St Austell PL26 6NA	01872 501955 juliamcintosh@yahoo.co.uk	961 411 on path	O T CP LSP DW £10.00 Summerhouse accommodation also available (Double)
52	National Trust Highertown Farm LANSALLOS C/O S & E Cornwall Office Lanhydrock, Bodmin PL30 4DE	01208 265211 jane.davey@nationaltrust.org.uk www.nationaltrust.org.uk	172 517 350 mts	T S CP DW £2.50 Contact National Trust local office at Lanhydrock
53	Mr A J Davey Camping Caradon Park Trelawne LOOE PL13 2NA	01503 272388 As Phone rachel@campingcaradon.fsnet.co.uk www.campingcaradon.co.uk	542 218 2.4 km	T S LY G CP LSP DW £6.50
53	Mr & Mrs R Haywood Talland Caravan Park TALLAND BAY Nr Looe PL13 2JA	01503 272715 01503 272224 www.tallandcaravanpark.co.uk	515 234 100 mts Apr-Oct	T S LY G CP LSP DW £5.00
54	Mr M Pickles Carbeil Caravan Park Treliddon Lane DOWNDERRY PL11 3LS	01503 250636 mark@picklesm.freeserve.co.uk www.carbeilholidaypark.co.uk	317 543 500 mts	T S LY GCP DW £5.00
56	Mr J Lovell Plymouth Backpackers Hotel 172 Citadel Road PLYMOUTH PL1 3BD	01752 225158 01752 207847 plymouthback@hotmail.com www.plymouthbackpackers.co.uk	473 540 on path	O D £10.00 Also 1 female En Suite Dorm sleeps 6
58	Mr J Tucker Mount Folly Farm BIGBURY ON SEA TQ7 4AR	01548 810267 as phone	661 447 on path	O T CP LSP DW £4.00 Open All Year
60	Mrs S M Squire Higher Rew Camping Park MALBOROUGH Kingsbridge TQ7 3DW	01548 842681 01548 843681 enquiries@higherrew.co.uk www.higherrew.co.uk	714 382 1.5 km	T S LY G CP DW £7.00 Easter-End Oct
60	Mrs F Stidston Bolberry House Farm Caravan & Camping Park BOLBERRY Nr Kingsbridge TQ7 3DY	01548 561251 as phone bolberry.house@virgin.net www.bolberryparks.co.uk	690 390 850 mts	T S LY G CP DW
60	Mr & Mrs B Sweetman Sun Park Caravan & Camping SOAR MILL COVE Nr Salcombe TQ7 3DS	01548 561378 As Phone sul-park.co.uk	708 378 1200 mts Easter - Sept	T S LY DW £8.00

Sect.	Name and Address	Tel. No. Fax. No. Web / Email	Map Ref. Distance from Path	Facilities Starting Price Opening Times
61	Mrs L Raeburn Malston Barton Sherford NEAR TORCROSS TQ7 2BB	01548 531794 01548 531694 david.raeburn@farmersweekly.net	774 452 5 km PD	O T S LY CP LSP KT PD £7.50 breakfast available £2.50; evening meal £7.50 B&B available
62	Mr P Keane Deer Park Dartmouth Road STOKE FLEMING TQ6 0RF	01803 770253 peter.keane@talk21.com www.deerparkinn.co.uk	864 491 1 km	T S LY CP DW £8.50 price based on 2 people
63	Mrs J Hosking Upton Manor Farm Camping St Mary's Road BRIXHAM TQ5 9QH	01803 882384 uptoncamp@aol.com www.uptonmanorfarm.co.uk	549 926 650 mts	T S LY G CP LSP DW £4.00 Spring Bank Hol to Mid Sept
64	Marine Park Holiday Centre Grange Road PAIGNTON TQ4 7JR	01803 843887 01803 845427 info@beverley-holidays.co.uk www.beverley-holidays.co.uk	888 587 1km	T S LY CP £9.50 EASTER-OCT
64	Beverley Park Holiday Park Goodrington Road PAIGNTON TQ4 7JE	888 588 01803 843887 01803 845427 info@beverley-holidays.co.uk www.beverley-holidays.co.uk	T S LY G CP 1.2 km Mar - Oct	£9.50
64	Mrs K Wedd Byslades Camping Park Totnes Road PAIGNTON TQ4 7PY	01803 555072 01803 555669 info@byslades.co.uk www.bysladestouringpark.co.uk	853 603 4 kms	T S LY G CP DW £6.00 No DW 19 Jul-1 Sept
65	Mrs J Hodgson Torquay Backpackers 119 Abbey Road TORQUAY TQ2 5NP	01803 299924 jane@torquaybackpackers.co.uk www.torquaybackpackers.co.uk	914 644 1 km	O D CP DW £9.00
66	Mrs M Jones Ladys Mile Holiday Park Week Lane Exeter Road DAWLISH WARREN EX7 0LX	01626 863411 01626 888689 info@ladysmile.co.uk www.ladysmile.co.uk	966 784 500 mts	O T S LY G DW £10.50
67	The National Trust Prattshayes Farmhouse LITTLEHAM Exmouth EX8 5DG	01395 276626 as phone	025 807 1.5 km	T S CP DW £4.00 Also open Spring Bank Holiday
68	Mr A Franks Oakdown Caravan Park Weston SIDMOUTH EX10 0PH	01297 680387 01297 680541 oakdown@btinternet.com www.bestcaravanpark.co.uk	167 902 2 km Apr to Oct	T S LY CP DW £9.00
69	Mr D. Boyce Salcombe Regis Caravan & Camping Park SALCOMBE REGIS Sidmouth EX10 0JH	01395 514303 as phone info@salcombe-regis.co.uk www.salcombe-regis.co.uk	151 892 1.5 km	T S LY G CP DW £7.85 15 Apr - 28 Oct

Sect.	Name and Address	Tel. No. Fax. No. Web / Email	Map Ref. Distance from Path	Facilities Starting Price Opening Times
69	Mr J M Salter Manor Farm Camping & Caravan Site Seaton Down Hill SEATON EX12 2JA	01297 21524	236 908 1km	T S LY CP DW £10.00 15 Mar to 31 Oct
69	Mr R K Webber Axmouth Camping Site Axe Farm SEATON EX12 4BG	01297 24707 axe.farm@ic24.net www.axefarm.co.uk	256 911 1 km	T S G CP DW £5.00 Mid Mar-Mid Oct
70	Mr & Mrs A Morgan Hook Farm Caravan & Camping Park Hook Farm Gore Lane UPLYME DT7 3UU	01297 442801 01297 442801 information@btconnect.com www.hookfarm-uplyme.co.uk	323 929 1.5 km	O T S LY G CP LSP DW £5.90 Open all Year
71	Mr R Loosmore Manor Farm Holiday Centre CHARMOUTH DT6 6QL	01297 560226 enq@manorfarmholidaycentre.co.uk www.manorfarmholidaycentre.co.uk	368 937 500 mts	O T S LY G CP LSP DW £8.00 Open All Year
71	Mrs J Ireland Newlands Camping Park CHARMOUTH DT6 6RB	01297 560259 01297 560787 enq@newlandsholidays.co.uk www.newlandsholidays.co.uk	373 935 500 mts	O T S LY G DW £10.00 Open All Year
73	Mr R Condliffe Freshwater Beach Holiday Park BURTON BRADSTOCK Nr Bridport DT6 4PT	01308 897317 01308 897336 enquiries@freshwaterbeach.co.uk www.freshwaterbeach.co.uk	898 479 200 mts	T S LY G CP DW £7.50 17 Mar - 12 Nov
74	Ms N Coombe Sea Barn Farm FLEET Weymouth DT3 4ED	01305 782218 01305 775396 wib@seabarn.fsnet.co.uk www.seabarnfarm.co.uk	619 807 400 mts	T S LY G CP LSP DW £9.00
74	Ms N Coombe West Fleet Holiday Farm FLEET Weymouth DT3 4EF	01305 782218 01305 775396 wib@seabarn.fsnet.co.uk www.westfleetholidays.co.uk	623 810 1200 mts	T S LY G CP LSP DW £10.00
78	Mr & Mrs J Wootton Toms Field Campsite & Shop Toms Field Road SWANAGE BH19 3HN	01929 427110 As Phone tomsfield@hotmail.com www.tomsfieldcamping.co.uk	995 785 1.5 km	T S LY G CP LSP DW £7.50 Mid Mar to Oct Bunk Barn also avail open all year £7
78	Mrs J M Scadden Ulwell Cottage Caravan Park ULWELL Swanage BH19 3DG	01929 422823 01929 421500 enq@ulwellcottagepark.co.uk www.ulwellcottagepark.co.uk	022 807 3 km	T S LY G CP DW 1 Mar - 7 Jan

YOUTH HOSTEL ASSOCIATION

There is an amazing variety of youth Hostels along the South West Coast Path, 20 in total and all offering comfortable, friendly accommodation. Prices start from £7.00 (U18) £10.25 (Adult) per night, including bed linen, the use of self-catering kitchens, drying rooms and cycle sheds. The YHA is a membership organisation, however non-members are welcome to join on arrival at the hostel. Membership enables you to take advantage of the 5000 Youth Hostels world wide, regular member's magazine 'Triangle', annual YHA Accommodation Guides and discounts at YHA Adventure Shops and local tourist attractions. YHA annual membership costs are currently: Under 18 - £6.75, adult - £13.50 and family (2 adults & 2 children) - £27.00. The meals are excellent value, at around £3.50 for breakfast, Packed Lunches £3.10 to £4.00 and 3 Course Evening Meals £5.10.

Book directly with the Youth Hostel of your choice of for further assistance, please contact YHA Customer Services, Tel: 0870 770 8868, or why not visit their website at www.YHA.org.uk

YHA, Trevelyan House, Dimple Road, Matlock, Derbyshire, DE4 3YH.
E.mail: customerservices@yha.co.uk.

YOUTH HOSTELS

Minehead Youth Hostel Alcombe Combe	MINEHEAD	TA24 6EW	Phone:0870 770 5968	Grid Ref: 973 442	
Lynton Youth Hostel Lynbridge	LYNTON	EX35 6AZ	Phone:0870 770 5942	Grid Ref: 720 487	
Elmscott Youth Hostel Hartland	HARTLAND	EX39 6ES	Phone:0870 770 5814	Grid Ref: 231 217	Self Catering Only
Boscastle Youth Hostel Palace Stables	BOSCASTLE	PL35 0HD	Phone:0870 770 5710	Grid Ref: 096 915	
Tintagel Youth Hostel Dunderhole Point	TINTAGEL	PL34 0DW	Phone:0870 770 6068	Grid Ref: 047 881	Self Catering Only
Treyarnon Bay Youth Tregonnan Treyarnon	PADSTOW	PL28 8JR	Phone:0870 770 6076	Grid Ref: 859 741	
Perranporth Youth Hostel Droskyn Point	PERRANPORTH	TR6 0GS	Phone:0870 770 5994	Grid Ref: 752 544	Self Catering Only
Land's End Youth Hostel Letcha Vean	ST JUST	TR19 7NT	Phone:0870 770 5906	Grid Ref: 364 305	
Penzance Youth Hostel Castle Horneck, Alverton	PENZANCE	TR20 8TF	Phone:0870 770 5992	Grid Ref: 457 302	
Coverack Youth Hostel Park Behan, School Hill	HELSTON	TR12 6SA	Phone:0870 770 5780	Grid Ref: 782 184	
Boswinger Youth Hostel Boswinger	GORRAN	PL26 6LL	Phone:0870 770 5712	Grid Ref: 991 411	
Golant Youth Hostel Penquite House, Golant	FOWEY	PL23 1LA	Phone:0870 770 5832	Grid Ref: 116 556	
Salcombe Youth Hostel Sharpitor	SALCOMBE	TQ8 8LW	Phone:0870 770 6016	Grid Ref: 728 374	
Maypool Youth Hostel Maypool House, Galmpton	BRIXHAM	TQ5 0ET	Phone:0870 770 5962	Grid Ref: 877 546	
Exeter Youth Hostel 47 Countess Wear Road	EXETER	EX2 6LR	Phone:0870 770 5826	Grid Ref: 942 897	
Beer Youth Hostel Bovey Combe, Townsend	SEATON	EX12 3LL	Phone:0870 770 5690	Grid Ref: 223 896	
Litton Cheney Youth Litton Cheney	DORCHESTER	DT2 9AT	Phone:0870 770 5922	Grid Ref: 548 900	Self Catering Only
Lulworth Cove Youth School Lane	WEST LULWORTH	BH20 5SA	Phone:0870 770 5940	Grid Ref: 832 806	
Portland Youth Hostel Hardy House, Castletown	PORTLAND	DT5 1BJ	Phone:0870 770 6000	Grid Ref: 685741	Self Catering Only
Swanage Youth Hostel Cluny Crescent	SWANAGE	BH19 2BS	Phone:0870 770 6058	Grid Ref: 031 785	

TOURIST INFORMATION CENTRES

MINEHEAD	17 Friday Street		TA24 5UB	Phone: 01643 702624	Fax: 01643 707166
LYNTON	Town Hall	Lee Road	EX35 6BT	Phone: 0845 660 3232	Fax: 01598 752755
COMBE MARTIN	Sea Cottage	Cross Street	EX34 0DH	Phone: 01271 883319	Fax: 01271 883319
ILFRACOMBE	The Landmark	The Sea Front	EX34 9BX	Phone: 01271 863001	Fax: 01271 862586
WOOLACOMBE	The Esplanade		EX34 7DL	Phone: 01271 870553	
BRAUNTON	The Bakehouse Centre	Caen Street	EX33 1AA	Phone: 01271 816400	Fax: 01271 816947
BARNSTAPLE	36 Boutport Street		EX31 1RX	Phone: 01271 375000	Fax: 01271 374037
BIDEFORD	Victoria Park	The Quay	EX39 2QQ	Phone: 01237 477676	Fax: 01237 421853
BUDE	Visitor Centre	The Crescent	EX23 8LE	Phone: 01288 354240	Fax: 01288 355769
PADSTOW	Red Brick Building	North Quay	PL28 8AF	Phone: 01841 533449	Fax: 01841 532356
NEWQUAY	Municipal Offices	Marcus Hill	TR7 1BD	Phone: 01637 854020	Fax: 01637 854030
PENZANCE	Station Road		TR18 2NF	Phone: 01736 362207	
FALMOUTH	28 Killigrew Street		TR11 3PN	Phone: 01326 312300	Fax: 01326 313457
FOWEY	4 Custom Hill House		PL23 1AB	Phone: 01726 833616	Fax: 01726 833616
ST IVES	The Guildhall	Street an Pol	TR26 2DS	Phone: 01736 796297	Fax: 01736 798309
LOOE	The Guildhall	Fore Street	PL13 1AA	Phone: 01503 262072	Fax: 01503 265426
PLYMOUTH	Island House	9 The Barbican	PL1 2LS	Phone: 01752 304849	Fax: 01752 257955
IVYBRIDGE	Leonards Road		PL21 0SL	Phone: 01752 897035	Fax: 01752 690660
SALCOMBE	Council Hall	Market Street	TQ8 8DE	Phone: 01548 843927	Fax: 01548 842736
DARTMOUTH	The Engine House	Mayors Avenue	TQ6 9YY	Phone: 01803 834224	Fax: 01803 835631
KINGSBRIDGE	The Quay		TQ7 1HS	Phone: 01548 853195	Fax: 01548 854185
BRIXHAM	The Old Market House	The Quay	TQ5 8TB	Phone: 01803 852861	Fax: 01803 852939
TORQUAY	Vaughan Parade		TQ2 5JG	Phone: 01803 297428	Fax: 01803 214885
PAIGNTON	The Esplanade		TQ4 6ED	Phone: 01803 558383	Fax: 01803 551959
TEIGNMOUTH	The Den	Sea Front	TQ14 8BE	Phone: 01626 215666	Fax: 01626 778333
DAWLISH	The Lawn		EX7 9EL	Phone: 01626 215665	Fax: 01626 865985
EXMOUTH	Alexandra Terrace		EX8 1NZ	Phone: 01395 222299	Fax: 01395 269911
BUDLEIGH SALTER	Fore Street		EX9 6NG	Phone: 01395 445275	Fax: 01395 442208
SIDMOUTH	Ham Lane		EX10 8XR	Phone: 01395 516441	Fax: 01395 519333
SEATON	The Underfleet		EX12 2TB	Phone: 01297 21660	Fax: 01297 21689
LYME REGIS	Guildhall Cottage	Church Street	DT7 3BS	Phone: 01297 442138	Fax: 01297 443773
BRIDPORT	32 South Street		DT6 3NY	Phone: 01308 424901	Fax: 01308 421060
WEYMOUTH	King's Statue	The Esplanade	DT4 7AN	Phone: 01305 785747	Fax: 01305 788092
SWANAGE	The White House	Shore Road	BH19 1LB	Phone: 01929 422885	Fax: 01929 423423
WAREHAM	Trinity Church	South Street	BH20 4LU	Phone: 01929 552740	Fax: 01929 554491
POOLE	Tourism Centre	The Quay	BH15 1BW	Phone: 01202 253253	Fax: 01202 684531

SOUTH WEST COAST PATH ASSOCIATION - HISTORY

We are sometimes asked what we have done and we set out below some of the things in which we have been involved in one way or another. We do as well send a steady flow of reports on path deficiencies, both as regards maintenance and the route of the path to the local authorities and the Countryside Agency.

1973   Official Formation in May.
Attendance Cornish Opening at Newquay.
Comments to Sports Council on proposed Countryside Park at Northam Burrows.
First Information Sheets produced.

1974   Evidence submitted to Mr Yepp for his report to the Countryside Commission on Long Distance Footpaths.
We welcomed Devon N.F.U. representation on our Committee.
Attendance at South Devon and Dorset Opening in September at Beer.
Registration as a Charity.
First Description issued.

1975   Mark Richard's book 'Walking the North Cornwall Coastal Path' published - a work in which we may fairly say we played a part.
Clematon Hill, Bigbury, small new section of Coast Path agreed at SWWA's instigation.
Article on SWW in 'Rucksack'.
Attendance at Opening of so-called Exmoor Coastal Path.
Bideford Public Enquiry - successful opposition to Golf Course on the Coastal Path at Abbotsham.
Hartland Point Success at last in getting path south from Hartland Point over Blagdon and Upright Cliffs. Walk over new Lulworth Range Walk.

1976   First Footpath Guide issued.
Thurlestone Diversion opposed.
Evidence submitted to House of Commons Expenditure Committee Environment sub-committee.
North Cliffs Improvements between Portreath and Hayle secured, thanks to National Trust.
Public Enquiry with R.A. at Kingswear on the section Kellys Cove to Man Sands.
Consulted by Devon County Council on path at Watermouth and Dorset County Council about Abbotsbury.
Goodbye to our first Chairman, Mr Walter - we lose a tower of strength.

1977   SWWA mentioned in the YH. Handbook.
Publications of Letts Guides in three volumes. The first satisfactory books to whole path in which we can say our information helped a little.
Attendance at Coverack Youth Hostel official opening.
Evidence presented to Lord Porchester's Exmoor Study.
Badges produced.
Evidence given to Devon County Council for Taw/Torridge Estuary Survey.

1978   First Printed Footpath guide.
Attendance at Westward Ho! Somerset/North Devon Opening.
Dean Quarry, St Keverne, Cornwall Opposition to diversion.
Pentewan Lack of Path submitted to Local Ombudsman.
Hartland New path seaward of Radar Station obtained, thanks to South West Way Association.

1979   Evidence given at Public Enquiries at Abbotsbury and Lulworth Cove.
Submission to Mr Himsworth for his report on Areas of Outstanding Natural Beauty.
First printed News Letters and Descriptions, and the first illustrated description.
Pine Haven to Port Quin gap submitted to Local Ombudsman.
Assistance to Letts for their Guide reprint.

1980   Result of 1976 Public Enquiry at Kingswear published.
Discussion Dean Quarry, St Keverne, Cornwall.
Dialogues with Countryside Commission about path deficiencies.
Alternative coastal path open Glenthorne Estate, Somerset and we submit proposals for rerouting in Exmoor National Park.
St Loy, Cornwall Special report submitted.
Attendance at Widmouth Head, North Devon, Public Enquiry.
Opinions expressed to Department of Environment on draft 'Wildlife and Countryside Bill'.

1981 Annual Guide 'State of the Path' section improved.
Attendance at second Kingswear Public Enquiry.
Countryside Commission decide that path wardenship will be greatly extended.
Duckpool, North Cornwall Bridge provided.
Path improvements at Watermouth; Braunton to Barnstaple; Dean Quarry; Clematon Hill;
Bigbury; Mothecombe and Maidencombe.

1982 Wardenship of coastal path in Cornwall completed.
Further openings at: Cleave Farm in North Cornwall, Pentewan with its unfortunate
execution and Mount Edgecombe in South Cornwall, Higher Brownstone Farm, Kingswear
and a short section west of Berry Head in South Devon.
Agreement was also reached for a high tide route at Mothecombe in South Devon.
The 1982 Guide incorporates a new `Itinerary Suggested' section.

1983 Opening of the Widmouth Head section in North Devon and a second long section in South
Devon between Kingswear and Man Sands.
Crackington Haven, North Cornwall Major improvements to the Path on the western side.
Cornwall's 10th Anniversary Walk.

1984 **New Section** A new section of the Path opened on the east bank of the mouth of the River
Dart close to Kingswear and giving access to Mill Bay Cove and a splendid stretch of coastal
walking.
Trebarwith Strand to Backways Cove in North Cornwall A coastal route opened.

1985 **Culbone - Foreland Point** The alternative coastal path at the Glenthorne Estate was
waymarked as the official route, which is a great improvement.
Pinehaven - Port Quin (North Cornwall) The new path was opened and is a vast
improvement, although the substantial fence and barbed wire detracts from the scene.

1986 **Minehead to Porlock Weir** New alternative path between North Hill and Hurlstone Point
signposted and waymarked.
Black Head, Cornwall Now purchased by the National Trust.

1987 **Barnstaple/Bideford/Northam** The new route completed along the railway lines and open.
Bude Attendance at Public Enquiry to prevent development adjacent to footpath.
Chynhalls Point Coast path moved to seaward of hotel.
Branscombe Attendance at Public Enquiry to urge true coast path instead of inland
route. Preferred route adopted.
Bidna/Northam Owing to breach in sea wall an acceptable diversion is negotiated.

1988 **Woody Bay to Trentishoe** Devon County Council adopts our recommended, nearer the coast
route as the official coast path.

1989 **Culbone** On site exploration with Countryside Commission and Exmoor National Park
Authority to discover an acceptable alternative to the long unnecessary Culbone diversion.
Chynhalls Cliff On site exploration for a more coastal trail.
Fire Beacon Point/Pentargon Cornwall County Council installs grand new path.
Wembury Attend public meeting at Down Thomas to successfully oppose erection of
locked gates across coast path by Royal Navy.
Strete Gate/Warren Cove Attend public meeting and give evidence to support proposals by
Countryside Commission and Devon County Council for an improved and more true coast
path.

1990 **Membership** Now over 1000.

1991 **Buckator** At our request Cornwall County Council re-route official path around the headland.
Worthy/Culbone On site explorations for a preferable diversion to that proposed by Exmoor
National Park Authority.
Strete Gate/Warren Cove Continuing our strong argument with Devon County Council for
a coast path.
Lyme Regis Continued pleas to Dorset County Council to reinstate the coast path along the
golf course.
We estimate the Coast Path to be about 613 miles (982 km) long.

1992 **Watcombe and Maidencombe** Our recommended route put in by Devon County Council.
Worthygate Wood Our suggested path installed by National Trust.
Commenced discussions with Countryside Commission to examine sections of coast
suitable for 'Set Aside'.

1993 **Foreland Point** Successful opposition to an application to close path on west side.
Buck's Mills Success with our request for a coast path avoiding the holiday complex.
Port Quin Our suggested path is installed by National Trust.
Write and produce the `trail description' in this book the 'Other Way Round'.

1994 Invited by the Countryside Commission to become a member of the South West Coast Path Steering Group to review the management of our coast path.
Association acquires a computer.

1995 Membership reaches 2000
Culbone section re-opened by Exmoor National Park.
Strete Gate/Warren Point - continuous pressure causes Devon County Council to explore again for a route that will provide an acceptable coast path.
Continuing involvement in the 'Coast Path Project'.
Association details on the Internet. See Web address on page 2.

1996 Path descriptions for the whole SWW written and printed.
Continuing involvement in the coast path project and production of the strategy document.
Lyme Regis - Golf Course Route reinstated by Dorset County Council.
Strete Gate/Warren Point - Devon County Council decides to install our preferred route but rejected by Countryside Commission.

1997 **Red River at Gwithian** A new footbridge put in by Cornwall County Council.
The SWCP Project published its strategy for the future management of the coast path.
The Association becomes a member of the SWCP Management Group.

1998 Our Silver Jubilee Year (25 years old). Application made, jointly with R.A. to Minister for the Environment requesting he use his powers to create a coast path between Strete Gate and Warren Point. Application refused.
Mountbatten Point, Plymouth opened as a coast path.
Jennycliff Plymouth City Council installs an off-road coast path.
South West Way Association launches its Silver Jubilee Appeal to raise funds towards markers at each end of the coast path.
South West Way Association produces a Development Plan for the next three years.

1999 Name changed to South West Coast Path Association.
Membership Secretary becomes known as Administrator.
Publications Officer appointed.
Continued involvement with celebratory markers at each end of the coast path.
A history of the coast path written and published.

2000 Global Positioning reveals the length of the coast path (1014 km - 630 miles) - it is Britain's only National Trail to exceed 1000 km.
Strete Gate / Warren Point - South West Coast Path Team undertakes a complete review of this section.
St German's Beacon - progress made in realising an acceptable coast path.
Crock Pits - Exmoor National Park installs a coastal route sought by us for many years.
Revised Path Descriptions now produced in-house.

2001 Eight Winter Cliff Falls Disrupt Line of Dorset coast path.
Celebratory marker installed at Minehead.
Whole coast path Closed for 3 months due to Foot and Mouth Crisis.
Introduction of Credit Card facilities for members.
11 August - Whole coast path walked on one day by Association members to celebrate the re-opening of the coast path.
Countryside Agency Board accept the review by the South West Coast Path Team that recommends vital coast path realignments between Strete Gate and Stoke Fleming.

2002 Introduction of Direct Debit facility.
Celebratory marker installed at South Haven Point.
St German's Beacon - True coastal route installed between Downderry & Portwrinkle.
Annual Award given to Chris Monk and his team at Cornwall County Council for their work on the new path at St German's Beacon.

2003   **South West Coast Path Association** is 30 years of age.

Easter Saturday - Association arranges 'Walk the whole path in one day' to celebrate the 25th anniversary of the official inclusion of the Somerset and North Devon sections into the South West Coast Path. The 70 sections all had walkers, 668 took part.

3000th Member – Rebecca Emery aged 13 years of Penzance

Youngest Yet – we receive news that Sarah Britton and Anna Radford, both aged 11, have completed the whole coast path.

Chynhalls Cliff – South West Coast Path Association's desired realignment is installed by Cornwall County Council.

Strete Gate to Warren Point – Countryside Agency accepts and agrees to fund the negotiated realignment.

Isle of Portland – Countryside Agency accepts the route around the Island.

Tregantle Cliff – South West Coast Path Association's desired realignment throughout the rifle ranges is installed by the MOD as a permissive path. As a result of this improvement, we award the MOD our Annual Award.

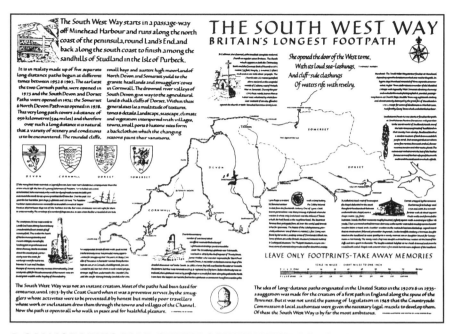

A CALLIGRAPHIC MAP OF THE SOUTH WEST COAST PATH

This quality produced calligraphic map of the South West Coast Path, Britain's longest footpath was designed, illustrated and written by James Skinner of Gloucester. He is a keen rambler and member of a number of walking organisations including the South West Coast Path Association, the Backpackers' Club and the Ramblers' Association.

James, and his wife Linda have spent many holidays walking the coast path - experiencing at first hand the incredible diversity of scenery. The South West Coast Path passes through five areas of outstanding natural beauty, numerous heritage coasts, through wild isolated countryside, across high cliffs and wide estuaries - yet touching small villages, towns and popular resorts.

The printed calligraphic map has been written entirely by hand complemented by fine pen and ink drawings illustrating many of the sights to be found whilst walking the path.

The **COLOUR** indicating the relief of the peninsular was achieved through using professional quality colour pencils. James has been interested in calligraphy since the mid 1980s when he attended a local summer school. More recently he has completed a full-time professional course in Calligraphy and Book-binding at Digby Stuart College, London. At present, James teaches the craft to adults at a variety of centres in his home county and the South West of England. This calligraphic map would make a superb gift, or an ideal memento for anyone having walked part or all of the path.

For every map ordered a donation will be made to the South West Coast Path Association - please mention this Guide when applying.

Overall size (approximately): 560mm deep x 760mm wide.

Image size : 464mm deep x 675mm wide.

ALL PRICES ARE INCLUSIVE OF POSTAGE AND PACKING
Calligraphic Map:- LAMINATED : UNLAMINATED - suitable for framing UK £9.95 USA $21; other overseas countries £12.50 (payable by sterling draft drawn on a London bank). Allow 28 days for delivery. Please make cheques payable to James Skinner and send to: James Calligraphy Services 49 Appleton Way Hucclecote. GLOUCESTER GL3 3RP England.

OFFA'S DYKE PATH - A MONUMENTAL TRAIL

Walkers on the Offa's Dyke Path glimpse the sea only twice as they progress from Sedbury Cliffs on the Severn estuary to Prestatyn on Liverpool Bay, or vice versa. In between their first and last day, however, they pass through a very varied landscape as they follow the approximate historic border of England and Wales. Unspoilt moorland, rolling hills and farmland are crossed by the path between the tourist areas of the Wye Valley and the North Wales coast. Across the plains of Gwent, over the Black Mountains, the river valleys of Radnor, the Severn and Dee valleys, the limestone hills round Llangollen and the Clwyddian ridges; the list of varied attractions is long. For nearly half the route, the Offa's Dyke ancient monument is a silent companion, sometimes almost eroded away, but at others an impressive 6 1/2 yards (6 metres) from ditch to the bank top as the earthwork rolls across the hills of the Clun area. Many ancient hill-forts, castles and abbeys lie on or near the route whose 177 miles (285 km) can be covered in a week, although most visitors will prefer a longer period in which to absorb its varied attractions.

Offa's Dyke Association was formed in 1969 as a pressure group to press for the establishment of the trail. When the route was officially opened in 1971, the Association continued its voluntary work by providing information services to walkers in the form of 'strip maps', route notes, guide books and its 'Where to Stay' accommodation and camping booklet. Pressure group activities continued to ensure the maintenance of the route, as its system of volunteers watched over lengths of the path.

Since 1982 the trail has been maintained by a professional service for which the Association lobbied. This has developed into the 'Offa's Dyke Management Service' financed by the Countryside Council for Wales and the Countryside Agency through Powys and Shropshire County Councils. ODA helps this body, with whom it shares premises at the recently opened Offa's Dyke Centre at Knighton, whilst also continuing to support walkers, run the Knighton TIC, and provide educational services based on the Offa's Dyke Interpretive Exhibition.

For details of membership and services offered, contact Offa's Dyke Association (SW), Knighton, Powys, LD1 1EN. Tel: 01547 528753. E-mail oda@offasdyke.demon.co.uk Website: www.offasdyke.demon.co.uk

Next Year's Updated Annual Guide
South West Coast Path Association Membership 2005

You may be one of those who have either bought this book from us or at a book shop. You can guarantee receipt of next year's updated, revised edition next March by joining the Association.

We, all volunteers, will update every section of this book, now in your hands, ready for a mail-out to members at the end of February 2005.

Membership rates are: Single UK £11.00; Joint UK £12.50; Non UK £16.00; Single Life £160.00; Joint Life £180.00.

Membership Application Form

I wish to join the South West Coast Path Association for the year 2005:

Name(s) ....

Address ....

....Post Code ....

Telephone: .... e-mail ....

Payment Details:

Payment made by: ☐ Cheque/Switch

☐ Amex   ☐ Visa/Mastercard   Expiry _____ / _____

Insert card/Switch Number on the line below   Issue No. _____

Gift Aid

Under the Gift Aid Scheme the Association can reclaim the income tax paid on any donation or membership sunscription received, provided you are a UK tax payer. If you would like to help us in this way then please indicate below and sign. All that we ask is if you cease to pay income tax in the future, please let us know.

I am a UK tax payer and would like the South West Coast Path Association to reclaim the tax paid on any subscriptions or donations I make to them.

Please sign here:	Date:
Signature(s)	

Please send completed form to: Liz Wallis, Administrator, South West Coast Path Association, Windlestraw, Penquit, Ermington, Devon, PL21 0LU, Tel/Fax: 01752 896237

INTRODUCTION TO THE SOUTH WEST COAST PATH ASSOCIATION

Whilst walking the path, or on any other occasion, should you meet someone interested in this book, the Association, or the coast path, do not worry if no one has a pencil and paper - just tear off one of these:

The South West Coast Path Association was formed 31 years ago to promote the interest of users of our coast path. We continue to press the authorities to maintain it properly and to complete the path. An annually updated guide to the whole 630 miles (1014 km) of the South West Coast Path is issued to members every Spring. They also receive newsletters that provide the latest news about the state of the path.

For information about membership and how to obtain this annual guide, contact:

Honorary Secretary , Eric Wallis, Windlestraw, Penquit, Ermington, Devon, PL21 0LU

T: 01752 896237   **F:** 01752 896237
E: info@swcp.org.uk   **W:** www.swcp.org.uk

The South West Coast Path Association was formed 31 years ago to promote the interest of users of our coast path. We continue to press the authorities to maintain it properly and to complete the path. An annually updated guide to the whole 630 miles (1014 km) of the South West Coast Path is issued to members every Spring. They also receive newsletters that provide the latest news about the state of the path.

For information about membership and how to obtain this annual guide, contact:

Honorary Secretary , Eric Wallis, Windlestraw, Penquit, Ermington, Devon, PL21 0LU

T: 01752 896237   **F:** 01752 896237
E: info@swcp.org.uk   **W:** www.swcp.org.uk

The South West Coast Path Association was formed 31 years ago to promote the interest of users of our coast path. We continue to press the authorities to maintain it properly and to complete the path. An annually updated guide to the whole 630 miles (1014 km) of the South West Coast Path is issued to members every Spring. They also receive newsletters that provide the latest news about the state of the path.

For information about membership and how to obtain this annual guide, contact:

Honorary Secretary , Eric Wallis, Windlestraw, Penquit, Ermington, Devon, PL21 0LU

T: 01752 896237   **F:** 01752 896237
E: info@swcp.org.uk   **W:** www.swcp.org.uk

The South West Coast Path Association was formed 31 years ago to promote the interest of users of our coast path. We continue to press the authorities to maintain it properly and to complete the path. An annually updated guide to the whole 630 miles (1014 km) of the South West Coast Path is issued to members every Spring. They also receive newsletters that provide the latest news about the state of the path.

For information about membership and how to obtain this annual guide, contact:

Honorary Secretary , Eric Wallis, Windlestraw, Penquit, Ermington, Devon, PL21 0LU

T: 01752 896237   **F:** 01752 896237
E: info@swcp.org.uk   **W:** www.swcp.org.uk